Syntactic development, its input and output

Syntactic development, its input and output

Anat Ninio

The Hebrew University of Jerusalem

OXFORD
UNIVERSITY PRESS

OXFORD
UNIVERSITY PRESS

Great Clarendon Street, Oxford OX2 6DP

Oxford University Press is a department of the University of Oxford.
It furthers the University's objective of excellence in research, scholarship,
and education by publishing worldwide in

Oxford New York

Auckland Cape Town Dar es Salaam Hong Kong Karachi
Kuala Lumpur Madrid Melbourne Mexico City Nairobi
New Delhi Shanghai Taipei Toronto

With offices in

Argentina Austria Brazil Chile Czech Republic France Greece
Guatemala Hungary Italy Japan Poland Portugal Singapore
South Korea Switzerland Thailand Turkey Ukraine Vietnam

Oxford is a registered trade mark of Oxford University Press
in the UK and in certain other countries

Published in the United States
by Oxford University Press Inc., New York

British Library Cataloging in Publication Data
Data available

Library of Congress Cataloging in Publication Data
Data available

Typeset in Minion by Glyph International, Bangalore, India
Printed in Great Britain
on acid-free paper by
CPI Antony Rowe, Chippenham, Wiltshire

ISBN 978–0–19–956596–2

10 9 8 7 6 5 4 3 2 1

Whilst every effort has been made to ensure that the contents of this book are as complete, accurate and
up-to-date as possible at the date of writing, Oxford University Press is not able to give any guarantee
or assurance that such is the case. Readers are urged to take appropriately qualified medical advice in
all cases. The information in this book is intended to be useful to the general reader, but should not be
used as a means of self-diagnosis or for the prescription of medication.

For Matan, Shira, Maya, and Eran

Acknowledgements

Thanks to the students, computer programmers, and research assistants who carried out the sometimes Sisyphean task of building the parental and child corpora from the original transcripts on the CHILDES archive and hand-coding them for grammatical relations: Yonat Drumlevitch, Michael Ely, Emily Lightstone, Shira Mady-Weitzman, Noa Schwarzbard, Nitzan Yaniv, and especially Livnat Herzig who was my right-hand assistant in the project's work. Without your patient and exacting labour on the close to two million words of the original transcripts, there would be no parsed corpus and no global patterns to be amazed by. I will be forever grateful for your willingness to be part of the team. I hope the results justify your efforts!

Many thanks to Catherine Snow and Brian MacWhinney for establishing and running the CHILDES archive. I am deeply indebted to all the individual researchers who contributed their observations to CHILDES, and, last but not least, to the parents and children who participated in the studies from which the data is taken. CHILDES is a truly revolutionary resource for research, and it makes all of us collaborators on the present project.

Special thanks are due to Liu Haitao for contributing to Chapter 2 the distribution of subject–verb, verb–object, and verb–indirect object tokens in *The Wall Street Journal* corpus of the Penn State Treebank which he calculated just for this book. I am indebted to Matan Ninio for computing the maximum likelihood estimates of power-law exponents for Chapter 5 using a software far beyond our competence to operate. I am very grateful to Shira Ninio and Uri Hershberg for technical help with the graphs, and for drawing the figure used for the cover design.

Patty Brooks, Liu Haitao, Uri Hershberg, Livnat Herzig, Tamar Keren-Portnoy, and Caroline Rowland read the manuscript and gave extensive and detailed comments. I could not have asked for better readers. I am extremely grateful for their support and for their constructive criticism. I am taking full responsibility for the errors that remain despite their good advice.

Thanks are due to Martin Baum and Charlotte Green of Oxford University Press for their help and support during the preparation of the manuscript.

Some parts of this material were presented in conferences, and in particular at the workshop on language development and language evolution at the ColRobot group of Collegium Budapest, Hungary, July 2006; Second Language

Culture and Mind conference (LCM 2) Integrating Perspectives and Methodologies in the Study of Language, Paris, July 2006; Psychometric Seminar Series of the National Institute for Testing and Evaluation, Jerusalem, January 2007; Biennial Meeting of the Society for Research in Child Development, Boston, MA, March 2007; Fifth European Conference on Complex Systems (ECCS 2008), Jerusalem, September 2008; Biennial Meeting of the Society for Research in Child Development, Denver, CO, April 2009; Problems in Linguistics Colloquium of the Department of Linguistics, The Hebrew University of Jerusalem, June 2009; Colloquium of the Department of Psychology, The Hebrew University of Jerusalem, November 2009; and the Biennial meeting of the Conference on Human Development, Fordham University, New York, April 2010. Thanks to the participants of those meetings and to Albert-László Barabási, Gershon Ben-Shakhar, Penelope Brown, Jerry Bruner, Yaniv Dover, Ram Frost, Steven Gillis, Gideon Goldenberg, Richard Hudson, Tali Kaufmann, Evan Kidd, Lorraine McCune, Bhuvana Narasimhan, Matan Ninio, Ari Rappoport, Izchak Schlesinger, Nitya Sethuraman, Sorin Solomon, Anna Stetsenko, Sigal Uziel-Karl, and Marilyn Vihman, for discussions, criticism, comments, and professional advice.

Various aspects of the research were partly supported under Grant GR2007-043 by the Center for Complexity Science (CCS) and Grant 200900206 by the Spencer Foundation.

Contents

Introduction

This book addresses the first stage of the development of syntax in young children acquiring English as their first language. This period is usually known as Roger Brown's Stage I (Brown, 1973), devoted to the development of simple sentences. Our goal was to understand normal expressive language development, namely, the first stage of syntax in children's spoken language. We hoped to gain a better understanding of how this knowledge is acquired through an exploration of the input to learning and its output, and the relation between the two.

In our study, parental speech is considered both the input to acquisition and the immediate goal of acquisition. Our method was to build two large corpora and employ methodology borrowed from Corpus-based Linguistics and Quantitative Linguistics in order to compare early child speech with parental speech, believing features of both, and their similarities and differences, illuminate the learning process.

Three features characterize our approach. First, our working hypothesis is that the basic units of acquisition are grammatical relations which can be defined as syntactic connections between pairs of words. In particular, we are assuming that children learn at the earliest stage of syntax to master the core relations of English which are the subject–verb, verb–object, and verb–indirect object relations. Accordingly, the book focuses on these three core grammatical relations, in preference to any other units and constructions of syntactic structure. For such basic word-combinations, we can leave open the theoretical question of whether these are atomic combinations generated by a Merger or Dependency operation, as assumed by current generative grammar (the Minimalist Program, Chomsky, 1995a) and by Dependency Theory (Hudson, 1990), or whether these are constructions of the kind proposed by Construction Grammars (e.g. Goldberg, 1995), albeit short ones consisting of just two constituents. Regardless of the specifics of the theoretical framework, we treat Stage I syntactic knowledge as lexical-specific, sharing this view with researchers who believe—as we do not—that at a later stage syntax becomes schematic and abstract. Fortunately, then, two-word grammatical relations can count both as Merge/Dependency couplets and as Argument Structure constructions; moreover, Stage I grammar is lexical specific in anybody's system (e.g. Tomasello, 2003), meaning that we can move on to exploring the details of early syntax without getting entangled in theoretical disagreements even before we started.

Second, our research strategy is derived from Corpus-based Linguistics, and consists of a search for both the fine details and the global characteristics of early child speech and of parental child-directed speech, based on large pooled speech corpora. Our belief is that a detailed investigation of the features of English as they are presented to young children in the linguistic input, and a comparison of the features of child speech with those of the parental register, can reveal important facts that illuminate the learning task as well as the processes of acquisition. We decided to build a large corpus comprising solely of parental child-directed speech for this study because existing large corpora, such as the Brown Corpus of American English (Francis and Kučera, 1979) contain exemplars of adult-directed, mostly written, English, and there are grounds to believe that child-directed parental speech forms a special speech register with its own unique characteristics. We used the English transcripts on the CHILDES (Child Language Data Exchange System) archive, but preferred to systematically construct a parental corpus instead of simply pooling all lines marked as uttered by adults in the observations. We also preferred to build a child corpus within clear parameters. In addition, we hand-parsed the corpora for grammatical relations instead of using the automatic parsing in CHILDES. The reasons for these decisions are explained in detail in the text. To summarize, this is a project that makes much use of the CHILDES archive but, true to the ideals of Corpus-based Linguistics, does all of its coding by hand.

Third, we are proposing a model of development that sees children as precocious social beings who crack the linguistic code by matching unknown linguistic forms with speaker's communicative intent which they interpret on the basis of the interactive context. Children are thought to be governed by the same pragmatic principles in choosing which items to learn to produce as are adults in choosing which items to say. We therefore predict that despite a smaller vocabulary, children's English will be very similar to parents' speech in its global features. The degree of similarity that we find will be used to evaluate the fit of the proposed model of development to empirical data. This model of development can be formalized in the terms of Complexity Theory, importing quantitative precision into the model-building. We consider language as a complex network, consisting of linguistic items such as words, and of speakers who produce words and sentences when they speak. New speakers are, thus, new nodes in an existing complex network. Children acquiring language are similar to new users linking into the World Wide Web: by linking into the Web, users become part of it. Hence, children learning to produce syntactic combinations do not reinvent language, nor do they internalize it;

instead, they link to a network of other speakers producing similar combinations. Like new users of the Web, children, too, are thought to be governed by the principle of Preferential Attachment, choosing the most frequent forms of expression in the input for each individual communicative need they learn to express in a multiword combination. Such a process causes the network to retain and even enhance its original global features prior to the new user joining it—and thus children's core syntax should be quite similar to parent's core syntax as far as global characteristics go.

It should be evident that the theoretical framework employed by us to conceptualize development includes, in addition to linguistics and cognitive-developmental psychology, also Complexity Theory (Barabási, 2002; Mainzer, 1996; and see also a special edition of *Science* edited by Gallagher and Appenzeller, 1999). Complexity Theory addresses the collective behaviours of complex systems. A complex system is one that is composed of many different components, in which there are multiple interactions between the components (Rind, 1999). These interactions are said to create a system with emergent features which are not completely explained on the basis of the behaviour of the individual parts. Complexity Theory takes a macroscopic view of systems, thus interested in those features which are only visible when the system is seen as an aggregate. On the macro-scale level, systems possess qualities which are undefinable at the level of individual components. Thus, a wave can be described by its wavelength and amplitude, but the individual atomic particles comprising the wave possess neither feature (Bak, 1997; Haken, 2000).

Interestingly, the study of complex systems is the reverse of the usual reductionist mode of doing science, in that the system is the focus of study rather than its parts. If the reductionist examination of parts is of any interest, this is only on condition that they help in understanding system-level behaviour (Phillips, 1999). One of the defining features of complex systems is self-organization, meaning that order emerges from the unplanned interaction of low-scale local events. The expectation that children's syntactic system will be similar to adults at the earliest stage of development is thus derived from a conception according to which complex systems such as language self-organize to some relatively stabile state. Given a basic similarity in the individual communicative events comprising of speech production in children and in their parents, it is expected that the children's language system will self-organize to a similar state as the parents' system possesses. Thus, if we are correct and children's learning is driven by similar forces to those driving adults' communication, the features of the children's syntactic system will replicate those of the adult system. Hence, similarity rather than discontinuities and jumps in global structural characteristics are expected during the formation of children's syntactic knowledge (*pace* Solé *et al.*, 2005). Rather than being impacted in some passive way by the linguistic input, children are thought to be responsible for the self-organization of their own language system and for causing it to be similar to that of adults in its global features.

The building of large pooled corpora of parental and child speech thus serves not merely to ensure reliable generalizations but also the theoretical goals of Complexity Theory. In this book, we shall submit the two speech corpora to a series of examinations for global features, testing the developmental hypothesis that the two will be closely similar.

It should be noted that the present work—similarly to Ninio (2006)—deals with the production of syntactic word combinations and does not directly treat comprehension. The model of development outlined above is for learning-to-say, and, presumably, saying some word-combination relies on understanding the syntactic know-how on which production rests. Comprehension taps the same know-how but, probably, in a lesser level of expertise and mastery (Hirsh-Pasek and Golinkoff, 1996; Roberts, 1983). Namely, we assume that comprehension is quantitatively, not qualitatively, different from production, and once we account for the mastery of productive syntax, we have also accounted for the development of comprehension.

Overview of the book

The book consists of five chapters, treating syntactic development from several different levels of analysis.

Chapter 1—Core syntactic relations—reviews the linguistic literature concerning syntactic atoms in two different types of linguistic theories: mainstream generative grammar and Construction Grammars. In the first approach, grammatical relations are defined as subtypes of the universal Merge operation of Chomsky's Minimalist Program or, alternately, of the Head-Dependent relation developed in Dependency Grammars (which is shown to be identical with the Merger operation). The grammatical relations subject–verb, verb–object, and verb–indirect objects constitute the clausal core. The motivation for positing such formal syntactic relations in linguistics is because they are defined solely by their coding properties and grammatical behaviour but dissociated from particular semantic roles. This defines core grammatical relations as purely formal components of the structure of clause, whose semantics is a lexical property of individual verbs. Alternative conceptions of syntactic units under Construction Grammars are then discussed, in particular the claim that grammatical relations are in fact meaningful linguistic signs, constituting abstract 'argument structure constructions' that possess uniform or at the least prototypical meaning. We shall tentatively treat the core grammatical relations as constructions, and will empirically test their meaningfulness or absence of it, in a later chapter.

Chapter 2—Registers and corpora—reviews the literature on child-directed speech which is a special register of English. It describes the methodology of the present project that involved the systematic construction of a large corpus of English parental speech addressed at young children and of a smaller corpus of early child speech, representing an age-dialect at Brown's Stage I grammar. After coding by hand for the three core grammatical relations subject–verb, verb–object, and verb–indirect object, the English corpus data reveals a surprising finding about the relationship of parental register and child dialect: the child dialect is almost exactly identical to the parental register in the distribution of the three grammatical relations in the clausal core, despite children's much smaller verbal repertoire. This means that in the composition of core syntax, the child dialect is identical to the parental register, modulo repertoire size. As there are obvious quantitative differences between child speech and parental speech, children need to continue to accumulate item-specific syntactic knowledge for quite a while until they catch up with the parental verbal lexicon. Regardless of the quantitative gap between child speech and parental register, children's speech at Stage I appears to have already caught up with parental speech at the least with respect to some global features.

Chapter 3—Verbs—focuses on the verb repertoires used by parents and by children to generate tokens of core grammar. We start by estimating the relative size of parents' and children's total syntactic verbal lexicon, checking if the smaller number of different verbs in children's speech stems only from the smaller speech sample we collected for them, as the estimates of type size are known to increase with the size of the sample on which estimates are based. To correct for sample size, we compare children's corpus to ten random samples of parental speech, identical in size to children's tokens. We find that even for identical number of tokens, children's verb repertoire is much smaller than that of parents, missing about 40% of verbs of the latter. Next, we ask about some basic features of the syntactic verb vocabulary. First, we analyse the combining verbs with respect to their articulatory or morphophonemic complexity, classifying them as either monosyllabic or polysyllabic; second, we classify the verbs for their historical origin, separating the native or Germanic sublexicon from the Latinate one. The results reveal that, surprisingly, both in parents and young children 98% of the tokens in the clausal core are generated by monosyllabic verbs, and 96% by verbs of native, Anglo-Saxon origin. Although polysyllabic verbs or verbs of Latinate origin are also used by parents, their combined weight in the token count is very slight. Children selectively use almost only the monosyllabic, native subset of the repertoire modelled by parents, apparently increasing thereby the morphophonetic and semantic simplicity of their verbs. Interestingly, the type differences do not affect the distribution of tokens by syllable length and origin in the two corpora, a statistic that again shows an identity in input and output.

Chapter 4—Input and output—reviews the syntactic patterns specific to the Anglo-Saxon verbal vocabulary in endstate English, including periphrastic constructions for tense, aspect, questioning and negation, and phrasal lexemes functioning as complex predicates. We next check to what extent parental speech contains such analytic constructions, and whether children take them up in their own speech. It appears that in parental as well as child language, the articulatory simplicity of Anglo-Saxon, monomorphemic verbs is paid for by the complexity of their syntax, which consists of analytic constructions, periphrastic combinations, and phrasal lexemes. Accordingly, a significant proportion of core grammatical relations do not have semantics as the verbs are copulas and auxiliaries or light verbs bleached of their semantics. This proportion is somehow higher in parents than in children, but, surprisingly, children do not seem to find analytic syntactic patterns especially difficult to learn. Checking parents' most frequent verbs in each grammatical relation, we find no support for the theory that these verbs possess the prototypical semantics of the constructions and can give it to the construction as it is built up by young children. In addition, we observe consistent multiple uses of individual verbs for two different grammatical uses or for a content-full and a grammatical use, within the same syntactic construction. These data emphatically support the conception of the three core grammatical relations subject–verb, verb–object, and verb–indirect object as formal structural roles without semantics of their own, rather than constituting meaningful 'argument structure constructions', either in the input or in the output. Such a syntactic system needs to be learned item by item; in addition, core syntactic knowledge does not seem to change its nature to schematic, abstract, and meaningful in adult speech either.

Brown (1973) called Stage I of grammar as the one concerned with the development of semantic roles and grammatical relations. Our study establishes this period as the stage at which genuine basic grammatical relations are mastered by young children, without the need or possibility to re-define syntax in terms of semantics. Semantic roles, while certainly important in any system of development, are best seen as verb-specific interpretations of syntactic relations, and not as substitutes for a purely formal syntax.

Chapter 5—Frequencies—turns to an examination of the overall pattern of verb frequencies in the input and output. We compared the token distribution of different verbs in the three syntactic patterns in parents' and children's corpora, computing rank-frequency distributions and drawing Zipf curves. In each case, the token frequencies distributed in an extremely skewed, power-law shaped distribution. Surprisingly, the exponents of the functions were identical for parents and children. The mechanism that may generate the overall identity of the output with the input is Preferential Attachment, proposed in the Complexity literature as the way power-law distributions in complex networks are sustained by newly joining items. In language acquisition this process probably takes the form of Pragmatic Matching whereby children learn unknown linguistic forms by matching them to speakers' communicative intent which they interpret on the basis of the interactive context. According to previous findings, children adopt for each specific communicative intent the form of verbal expression most frequently used by parents for that specific intent, with less frequent forms of expression fast dropping in probability of being taken up. To use this mechanism, children should be able to learn any linguistic form that captures their interest, regardless of its absolute frequency in the input. We computed the input frequency per million words for each verb children use. It appears that 35–50% of all verbs used by children in the three core grammatical relations are surprisingly rare in the input, occurring less than 20 times in a million words. Children are indeed able to learn item-specific syntax on the basis of very little input. A summary comparison of children's early syntax with that of parents shows that already by Stage I, children are similar to parents in the global features of their core syntax. However, children's syntactic system is smaller; children need to learn longer and more complex verbs in grammatical combinations to catch up even with the simplified register of parental speech.

We tested the possibility that children learn their large syntactic verb vocabulary into 'frame-and-slot' formulae centred not on verbs but on pronouns, as sometimes proposed in the literature. Checking both longitudinal acquisition data and our own corpus of Stage I syntax, we found unequivocally that the spread of syntactic constructions over a large verb vocabulary is not due to children's inserting the new verbs into pronoun-centred formula such as 'I + X'. Instead of a few pronouns, we found a great variety of different noun-phrases used by the children as the noun-complements of verbs in syntactic combinations. This means children learn verbs with their semantic and syntactic valency, and not statistics-derived formulae such as the pronoun-centred pattern. Our developmental study thus supports the choice of the Minimalist Program and of Dependency Grammar as the linguistic theories providing the most sustainable framework for developmental research.

Because of the affinity of this project with Complexity Theory, questions of structure are a constant background to the treatment of development.

A concept that makes an appearance in various different contexts and at different levels of analysis is that of the core of a set, class, or system. The topic of the present work is the three grammatical relations at the clausal core; there are many peripheral relations that also contribute to the clause's structure but we thought that a study of how children acquire syntactic knowledge should start with an exploration of their mastery of the clausal core. The distribution of the tokens of three grammatical relations in natural speech supports this decision, with relative frequency replicating the ranking in a hierarchy of centrality. Second, we concentrated on the acquisition of English, a language that has as its core the native, Anglo-Saxon vocabulary and its special grammar. Our findings depict parental and child speech as a natural 'Basic English', a 'restricted language' that consists almost exclusively of the native core; this is the language used by parents to communicate with young children and this is the language young children learn as their first approximation to English. Third, we found a consistent distinction between more central, frequent verbs and less frequent ones even within the Anglo-Saxon lexicon; the central set is a core vocabulary, with special grammatical and semantic characteristics. That is, the deeper we explore the language system, the more we continue to find a repetition of its structural make-up, with core within core carrying the most important, basic tasks of structure building. Syntactic development begins with the mastery of the innermost core of the English language; these are the foundations on which the rest of the system is constructed as children become proficient speakers of their native language.

Chapter 1

Core syntactic relations

1.1 Basics of syntax

In this book we explore the beginnings of syntactic development in young children, focusing on the three core grammatical relations that serve as the basis to the syntactic structure of clauses in English: subject–verb (SV), verb–object (VO), and verb–indirect object (VI). These grammatical relations, also called syntactic functions, case relations, and similar, are the building blocks of sentences, and serve as primitive units of syntax in the great majority of theories of syntactic structure. There are two ways to look at them, and theories are split on this issue: are they meaningful constructions possessing prototypical semantics, that can and should be acquired by children on a general or abstract level so they can be used to generate an infinite number of exemplars using different verbs inserted into the construction; or are they meaningless formal patterns used in a purely formal, autonomous system of building up the structure of sentences, which can be used for certain individual verbs according to a priori specifications to be learned on a lexical-specific manner?

The first alternative is the one proposed by mainstream generative grammars such as the Minimalist Program (Chomsky, 1995a) or Dependency Grammars (e.g. Hudson, 1990; Mel'cuk, 1988), the second by Construction Grammars and Cognitive Grammar (e.g. Goldberg, 2005; Langacker, 1987).[1] We do not have to decide a priori which alternative we take as our theoretical umbrella, as the methodology of the study is identical either way. We shall focus in our research on all formally defined exemplars of the three core grammatical relations we find in the data set we use (large corpora of parental and child speech) and explore their various features, whether or not they turn out to be, on examination, meaningless formal patterns homogeneous only in their coding features, or else meaningful constructions possessing a prototypical semantics in parental and child speech. Thus, for the time being we shall leave the question of their meaningfulness open, to be checked as part of the research goals of this project.

Because the linguistics issue is of such crucial importance for the construction of a theory of the development of syntax, the present chapter is devoted to a summary presentation of the different conceptualization of syntax and its units in the two types of theories. Never has this task been more necessary than these days when mainstream theoretical linguistics has just undergone a revolutionary change, turning upside down all our presuppositions on what, exactly, are children supposed to be developing when they learn to generate grammatical sentences. If at the start of the scientific study of language development, usually counted from the seminal publications of the 1960s, it was taken for granted that adult syntax is organized somewhere along the lines of Chomsky's Standard Theory (1957, 1965), consisting of abstract phrase-structure rules, deep structure and surface structure, and transformations mapping the one to the other, at the present moment practically nothing has remained in Chomskian theorizing from all that. For an empiricist like myself, this is good news. As Chomsky is unquestionably the most influential theoretical linguist of our times, it is a reason for rejoicing that his thinking about syntax has came up with a version that, for the first time ever, allows children to actually learn syntax from the language addressed to them by their parents and others in their environment. We shall start by summarizing the relevant elements of current generative grammar, allocating them, as it is customary, the status of a psychologically real cognitive apparatus people actually use when generating sentences. This does not mean, of course, that there are no other theories of syntax and that researchers should not continue to shop around in the arsenals of theoretical linguistics for a theory that seems to them best suited to developmental psycholinguistic concerns. Indeed, we shall continue with a detailed exposition of an alternative to the Chomskian theory in the form of Construction Grammars, to be considered as a possible framework for developmental theorizing.

1.1.1 Why not a-theoretical conceptualizations of multiword utterances?

One alternative that is rejected out of hand in this particular monograph is to ignore theoretical linguistics altogether and to work, instead, with a kind of personal-intuitive conceptualization of multiword utterances that is sometimes seen in developmental work. The risk in such a move is that the resultant alternative syntactic system might not withstand closer scrutiny for coherence. As an example, let us take a recent study in which syntactic frames are defined by the first two words of a sentence, followed by some kind of filler material (Cameron-Faulkner *et al.*, 2003). For instance, one of these frames consists of yes/no questions, starting with the words '*Are you*', followed by the words forming the rest of the sentence; the total frame with the empty slot is '*Are you ___?*' or maybe '*Are you X?*', for any X. The motivation for these kinds of slot-and-filler frames is the researchers' strong impression that there are recurrent formats in the collection of sentences uttered by parents to young children and their feeling that some frequency-based criterion might identify the operative frames. These, in turn, are thought to be the units of learning for young children, who shorten the way to the generation of sentences by being given sentence-size frames with empty slots to fill. In the Cameron-Faulkner *et al.* study the intuitive choice fell on the first one to three words or morphemes of a sentence as the fixed material that seemed to the investigators to define recurrent patterns.[2] If at least one mother produced four or more sentences that had such fixed beginning with some continuation, the relevant pattern was deemed a 'frame' for the sake of this study and further analysed, tabulated, or compared with children's productions.

The problem, is of course, that '*Are you*' does not open a particular slot that children can learn from maternal speech to fill: it represents at least three (if not more) quite different grammatical patterns which are followed by quite different types of expressions, depending on which one of the three was meant by the speaker (Quirk *et al.*, 1985). The verb *to be* is used either as a copula, in which case it is followed by a predicate complement which is a noun, adjective, or adverb and the phrases they head (as in '*Are you hungry/my little boy/there/ under the bed?*'), or it is a tense/aspect auxiliary verb, followed by Verb-*ing*, namely, by a non-finite verb in the progressive participle form and the phrase it heads (as in '*Are you running away from me/looking at the camera/dreaming/ sulking?*'), or it can be a passive auxiliary verb, followed by a past participle (as in '*Are you bothered by the noise/invited to the party?*'). Obviously, it is impossible to learn '*Are you __?*' as a frame with two fixed words and a slot to fill just anyhow, as the so-called 'slot' has its own specifications and these are seriously divergent in different cases. There is no freely fillable X-slot following '*Are you*'; filling it needs distinguishing between the three uses, meaning-wise as well as by their form. It would little help a child to learn such a formula, as it is neither semantically homogeneous nor does it get a single set of complements (aka slot-fillers) in different uses.[3]

The linguistic objection to the '*Are you __?*' frame is of course much more general. I think all structuralist linguists would say that being the first and second words of some sentence does not define a linguistically coherent unit. A sacred principle of linguistics, formulated, I am sure, after much trial and error, is that units of grammar are to be defined not by their positioning in a linear string, but by their structural functioning. Two or three words side by side do not a grammatical pattern make. In order to go against the grain of theoretical linguistics, the patterns posited by us developmentalists need to withstand all professional scrutiny, which is not the case with the two-word-defined patterns in the Cameron-Faulkner study. We pointed out above that the same two-word string can represent three quite different patterns; the opposite problem also exists which is that there is nothing very special about these two particular words, as there are other words that can start a sentence and represent very similar patterns. In our case, 'Are you __?' is in fact identical in functioning to 'Are we __?' and 'Are they __?', and this is just the shortlist if we wish to stay with this irregular form of the verb be. From a syntactic point of view, the difference in the personal pronoun serving as the subject is irrelevant to the grammatical pattern and makes distinctions where none exist. Isolating 'Are you __?' as the grammatical unit children learn ignores the inherent identity with 'Are we __?' and 'Are they __?' (even if we forget for a moment 'Is he/am I' and so on), and errs in defining the knowledge children are to acquire if they are to master the construction of yes/no questions with are. That knowledge needs to include the function of the subject-pronoun in the grammatical pattern, namely, the fact that you is also a variable element and it can alternate in a paradigm with we and they, if appropriate. The frames based on the first two words of sentences define neither some unique grammatical pattern (there are at least two different ones in this case) nor a well-defined pattern as it is inherently identical with patterns using different subjects. Theoretical linguistics would assert that the first two words of a sentence and the following slot do not successfully define a piece of grammar that children can use to produce their own multiword utterances. The same is true for other kinds of distributionally selected frames based on fixed words in fixed positions that has been proposed in the field (e.g. Bannard et al., 2009; Pine et al., 1998).

I believe it is risky to turn our backs on theoretical linguistics, and to formulate a model of syntactic structure for developmental studies in other terms than the ones suggested by it. This leaves quite a large degree of freedom for developmentalists to pick their own version of grammar from among the many different theories proposed by grammarians, whether some version of Construction Grammar, Lexical Functional Grammar, Head-Driven Phrase Structure Grammar, and so on, or, as defined below (section 1.2.1), a combination of Chomsky' Minimalist Program with Dependency Grammar. Others may disagree with me, of course, but I see our task as learning what the linguists say, our expertise being the tracing of developmental processes rather than original thinking in the field of theoretical linguistics. Ultimately, the fate of distribution-based slot-and-frame patterns will be decided by their success in accounting for developmental data. As we shall be analysing large parental and child corpora, we can test this question on empirical data (see Chapter 5).

All this said, we can now turn to a more detailed exposition of our chosen duo of theoretical frameworks, starting with the characterization of syntactic structure in the Minimalist Program and Dependency Grammars by the operation Merge/Dependency. As the book concerns syntactic development in young children in the first stages of multiword speech, it is necessary to begin at the beginning, namely, to define the very building blocks of syntax in the Chomskian and Dependency Grammar systems.

1.2 Syntactic atoms in mainstream generative grammars

1.2.1 Merge/dependency

In the definition of syntactic atoms, fundamental principles are shared by two major linguistic theories which are Chomsky's latest version of generative grammar, namely, the Minimalist Program (Chomsky, 1995a), and Dependency Grammar (Hudson, 1984; Mel'cuk, 1979; Tesnière, 1959).[4] The two theories propose that syntactic connectivity implements a single asymmetrical unification operation, the binary Merge/Dependency relation between two words.

Chomsky defines Merge as the major building block of syntactic structure. It is an operation creating a new syntactic unit from the unification of two old ones (Chomsky, 2001, p. 4). Merge combines two elements in an asymmetrical process in which one element, the Head, provides the properties for the resultant combination. The Head is also used as the label of the combination, so the same label is used both for one of the combining units and for the resulting combination. A typical tree-structure illustrating Merge is (1), representing the phrase 'saw it' as in 'The man saw it' (based on Chomsky's (1995a) example (11), p. 247):

(1)

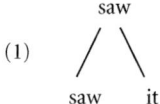

The recursive application of the operation Merge creates the complete hierarchical structure of the sentence. Potentially, it can generate an infinitely large syntactic structure.

Like Merge, Dependency is an asymmetrical operation between two syntactic elements, in which the combination shares the grammatical features of the Head and not of the Dependent unit entering the combination (Hudson, 1990; Mel'cuk 1988; Tesnière, 1959). For example, if the Head of the combination is a noun (wine) and the Dependent is a modifying adjective (red), the combination (red wine) will be a noun-phrase, which can occur in the same environments as its Head-noun, such as being the object of a verb. Namely, in traditional terminology, a Merge/Dependency combination is endocentric (Bloomfield, 1933, p. 194): it inherits the distributional properties of its

Head-word, so that the combination is distributionally equivalent to the Head. X' theory terminology, the phrase X' is the projection of the Head-daughter X. In Hudson's terminology, the combination inherits its external syntactic relations from its Head-word (1990, p. 106).

The difference between Merge and Dependency is one of notation: in the Dependency system, there are no nodes representing the results of combinations, as there is in the depiction of the Merge operation.

The tree-structure (2) represents the same phrase 'saw it' as (1), in a Dependency-type notation:

(2)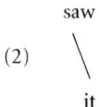

The difference is that the Dependency tree only uses one single node to represent both the Head unit and the resultant combination. The single node labelled 'saw' is to be seen both as the Head element 'saw' and the combination of 'saw' and 'it'. It is obvious that the two-node tree in (2) is more parsimonious than the three-node Merge tree of (1) and it is also obvious that (1) can always be collapsed into (2). In fact, computer theorists such as Aho *et al.* (1986) who use Chomsky's 'Rewrite Rules' as the basic method for defining the 'syntax' of programs for compilers, collapse Chomskian trees into Dependency trees as a matter of routine.

The Merge/Dependency operation is a word-based relation, bringing together in a syntactic unification two words of the sentence. Thus, the syntactic atom of these two major theories of syntax is a two-word syntactic couplet, made of a Head word and a Dependent word, where, intuitively, the Head word receives the Dependent word as its complement or modifier. This type of combination, iterated over all the words of the sentence, creates the hierarchically organized structure of the sentence.

1.2.1.1 Word meaning and syntax

For a developmentalist project, probably the major advantage of working with Merge/Dependency is the inherent relation it posits between syntax and the meaning of the words participating in the syntactic combination. In a combination such as 'saw it', analysed above as an example of the Head word *saw* getting the pronoun *it* as its Dependent, there is an inherent reason why *it* is a dependent of saw: *to see* means to perceive some visible object, and the word *it* refers to the present object of vision. The Merge/Dependency relation is not arbitrary or random; apart for some exceptional cases, it is always the formal expression of a semantic relation between the Head and the Dependent words.

Learning the meaning of the verb '*to see*' means learning that there is something that has been or will be seen.

Learning word meanings is a fundamental component of learning their syntax, including the fact that the Dependent is a variable that needs to be 'evaluated' separately. Ninio (1988) makes the point that learning the meaning of a word is incomplete unless its syntactic potential is understood on the semantic level:

> That "sit" takes a "sitter" argument is a fact about the semantics of this word: The word sit is meaningless unless it is understood to entail that there is someone to do the sitting, and, moreover, the word is not understood correctly if it is not understood that many different persons may do the sitting.
>
> Ninio (1988, p. 111)

Syntactic development builds on this kind of knowledge of the word's semantics, by offering a way to express the 'thing seen' or the 'person doing the sitting' in a separate word or phrase. In the Merge/Dependency conceptualization, syntax is not a set of arbitrary abstract rules and regulations but, rather, a very concrete extension of words' meaning. In particular, children do not need to act like (mindless) super-computers and try to abstract repeating statistical patterns from multiword utterances, hoping they will stumble by chance on some useful grammatical combination. In our system, children start with meaningful words (like *sit*) whose meaning include a requirement for a semantic complement (the identity of the 'sitter'), and syntax is there merely to lead them to the relevant expression.

The above is an intuitive phrasing of the inherently semantic basis of syntax in the Merge/Dependency system. In sections 1.2.2 and 1.2.3 we shall discuss in more precise terms the relationship of syntax to semantics in mainstream generative linguistic theories.

1.2.2 The semantic function of the dependency relation

Although the Merge/Dependency relation has no associated semantics in the usual thematic sense of this term, it does perform a unitary semantic function. The semantic function of the Merge/Dependency combination mirrors its syntax: just as the word-combination gets its syntactic properties from the Head word, it also gets its sense from the Head word.

To remind ourselves, the grammatical properties inherited from the Head are the external syntactic or distributional properties: if the Head is a noun, the combination will be a noun-phrase, which can occur in the same environments as its Head word, such as being the subject of a verb. The semantic function of the asymmetrical Merge/Dependency operation is the creation of the equally asymmetrical hyponymy relation between the Head–Dependent word-combination and the Head word: the former is a narrowing down, refining or special case of the latter. Thus, the Merge/Dependency operation is a universal general-specific combination, with the Dependent serving as a modifier of the Head word, specifying its sense and generating a hyponym.

Hudson (1990) says:

> 1. C [construction containing Head and at least one other word] refers to a hyponym of what H refers to; e.g. *big book* refers to a kind of book, *jam sandwich* refers to a kind of sandwich, *Leaves fall in the autumn* refers to a kind of falling, in which the faller is leaves and the time is the autumn.
>
> Hudson (1990, p. 106)

Namely, the effect on meaning is the semantic equivalent of the syntactic effect of Merge/Dependency which is that the combination it creates is distributionally equivalent to the Head. We might say that syntactic word-combinations are languages' systematic procedure for using words to further specify the meaning of other words. Syntax tells us which word does the specifying service to which other word; in every case, a syntactic Dependent modifies its Head. Intuitively, we need regulated formal or syntactic connectivity in order to be able to figure out which word modifies which other word in a multiword sentence, without being overwhelmed by the sheer number of combinatory possibilities.

This does not mean that simply being the Dependent of some Head word tells us exactly what part of the meaning of the Head word is being modified. A semantically complex word such as a verb may have several different semantic arguments—its agent of action, its undergoer, and so on—and it can also take many different types of adverbial adjuncts. Just being a dependent does not tell us which component of the Head word is being modified and further specified by it. This information is provided by the differentially encoded types of dependents, standing in particular grammatical relations with the Head and filling different syntactic functions. Grammatical relations will be the theme of the next section 1.3 and we shall elaborate on this topic there.

1.2.3 Valency

Chomskian theory in its two latest versions, the Government-Binding theory and the Minimalist Program (Chomsky, 1981, 1995a) is a radically lexicalist theory. This means that syntactic connections, or the phrase structure of a sentence, are thought to be projected from the lexicon. Words with syntactic potential such as verbs and other predicates are said to possess logical-semantic arguments; they also subcategorize syntactically for certain syntactic complements that express the semantic arguments in the correct interpretable form. In traditional terminology, such stored information about the combinatory properties of words, semantic as well as syntactic, is the word's *valency* or *valence* (Allerton, 1982; Tesnière, 1959). Both types of valency information are stored in each word's lexical entry, alongside the sound, meaning, and morphological class of the word. Most current linguistic theories acknowledge stored combinatory potentials of words, sometimes using for it terms such as 'argument structure', 'grid', 'logical-functional structure', 'predicate-argument structure', 'subcategorization list' and so forth. For a literature review, see Hudson (1990).[5] There are two kinds of valency information in the lexicon as syntactic form is in general autonomous of semantics as the two are mapped to each other by many-many mapping, so that syntactic devices, such as case-marked syntactic roles, can have and do have many different semantic meanings in terms of thematic roles.

The lexicon might, however, store not only single words or lexemes but also the meaning of idiomatic phrases or clauses whose meaning cannot be predicted from those of their individual components.

As we saw above, in Chomskian as well as Dependency formalism, the meaning of a syntactic combination is computed in a preordained way from the meanings of its Head word and Dependent word. A major premise of mainstream linguistics is that the meaning of word-combinations is compositional, computed from the lexical meaning of the lexemes combined, when syntax determines the way the two should be combined, whether in a complementing or adjunction relation (Frege, 1892/1960). This implies that while the meaning of words is to be stored, the meaning of multiword combinations is to be computed ad hoc, and it is not given a priori. This is the principle of *compositionality*, which is the semantic counterpart of syntactic autonomy.

However, this principle has to be weakened somehow to account for the existence of phrasal predicates, idioms, and coerced complements, in which cases the meaning of a word-combination is not predictable from the lexical meaning of their components and thus also needs to be stored in the lexicon. We shall deal with this issue in Chapter 4 in more detail. Here it suffices to say that storing the meaning of certain specific word-combinations in the lexicon does not seriously threaten the autonomy of syntax from semantics, nor necessitates the abandoning of words as syntactic atoms and the Merge/Dependency operation as the universal combining operation of syntax. As has been pointed out, idioms may have unpredictable meaning but their syntax is indistinguishable from that of word-combinations derived by regular phrasal rules (Culicover and Jackendoff, 2005, p. 37; Fraser, 1970; Sag *et al.*, 2002). The correction to syntactic theory should be a weakening of the assumption that the Merge/Dependency operation always leaves the Head total freedom to choose its Dependent, as in the mathematical 'functional application' it has been compared to (e.g. Steedman, 1988). Mostly, syntactic composition operates freely with variables as if the predicate word were a mathematic function $f(x)$ able to get any x, but sometimes some set value of the Dependent is given in the lexicon, with the specific semantics of the word-combination listed. This does not mean that the phrase is not homomorphic with a compositionally built one and thus the regular syntactic combination does not apply to it. On the contrary: many idioms and other semantically unpredictable word-combinations such as phrasal verbs allow variation in the actual words used or in the word-order of the idiom, as well as allow the insertion of non-idiomatic elements into the construction (Bolinger, 1975 and many others).[6] All these are features of free syntactic combinations, showing that idioms may be dissimilar in the way their semantics is computed and their meaning may need to be listed in the lexicon, but they are not dissimilar to other word-combinations in the way their syntactic structure is regulated nor the way they fit into the overall syntactic structure of their sentences. In any case, syntax stays atomic and lexical, and does not change its units to a priori prepared phrasal or sentential constructions. Selection restrictions on arguments are not at all unusual in syntax, and all the grammatical prepositions introducing indirect and oblique objects—*to, on, in, with,* and so on—are determined by the verb to which they serve as syntactic dependent, for instance, in such a clause as '*John relies on his family*'. In the case of idioms, we might say this is a marked case in which a verb selects a particular noun or even employs a deeper selection restriction affecting also the Dependent of its Dependent (Baltin, 1989). Nevertheless, these cases, too, can be accommodated by a generative syntax.

1.2.4 Minimalism

The beauty of the Minimalist Program as well as Dependency Grammars is in their parsimony: they use a very slim theoretical apparatus to generate syntax. Both kinds of theory build up the syntactic structure of sentences with the help of the recursive employment of the Merge/Dependency operation, with a very minimal addition of some movement rules.[7] In fact, this is all there is. The same universal combinatory operation combines all pairs of words syntactically related in a sentence, and it generates the sentence with its bare syntactic structure (Chomsky, 1995b). For readers used to the elaborate machinery of Chomsky's Standard Theory, this feature of the Minimalist Program must have come as a great surprise. The most conspicuous feature of this theory of syntax is that it lacks rules mentioning units larger than words, such as phrases and clauses; namely, there are no phrase structure rules in Minimalist syntax. X-bar theory, with its bar levels, is also removed from the theoretical apparatus. As Chomsky says in this canonical exposition of what is 'Bare Phrase Structure' in the Minimalist Program:

> The structures stipulated in earlier versions are either missing or reformulated in elementary terms satisfying minimalist conditions, with no objects beyond lexical features.
>
> Chomsky (1995b, p. 403)

In a later text summarizing the theory, Chomsky makes a list for the reader of the units his theory is working with:

> The language therefore involves three kinds of elements:
>
> ♦ the properties of sound and meaning, called "features";
> ♦ the items that are assembled from these properties, called "lexical items"; and
> ♦ the complex expressions constructed from these "atomic" units.
>
> It follows that the computational system that generates expressions has two basic operations: one assembles features into lexical items, the second forms larger syntactic objects out of those already constructed, beginning with lexical items.
>
> [...]
>
> Optimal design would introduce no new features in the course of computation. There should be no indices or phrasal units and no bar levels (hence no phrase-structure rules or X-bar theory; see Chomsky 1995c).
>
> Chomsky (2000, p. 10–11)

His reference in this quote is to the basic text of the theory, the 1995 book *The minimalist program* in which he lays down the core minimalist assumptions, one of which is the Inclusiveness Condition:

> No new objects are added in the course of computation apart from rearrangements of lexical properties (in particular, no indices, bar levels in the sense of X-bar theory, etc.).
>
> Chomsky (1995a, p. 228)

In addition to phrases as formal units of the grammar, the Minimalist Program gets rid of multiple levels of syntactic structure and a host of other abstract principles and sub-theories, admitting that their use was an error:

> A particular expression generated by the language contains a phonetic representation that is legible to the sensorimotor systems, and a semantic representation that is legible to conceptual and other systems of thought and action.
>
> One question is whether there are levels other than the interface levels: Are there levels "internal" to the language, in particular, the levels of deep and surface structure that have been postulated in modern work? (see, for example, Chomsky, 1965; 1981a; 1986). The minimalist program seeks to show that everything that has been accounted for in terms of these levels has been misdescribed, and is as well or better understood in terms of legibility conditions at the interface: for those of you who know the technical literature, that means the projection principle, binding theory, Case theory, the chain condition, and so on.
>
> Chomsky (2000, p. 10)

After removing the superfluous theoretical apparatus, the remaining grammar consists of lexical items with their sound, meaning and morphosyntactic features, and a combining operation that arranges them into interpretable sentences. This seems a very simple system and not at all difficult to learn, and Chomsky is not reluctant to say so:

[On such assumptions,] we expect that languages are "learnable," because there is little to learn.

Chomsky (2000, p. 124)

The attraction of generative theory is its simplicity, when all a child needs to learn is individual lexical items and the Merge/Dependency operation that combines them into structured strings. Under these presuppositions there is no need for children to master abstract rules, phrasal rules, constructions, or any combinatory operation that uses units other than lexical items. They do need to learn, however, how to express the syntactic relation between two words in a formally marked manner, in each particular case. This is the task of case roles, to be discussed in the following section.

1.3 **Grammatical relations**

As we said earlier, Merge/Dependency is a universal combinatory principle underlying all syntactic structure. Children need to understand this principle in order to combine any two words that stand in a syntactic relation, namely, one is a predicate and the other is its grammatically formatted argument. It is not enough, however, to get a grip on this general principle in order for children to master syntax. In order to learn to express syntactic relations, children need to get to know how to encode certain specific, *embodied* grammatical relations and not just the abstraction Merge/Dependency. In other words, Merge/Dependency couples do not exist as abstractions but, rather, come in a variety of forms and shapes. Children need to learn how to express each of them, and this learning is the topic of the present monograph.

As we said, there is not just one kind of (embodied) Merge/Dependency couple but, in every language, there is a large set of distinct Merge/Dependency relations, distinguished by their grammatical features. Different types of Head words (for instance, verbs, nouns, or prepositions), different types of Dependent words, different kinds of encodings and grammatical behaviours make for non-identical Merge/Dependency couplets. In linguistic terminology, these distinct subtypes of the Merge/Dependency relation are called *grammatical relations* (Givón, 1997; Hudson, 1990) and sometimes *syntactic relations* or *functions* (Matthews, 2007).[8,9]

The Merge/Dependency relation between a Head word and a Dependent word is the universal syntactic relation, and the complete structure of sentences is built up from its iterative application. However, despite its fundamental identity on an abstract, theoretical, or let's say mathematical, level, not all Merge/Dependency couples are identical as linguistic entities, but, rather, there are several subtypes with important differences between them.

The first subdivision is according to the general roles of the logical-semantic predicate and argument in the syntactic combination. When the predicate is the syntactic Head and the semantic-logical argument is the syntactic Dependent, we speak of complementation. For example, the syntactic direct object is by definition one of the logical-semantic arguments of the verb, as in the sentence '*I saw John*', 'John' is the syntactic object of the verb 'see', and it is also a semantic-logical argument of the same verb. In these cases, we speak of the general type of syntactic relation as *complementation.* However, in a relative clause the verb may serve not as the syntactic Head but as the syntactic Dependent of its own logico-semantic argument, as in the sentence 'The man I saw in the yard was very tall'. The verb 'see' still gets the person seen as its logico-semantic argument but the syntactic relation they participate in is one of *adjunction, modification,* or *attribution,* not of complementation. The adjunct type of relation also exists between a prenominal adjective and a common noun, as in the phrase 'red shoes' in the sentence '*I bought a pair of red shoes*', as well as between an adverbial and a verb it modifies, as in the sentence, '*The coin span fast until it fell off the table*', where the adverb 'fast' modifies the inflected verb 'span'.

We saw already that there is a fundamental difference between the grammatical functioning of complements and adjuncts, when complements are required by the Head word to provide some information otherwise felt as missing (e.g. they tell us whom the speaker saw), whereas adjuncts are optional and the Head word can function without their additional information perfectly well. Complements are obligatory, adjuncts are not, and this of course stems from the different relationship between the predicate and its logico-semantic argument in the two cases.

There are, however, further differences within subtypes of complements and of adjuncts, based on their form and function. Beyond the basic distinction between complements and adjuncts, it is customary to make further distinctions based both on the form of the Head and the Dependent and on the grammatical functioning of the combination. Here we arrive at the level of differentiation entitled grammatical relations.

1.3.1 Form and function of grammatical relations

Unit of language—words, morphemes, and Merge/Dependency couples—possess two sides, their form and their function. Grammatical relations are also defined by two sets of properties: their form, or, as Keenan (1976) and many linguists say, their coding properties, and their grammatical functioning, or, in Keenan's term, their behavioural properties. These properties will be defined shortly in more detail. While coding properties identify a term in the clause as some specific grammatical relation, behavioural properties tell us how these terms function in the grammar.

Both so-called traditional grammar as well as present-day mainstream theoretical linguistics, including the major theories Dependency Grammar (Hudson, 1984, 1990; Tesnière, 1959), Lexical Functional Grammar (Bresnan, 1982),[10] Relational Grammar (Perlmutter, 1983), and more use grammatical relations as atoms or primitives of syntactic structure.[11] In Chomsky's Principles and Parameters Theory there is an equivalent construct under the name of 'structural case' (Chomsky, 1981; and see also Alsina, 2001).[12]

Grammatical relations are also among the most extensively explored subjects in typological linguistics, their variance forming a so-called alignment typology. According to theory widely held, grammatical relations are universal and are to be found in all languages, although languages differ in the way major semantic and pragmatic elements of the clause are mapped into such grammatically homogeneous categories. However, the details of alignment differ: languages are said to fall into a few typological kinds such as nominative-accusative, ergative, active, Philippine type, and so on, according to their sets of grammatical relations. For a review, see Andrews (1985).

In English as in other nominative-accusative languages, grammatical relations are such familiar syntactic functions as subject–verb, verb–direct object, verb–indirect object, modifier–noun, verb–adverbial and so on, defined by coding and behavioural properties.

1.3.2 Properties of grammatical relations

Following Keenan (1976), it is customary to see grammatical relations as clusters of properties of two types: coding properties and behavioural or functional properties. Coding properties are the form by which expressions serving in various grammatical roles are encoded or marked. Behavioural or functional properties are the syntactic functions targeting expressions serving in given grammatical roles (see also Givón, 1997; Manning, 1996).

1.3.2.1 Coding properties

The idea behind the postulation of a universal Merge/Dependency relation is that syntagmatic connectivity in sentences is founded on the basis of lexically given logical characteristics of predicate words. However, the lexicon leaves open the question of how the relevant predicate functions in the present sentence, and where to find the value for its variable elements. We need syntactic rules that would instruct the speaker and the listener how to connect the predicate with its semantic arguments. Coding properties of grammatical relation do the work of connecting between predicates and arguments, when the two form a given type of syntactic connection. Their role is to provide, for each predicate, the 'address' of the word carrying the value for each of its logical arguments, dependent on the particular grammatical relation the two stand in. In the case of valency complements (also called core arguments), the logical argument of a predicate is its syntactic Dependent, as in the case of a verb's subject, object, and indirect object. In the case of adjuncts in an attributive relation, the relationship is in the opposite direction for semantics and syntax, and the logical argument of a predicate is its syntactic Head, as in the case of an adjective modifying a noun or a verb modifying a noun by means of a relative clause. In these cases, the syntactic relation 'reverses' the logical or semantic predicate-argument relation. (For more details, see Hudson, 1984; Ninio, 1995; Venneman, 1977.)[13]

Each different syntactic realization of the predicate-argument relation is a unique grammatical relation, marked by its own 'packaging' or 'addressing' devices. If some syntactic relation 'alternates' among two or more formal expressions, as in the case of the well-discussed dative alternation or *fill*-alternation (Levin, 1993), each alternative can be seen as the expression of the same predicate-argument relation with its unique 'address'. In addition, verbs can possess several different sets of logical-semantic arguments, given that there is a degree of lability in their meaning and valency. For example, some verbs can be used both as intransitive verbs in a so-called 'middle' pattern, as well as in a transitive version, for instance, the verb 'float'. In English, most if not all verbs can appear in multiple valency patterns, and see Hornby (1945) for a seminal exploration of this phenomenon.

The repertoire of grammatical relations and the details of their 'packaging' or 'addressing' is a language-specific component of grammar. Overall, there is a limited number of different 'addressing' devices. First, the LINEAR POSITIONING of Dependents relative to Heads in the sentence-string may be specified, or their word-order in the clause in general. Second, there might be a redundant encoding of dependent information on (or next to) the Head word, as in CROSSMARKING (aka AGREEMENT) or PRONOUN CLITICS.[14] Third, Head words like verbs may be marked for the existence of various kinds of dependents such as an OVERT MORPHOLOGICAL MARKING of transitivity. Fourth, dependents may be marked for their grammatical role vis-à-vis the Head by nominal CASE MORPHOLOGY or ADPOSITIONAL CASE MARKERS.[15]

We might see these 'packaging devices' as a language's way to identify a unique type of dependent in the clause. Although as a rule such 'grammatical roles' do not possess a homogeneous meaning (and see section 1.4.2), they do serve as targets to a uniform set of grammatical functions. This is what is called their behavioural properties.

1.3.2.2 Behavioural properties

Behavioural or functional properties of grammatical relations are syntactic functions that refer to expressions serving in given grammatical roles. The functions may target such expressions in the definition of their range of application, in some cases restricting the pattern to some grammatical roles such as subjects or objects only.

A central example of syntactic patterns that target subjects rather than expressions serving in any other grammatical role, in English as well as other languages, is their behaviour in multiclausal sentences. Subjects are as a rule omitted in one of the clauses of most kinds of multiclausal sentence patterns, whether involving clause coordination or subordination. In these cases, the omitted subject is to be understood as co-referential with the existing subject of the other clause, and this regardless of the semantic roles involved in the two clauses.

Two very prominent examples of such multiclausal behaviours are described here in some detail. One is the control of co-reference across conjunctions (Anderson, 1976; Comrie, 1989). The subject—and only the subject—of coordinated clauses can and should be omitted in the second coordinate, as in (3).

(3)
    a. John bought a painting and loaned it to the museum.
    b. *John bought a painting and he loaned to the museum.

In (3)a the co-referential subject 'John' is omitted from the second coordinate, and the co-referential object 'painting' is referred to with the pronoun 'it'. This makes for a grammatical sentence. (In fact, if the subject 'John' is repeated in the second conjoined clause, the sentence is odd and people will tend to interpret it as if there are two different 'John's involved.) In (3)b. the co-referential subject 'John' is referred to in the second coordinate by the pronoun 'he', and the co-referential object 'painting' is omitted. This is an unacceptable sentence, marked, as usual in linguistic texts, by a star.

The second type of pattern restricted in English to subjects is also a kind of co-referential omission.[16] When there is in a sentence some kind of non-finite verb form, such as a gerund or an infinitive, serving as a complement to some main or matrix verb, the omitted subject of the lower verb can only be co-referential with the subject of the upper or matrix verb, never with its object or with any other expression in the sentence (Andrews, 1985). For example, in (4)a and (4)b we see two examples of the so-called 'equi' pattern:

(4)
    a. John tried to sleep.
    b. Mary promised Fred to talk to John.

In (4)a the sleeper can only be John, not any other person, and in (4)b, Mary can only have promised that she would talk to John, not that Fred would (see also Pollard and Sag, 1987; Steedman 1988).

Similarly, in the 'raising' pattern exemplified by (5),

(5) John seems to like Mary.

it is necessarily John who is said to like Mary, not any other person.
The same is true for participles and gerunds, as in (6)a–c:

(6)
    a. The children are going home soon.
    b. I've seen worse movies.
    c. We considered selling the house.

For more subject properties, see Comrie (1989, pp. 104–23).

Not only subjects but direct and indirect objects, too, have coding and behavioural properties, such as their positioning, case marking, conjoint omission possibilities, relativization strategies, and so on.[17] Although two-clausal behavioural properties of subjects and objects are too complicated to be relevant for young children just beginning to learn the basics of English syntax, it may not be so for coding properties, and for such behaviours as the control of non-finite verbs' understood subjects. It is to be seen which properties are actually mastered in the first period of syntactic development.

1.4 Nucleus, core, and periphery of clauses

There is a strong tradition in linguistics that there is a profitable distinction to be made between a few core grammatical relations in sentences and a larger number of more peripheral ones.

In general, a clause is thought to be built around a *nucleus* comprising of its main predicate. In English the main predicate is inevitably a finite, inflected verb. This verb is the syntactic *root* of the clause, and all other words are its direct dependents, or the dependents of its dependents. Namely, the finite verb is the highest element in the syntactic tree, the one that does not have a Head and it is the Head, and indirectly, the 'parent' of all other words in the clause. Thus, the main verb is the universal organizer of clausal structure, and its obligatory complements provide the skeleton of the clause (Algeo, 1995; Foley and Van Valin, 1984; Hudson, 1984; Mel'cuk, 1988; Seiler, 1988; Tesnière, 1959). In some cases, other, secondary predicates, whether non-finite verbs, particles, adjectives, and so on, join the main verb and generate a complex predicate (Alsina *et al.*, 1997; Foley and Olson, 1985; and see Chapter 4). Strictly speaking, then, it is the finite, inflected verb and the predicate complex it heads, that together form the main predicate of the clause and can be said to be its nucleus.

Semantically, we might say that the verb-nucleus is what the clause is about, all the rest of the elements of the clause are just elaborations on it. This is also reflected in the syntactic relations between the clausal nucleus and other expressions, forming a tree-structure. The finite verb is the highest node or 'root' of the tree, dependent on no expression. However, apart from the root, consisting of the main verb or main predicate, all other expressions in the clause are dependent on some Head expression, ultimately related back to the main verb. Namely, apart from the nucleus, the rest of the clause is formed by the direct and indirect dependents (subordinates) of the main predicate, customarily divided into two categories, core and periphery (Foley and Van Valin, 1984).

The *core* of the clause contains the direct valency-derived complements of the main verb or main predicate (Dik, 1978; Givón, 1997; Pike and Pike, 1982). These are obligatory complements expressing valency arguments of the main verb. These valency-dictated elaborations are semantically required, often syntactically obligatory, hence they are closer than other dependents to the root-verb. Thus, the core contains the expression of the logical-semantic arguments of the verb, their reading determined a priori by the verb's lexical semantics. Information about the syntactic expression of such dependents is therefore stored in the lexicon, and it is said that the verb subcategorizes for them. In some languages, this means that the overt expression of these syntactic dependents in the clause is obligatory and they cannot be omitted. In other languages, the syntactic expression of valency-arguments is more flexible; however, they are still felt to be semantically required and their 'value' has to be provided at the least by some accepted default mechanism such as previous mention.

Any dependent of the verb that is not a valency argument, such as adverbial adjuncts (also called the verbs' satellites), are on the *periphery* or margin of the clause (Dik, 1978; Foley and Van Valin, 1984; Pike and Pike, 1982).

In the linguistic literature core arguments are also called actants or terms. The name 'actant' comes from Tesnière's (1959) conceptualization of the clause as the description of an event in which the verb depicts an action and the core arguments are the main actors in the event. He saw all but the core arguments as peripheral depictors of the circumstances in which the action took place, therefore calling the later 'circumstants' (see also Seiler, 1988).

It is possible to define the core of the clause by pragmatic criteria and authors such as Van Valin (2004) justify this layered concept of the clause by such criteria as relative topicality and perspective of the sentence. We shall, however, stay with a purely formal definition and define the core by syntactic-grammatical properties, namely, by their coding and behavioural properties.

Core dependents are distinguished by coding properties that reflect their direct relationship with the verb. It is well-documented that universally, the verbal agreement or cross-referencing system is exclusively reserved for core arguments such as subject, object, and indirect object (Andrews, 1985; Goldenberg, 1985; Johnson, 1977; Keenan, 1984; Schachter, 1977). Adjuncts and peripheral elements of the clause are not, as a rule, cross-referenced on the verb.

In a complementary pattern, the core complements of verbs tend to be expressed as bare noun-phrases, without morphological case marking or without being prepositionally marked. Namely, they tend to be in the unmarked nominative case and not to have prepositions or post-positions marking their syntactic role (Andrews, 1985). The absence of prepositions or post-positions means that core complements will be in a direct syntactic relationship with the verb, without the mediation of grammatical linking elements. As a universal tendency, core arguments are direct, and peripherals are oblique arguments of the verb. Taking directness of relation as a criterion, all oblique or non-direct dependents of the verb are on the periphery of the clause, even if the verb possesses a valency requirement for them. This includes also prepositional and oblique objects as belonging to the periphery of the clause, alongside adverbial adjuncts of the verb.

In the present study we shall adopt this criterion, thus viewing the core as containing only the grammatical relations subject, direct object, and indirect object expressed as a preposition-less object.

As for grammatical behaviour, there is a host of syntactic patterns reserved for core arguments. For example, in many languages only subjects may relativize, topicalize, be clefted, or be questioned (e.g. Keenan and Comrie, 1977). Similarly, in many languages only core objects may passivize (Foley and Van Valin, 1985). Beyond the particular patterns associated with core relations, a general behavioural property stands out. In general, expressions encoded as core grammatical relations tend to participate in a larger number of grammatical patterns and processes than peripheral elements, whether these involve anaphoric control of omitted dependents (as in conjunction deletion, see below) or valency-changing operations like causativization or passivization which change the syntactic expression of semantic arguments in the sentence. In the terminology of Relational Grammar, 'terms' (aka core complements) are syntactically active, while non-terms (and adjuncts) are inert (Perlmutter and Postal, 1983).

1.4.1 Hierarchy of grammatical relations

In English, as in nominative-accusative languages in general, the consensus among linguists is that there are three core grammatical relations: the subject–verb, verb–direct object, and verb–indirect object relations (e.g. Foley and Van Valin, 1985). The placement of these three in the core is graded. On any of the criteria we used to define the category of core relations, different dependents of the verb form a hierarchy of answering to form. The usual hierarchy is basically the one used in Relational Grammar (e.g. Johnson, 1977), namely (7),

(7) subject > direct object > indirect object > other elements.

The hierarchy is thought to represent the order of semantic composition of arguments with the verb, in reverse. The argument lowest in the hierarchy combines with the verb first, the sequence continuing with the next lowest element, with the subject—the 'first argument'—the last, after the verb's other arguments are made definite and added to the semantics of the verb (Marantz, 1984).[18] The evidence for order of composition are phenomena known as 'semantic tailoring' by which the semantics of a predicate are determined in interaction with its dependents, but not vice versa (Allerton, 1982). Marantz and others also use a related phenomenon of subject/object asymmetry in idiom formation as evidence for the compositional interpretation of the argument hierarchy, as object idioms are much more frequent in English than subject-idioms.

The hierarchy in (6) is quite similar to the upper part of the Accessibility Hierarchy of Keenan and Comrie (1977) that describes the probability of expressions to be relativized (and see also Pollard and Sag, 1987). In fact, it is possible to build the same hierarchy by the ease by which different arguments and other dependents of the verb are accessible for syntactic constructions involving 'factorizing' (Kiparsky, 1968, p. 34, note 4) such as relativization, topicalization, fronted wh-question formation, cleft, coordination with co-reference deletion, gapping, and so forth. Namely, the hierarchy represents some kind of relative distance of the dependent term from the verb, with subjects being the best separated conceptually.

The lower a term on this hierarchy, the less likely it is to be in the core in a given nominative/accusative language. In English, subjects and direct objects are undoubtedly in the core. However, indirect objects are problem cases. Indirect objects possess—in English—two forms of expression: that of a direct object (in the so-called double object construction), and that of a prepositional object with the case-marked preposition *to*. Given that the two forms of expression connect to the same semantic valency component of the verbs and thus can very often alternate without discernable difference in semantics, may be just conditional on how 'heavy' the relevant noun-phrase is, it feels somehow arbitrary to exclude one of the expressions from the core and admit the other. However, if we did accept the prepositional indirect object as part of the core, it would be difficult to close the door on other oblique or prepositional objects (see also Andrews, 1985, p. 127).[19,20] At the end of the day, the winning consideration was that in this study, the core should contain only grammatical relations which can be potentially expressed by two words, consisting of the verb and a pronoun complement. To be on the safe side, we did code for prepositional indirect object as well, and can, if necessary, examine the sentences we thus left in limbo.

Assuming that the hierarchy of grammatical relations represents some psychologically real relative priority in terms of relevance or pragmatic pertinence, we expect that it will be reflected in tendencies of syntactic development. If children prefer core elements over peripheral ones and higher-ranking terms over lower-ranking ones, we might in general make the prediction that children will concentrate on subjects more than on objects, with indirect objects a disfavoured third.

1.4.2 Syntax and semantics: neutralization of semantic distinctions in grammatical relations

As mentioned earlier in section 1.3.2, in mainstream generative linguistics grammatical relations are not thought to have defining semantic properties. On the contrary, the motivation for positing such terms as subject or object is precisely because they are needed to label some purely formal and behavioural categories which are not semantically homogeneous. This is especially so regarding the core grammatical relations we are focusing on. Probably, when linguists claim syntax is fundamentally autonomous as there is no one-to-one mapping of form to meaning (e.g. Jackendoff, 1997), they mostly refer to the fact that core grammatical relations are not associated with any particular meaning.

One of the defining properties of core grammatical relations is their wide semantic range, or, as it is called in some linguistic terminology, their restricted neutralization of semantic distinctions (Andrews, 1985; Dik, 1997; Kibrik, 1997; Lyons, 1968, p. 439; Van Valin, 1993; Van Valin and LaPolla, 1997). This is true for the three grammatical relations subject, object, and indirect object considered here to be in the core of the clause. Van Valin's Role and Reference Grammar, for example, points out that grammatical relations neutralize the semantic macro-roles Actor and Undergoer, so that, for instance, the entity encoded as subject can be either.

Givón (1997), who talks about the dissociation of grammatical case roles from semantic roles rather than neutralization of the latter, lists the multiple semantic roles of subjects and direct objects in English to illustrate the point:

> To demonstrate, even in the most superficial way, that a case-role is grammatical rather than semantic, one must demonstrate its dissociation from semantic roles. That is, one must show that it admits more than one semantic case-role. For a nominative

language such as English, with unmarked subject and direct object, such a demonstration is relatively easy. Consider:

(1) Multiple semantic roles of the grammatical subject:
   a. Patient of state:
      She is tall
   b. Patient of change:
      She is falling asleep
   c. Dative:
      She is dreaming
   d. Agent:
      She is writing a letter
(2) Multiple semantic roles of the grammatical object:
   a. Patient of state:
      He saw her
   b. Patient of change:
      He pushed her
   c. Ablative:
      He approached her
   d. Allative:
      He left her
   e. Ingressive:
      He entered the house
   f. Dative:
      He gave her a book
   g. Benefactive:
      He built her a house

Givón (1997, p. 2–3)

Schlesinger (1995) reviews some of the linguistic literature on semantics of direct objects in a chapter devoted to this topic and concludes that objects possess a practically infinite variety of semantic roles. If we want to consider a whole sentence-level construction rather than individual case roles, it should be mentioned that the subject–verb–object (SVO) pattern is similarly associated with a wide variety of meanings (Dowty, 1991).

Lastly, the double-object construction of the ditransitive, which is often considered to be prototypically reserved for meanings associated with the transfer of possession, in actuality has, in English, quite a variety of different semantics, as pointed out by Jackendoff (1997, p. 175).

The semantic variety might be more pronounced in the core relations than in the more marginal or peripheral ones. Andrews (1985, p. 82) generalizes that the case roles of core grammatical relations, the so-called 'syntactic cases' always imply a great degree of semantic variability, and should best be viewed as expressing some abstract grammatical relation, not necessarily correlated with semantic roles or any other aspect of meaning. By contrast, the other, 'semantic cases', may indeed be semantically homogeneous. In fact, most theoreticians we listed, and Andrews among them, are unwilling to acknowledge the existence of grammatical relations proper in a language unless the same category cannot be defined on a shared semantic or pragmatic basis. Our special interest in core grammatical relations, therefore, targets that part of English grammar in which there is, by definition, a dissociation of abstract syntactic entities from classes with homogeneous semantics.

It is still possible, as claimed by Goldberg (1995) and associates, that this dissociation is not in fact a feature of parental speech to young children laying the foundations of syntax, inviting a different conceptualization of syntax as more accurate for developmental modelling. We turn now to such a theory, namely, to Construction Grammar.

1.5 Conception of syntax in Construction Grammars

1.5.1 The concept of construction within Construction Grammars

Construction Grammars (CxGs) are a family of theories that treat not only morphemes and words but also syntactic strings of words as meaningful linguistic signs, possessing an associated form and meaning. Most importantly for our purposes, such theories acknowledge the existence in grammar of phrasal constructions which are syntactic templates paired with conventionalized semantics (Croft, 2001; Fillmore et al., 1988; Goldberg, 1995, 2003). In such theories of grammar, constructions are seen as the basic units of syntax, and not words, which are the atomic syntactic units in mainstream generative grammars. As constructions are stored syntactic templates, they are not built up from atomic components by a recursively applied operation such as Merge/Dependency. Instead, grammar is an inventory of lexically stored constructions.

It is clear that CxGs do not posit an autonomous syntax separate from semantics, a principle which is a cornerstone of Chomsky's Minimalist Theory and Hudson's Dependency Grammar as well as of other generative theories that build up syntactic structure from atomic elements. On the contrary, the major characteristic attributed to constructions is that they are meaningful linguistic signs in which form and meaning is coupled. This defines afresh the architecture of grammar in that constructions are seen as the basic organizational units of grammar, rather than forms (syntax) and meanings (semantics) separately.

The question is, what counts as a construction? The CxG approach was originally developed in order to handle idiomatic word-combinations whose meaning is impossible to arrive at by composing the meanings of the individual lexemes according to the rules of syntax. The major motivation was the existence, in language, of idioms (such as *take a break*) and ad hoc or coerced complements (such as *Bake me a cake!*) in which the phrasal meaning or the presence of a complement in the phrase is not predictable from the participant verb's semantic and syntactic valency. In a more restricted version of this theory (e.g. Goldberg, 1995; Jackendoff, 1996) the definition of a meaningful phrasal construction is indeed confined to idiomatic multiword combinations that need to be stored with their otherwise unpredictable meaning in the lexicon, but otherwise phrase structure is built up from atomic components, in the manner of mainstream generative grammars. If the restricted version is adopted, we are back at Minimalism, Dependency Grammar, and the Merge/Dependency operation for the treatment of the three core grammatical relations. Under this version, free, fully productive combinations such as SV, VO, and VI would be projected from the verbs' valency, and the combination would not qualify as a 'construction' as the meaning of the phrase is fully compositional and can be derived from the component words' meaning and their syntactic relationship.

More interesting for us is a more radical version of CxG that claims that all syntactic word-combinations, including fully productive and compositional ones, are meaningful constructions (Croft, 2001, 2003; Goldberg, 1996, 2003, 2005; and see also Langacker, 1987). For instance, Goldberg (2005) defines constructions as:

> learned pairings of form with semantic or discourse function, including morphemes or words, idioms, partially lexically filled and fully general phrasal patterns.
>
> Goldberg (2005, p. 5)

The inclusive view of constructions as comprising the totality of language is made clear in the following:

> What makes a theory that allows constructions to exist a "construction-based theory" is the idea that the network of constructions captures our grammatical knowledge of language in toto, i.e. it's constructions all the way down.
>
> Goldberg (2005, p. 18)

The inclusion of syntactic templates with compositional meaning in the category of constructions is emphasized in particular for the case of frequently observed form-function correspondences, as in the citation from Goldberg and Jackendoff (2004):

> [...] stored (typically highly frequent) regularities between form and meaning are considered constructions even if they are fully compositional.
>
> Goldberg and Jackendoff (2004, p. 533)

This point is essential for Goldberg's theory of the origin and development of phrasal constructions that also has a serious implication for the acquisition of syntax in young children, as we shall see presently (section 1.5.3)

First, however, we should make clear what the model of combinatory operations producing syntactic phrases is, according to the more inclusive version of CxG. Recall, the major premise of mainstream linguistics is that the meaning of word-combinations is compositional, computed from the lexical meaning of the lexemes combined, when syntax determines the way they are combined, whether in a complementing or adjunction relation (Frege, 1892/1960). According to CxG, however, meaning is not a feature of lexemes nor of syntactic roles but, instead, of the constructions into which lexemes are placed. Namely, the meaning of word-combinations is not based on the composition of the a priori lexical meaning of the predicate word and the argument expression, directed by their syntax, but, instead, it is a feature of the construction in which the words are placed in a manner reminiscent of 'lexical insertion' in earlier Chomskian theories.

In other words, all word combinations, including the completely productive ones, are said to consist of the combination of several different lexical items with a syntactic template which is the construction, the latter contributing not just the form but also the meaning to the combination. In fact this implies that verbs do not possess semantic and syntactic valency, both being stored separately in the form of an abstract format to which the individual concrete verb is inserted. Goldberg says:

> Even basic sentence patterns of a language can be understood to involve constructions. That is, the main verb can be understood to combine with an argument-structure construction (eg transitive, intransitive, ditransitive constructions, etc.). The alternative is to assume that the form and general interpretation of basic sentence patterns are determined by semantic and/or syntactic information specified by the main verb (Grimshaw 1990; Levin and Rappaport Hovav 1995; Pinker 1989). [...] However, [...] in general the interpretation and form of sentence patterns of a language are not reliably determined by independent specifications of the main verb.
>
> Goldberg (2005, p. 6)

Thus, in the present version of CxG proposed by Goldberg (2005), there is a deep difference in the architecture of grammar, relative to mainstream generative theories. Syntactic constructions are meaningful and stored as abstract templates together with their schematic meaning interpretation, while the words composing them, such as verbs, do not have syntactic and semantic valency, and they are stored with a rather underspecified lexical semantics that can accommodate itself to the various construction-based meaning. Thus, valency is exchanged by the construction.

This perception is proposed as an alternative to the generative grammar of Chomsky's Minimalist Program and Dependency Grammar: instead of having a stored lexical valency that prescribes a priori how verbs combine with complements and what the meaning of the combination is, in this conception, verbs combine almost freely with a wide range of constructions, each carrying the form of the word-combination as well as its prototypical meaning. What is relevant for our purposes is that under the present version of CxG, the syntactic combinations of verbs including the three core grammatical relations subject–verb, verb–object, and verb–indirect object are also considered meaningful constructions, or, in the term often used in this literature, 'argument structure constructions'.

I want to emphasize that two things are different in CxG from the mainstream generative conception presented above: the separation of meaning from the lexema and its attribution to the construction; and the abstractness of constructions. The two are connected: a lexicalist syntax associates valency with particular lexemas, which therefore possess a priori potentials to appear in different semantic versions in different formal constructions; and, as structure is built up from individual verbs and their valency, phrasal meaning is always concrete and computed relative to the combinations' particular building blocks.

To summarize, CxG is certainly a different theory of syntax than the generative systems presented above, in three major aspects:

The first major difference is in the conceptualization of units of syntax and the manner by which syntactic structure is built. In generative syntax, the units of syntax are atomic—they are single words and the combination operation Merge/Dependency is binary, combining word with word. The structure of multiword strings is built up by the recursive application of the binary combining operation, which makes possible the generation of an infinite length and variety of different sentences to which it is always possible to add another component, hence the theories are called generative. In CxG the units are the multiword phrases, clauses, and sentences which are not built up from smaller components but are stored as multiword Gestalts. The lack of recursion and the absence of generative means of building up structure from atoms, means that any difference between two sentences implies there are two different constructions stored in the lexicon, each sentence accounted for by a different template.

The second difference is in Merge/Dependency being an asymmetrical relationship which does not exist in CxG.

The Merge/Dependency combination is asymmetrical, driven by the stored lexical-specific valency of the verb, with the nominals fulfilling dependent roles according to the verb's a priori requirements. By contrast, in the present version of CxG, syntactic units are multiword constructions without an internal structure of combining components, merely possessing variable slots for various elements. As verbs do not determine the form and meaning of the construction, there is no asymmetry in their contribution to the combination, as claimed by valency-based generative grammars. The construction which is a multiword scheme has an open slot for the verb as well as for its complements, in a symmetrical fashion.

The third difference is that these abstract multiword formats are said to be meaningful linguistic signs, possessing their own semantics which they contribute to the phrase or clause, with concrete words merely contributing word-semantics but not the meaning of relationships among the components of the phrase or clause. By contrast, in the generative systems such as Minimalism or Dependency Grammar, types of syntactic phrases have only some specific form but no meaning of their own. The complete meaning of the phrase or clause is determined in a compositional fashion from the lexical semantics of the combining words, with the Head of the combination—in simple sentences, the verb—determining also the semantic role of its various nominal complements, as, for example, agents or objects of the action referred to by the verb.

1.5.2 Core syntax a possible problem for CxG

One problem raised by the comprehensive theory of constructions in CxG is that it is difficult to claim that the basic transitive and intransitive constructions of English indeed possess a prototypical semantics. This is so whether we consider the maximal multielement sentential form (e.g. SVO but also SV and VO if they constitute the whole clause) or the phrasal constructions called grammatical relations (e.g. SV and VO, if they are constituents of more complex sentences). As we said above (section 1.4.2), the syntactic categories subject, object, and indirect object were posited in linguistics precisely because they are identically coded elements in sentences that do not possess a definite semantic role.

This means, of course, that grammatical relations at the core, namely, subject–verb, verb–object, and verb–indirect object combinations, which are defined, as we saw, because they neutralize semantics and are defined merely by their formal homogeneity, appear to pose a problem for CxG. One possibility is that although there is much merit to a construction-based theory of grammar, it should also acknowledge that some syntactic patterns (i.e. the core grammatical relations) are not constructions, and should allow parts of syntax to be built in the atomic generative way, regardless of semantics. Such suggestions were made by Jackendoff (1997) and Ariel (2008), otherwise sympathetic to the CxG project. For instance, Jackendoff argues that basic phrase structure, structural case marking, and agreement are syntactically autonomous, and the relevant phenomena are better not included among the meaningful constructions covered by the theory.[21]

However, it is still possible that there is a much tighter form–function correspondence in parental speech to young children, and in children's own early productions, establishing the hypothetical basic meaningful constructions for the three core grammatical relations, too. This question has not yet been tested in studies published by Goldberg and colleagues as they concentrated on more elaborate constructions such as Caused Motion or the full ditransitive (e.g. Goldberg, 2005). As we shall be analysing large parental and child corpora, we can test this question on empirical data (Chapter 4). We shall return to this possibility in section 1.5.4.

1.5.3 Implications for a model of syntactic development

Although there are a number of projects in developmental psycholinguistics that use the Minimalist Program or Dependency Theory as their theoretical umbrella (e.g. Ninio, 2006; Sagae *et al.*, 2004a),[22] there are quite a few researchers who work within the framework of CxG.

The choice of CxG as a theoretical framework has different implications for a theory of syntactic development than the choice of mainstream generative syntax, as it defines different units and different kinds of syntactic combinations. Most importantly, CxG implies that grammar consists of abstract phrasal templates with attached meanings as basic units of syntax, which children are to form during development. In the developmental literature, this theory has informed a view according to which children start syntactic development by acquiring a number of item-specific verbal patterns or 'verb-islands' (Tomasello, 1992), but after accumulating a quantity of these, form abstract 'Argument Structure Constructions' consisting of phrasal, clausal, or sentence-sized subcategorization formulae centred on categories of verbs, possessing a uniform semantics. Following the formation of such a schematic syntactic formula and learning its associated meaning, children are said to use it as a template to generate many different sentences with many different verbs whose syntax they do not learn on a lexical specific way (e.g. Goldberg, 2005; Goldberg *et al.*, 2004; Tomasello, 2003, 2006; and see chapters in Clark and Kelly, 2006).

By contrast, a lexicalist syntactic theory such as Chomsky's Minimalist Program (1995a) absolves children from any other learning but of individual verbs with their item-specific syntax and semantics (see section 1.2.1). Under such a theory, there is no need for children to master abstract or phrasal rules, constructions or their prototypical semantics, or any syntactic operation that uses units other than lexical items. In actuality, a lexicalist linguistic theory defines syntactic development as comprising only the presumed item-specific learning characterizing the first stage of development in the developmental model offered by researchers working in the CxG tradition. Generalization to novel items would be based on analogy with already learned items rather than on an abstracted template (see Ninio, 2006, chapter 4 for a proposal in this spirit).

As the children we are investigating in the present project are three years old or younger, namely, at the start of verbal word-combinations, both kinds of theories place them in the period of item-specific learning; a lexicalist theory, because for it all learning is item-specific in any case, and a CxG-based theory, because for it this is a pre-constructions period when children are supposed to merely accumulate a set of unrelated 'verb-islands' (Tomasello, 2000, 2003). Paradoxically, a lexicalist theory would attribute to children at this stage a better-integrated grammar than would a CxG-based theory, as in a lexicalist theory the lexical-specific syntactic rules are not isolated 'islands' but, rather, they form the integrated syntactic system, whether in adults or in children. This issue will be further discussed in Chapters 2 and 5 of this book.

1.5.4 Establishment of the semantics of constructions

An important component of a theory of CxG concerns the establishment of the semantics associated with formal templates. Goldberg (1995, 2005) offered a testable model of the formation of constructions that serves a dual purpose: it is a learning process by which children acquire abstract phrasal or clausal constructions with their prototypical meaning so that afterwards they can use the meaningful construction template to generate sentences with a variety of different verbs and nouns; and it is also the process that explains how a given phrasal or clausal pattern such as the abstract V–NP–NP format of the ditransitive acquires the prototypical semantics associated with it. According to the claims of this hypothesis, such verbal constructions appear in child-directed speech (CDS) or parental speech with a single very frequent verb, which then gives its own semantics to the constructions. Data supporting this model have been published, using such constructions as the ditransitive, intransitive motion, and caused motion constructions. In all cases, the constructions explored were sentential templates (aka argument structure constructions), consisting of multiple constituents including the verb, its complements, and mostly also some adjuncts. A typical example taken from Goldberg *et al.* (2004) is the Caused Motion construction, whose formal template consists of an optional subject (X), a verb, an object-NP (Y), and a locative expression of some kind, whether a particle, prepositional phrase, an adverb, or any combination of them (Z). As an example of sentences coded as exemplars of this pattern, the article gives the sentence '*What did she put in his eyes?*' said by a mother, showing that order of elements was ignored. We can add some sentences given as examples of what children said, in another part of the study: '*pour some milk in it*', '*throw diaper away!*', '*put another ball in here*', and '*want you in the house*'. The meaning of this construction is said to be 'X causes Y to move Z'. The examples certainly demonstrate that in coding, the researchers did not select a priori for the constructional meaning but for the formal features, as '*want you in the house*' is not, semantically, caused motion. In this study it was found that mothers taken from the Bates *et al.* (1988) corpus express this construction with 43 different verbs, and they use the verb *put* in 38% of the tokens of this construction, which consisted of 99 of a total of 259 exemplars, thus supporting the hypothesis that the single most frequently used verb contributes its semantics to the construction.

It is possible that the rather elaborate constructions usually presented in CxG texts as examples of meaningful patterns with a semantic prototype, are indeed homogeneous semantically, for example, the construction consisting of SVO plus a locative adverb, said to represent Caused Motion. However, if this theory is correct, it should apply also to the core grammatical relations subject–verb, verb–object, and verb–indirect object, our constructions of interest. In the several publications reporting on research regarding the establishment of the prototypical semantics of syntactic constructions (including Goldberg, 1995, 2005; Goldberg *et al.*, 2004; Sethuraman and Goodman, 2004) there is no exploration of the core grammatical relations SV, VO, and VI, whether as phrasal or clausal patterns. If constructions are 'all the way down', they should also include the single-complement SV, VO, and VI patterns. It is interesting to ask whether these constructions behave as the more complicated multielement ones studied in previous studies, namely, whether they possess a prototypical semantics which is the lexical semantics of the verb most frequently used by parents addressing young children. These word-combinations are the most basic, simplest, and most necessary constructions for early child language; if the claims of Construction Grammar as to the units and processes of syntactic development are to apply to early stage of acquisition, we should find the expected high degree of form–function correspondence in parental language for core grammatical relations, too. As we will use a large corpus of parental speech and child speech in this project, we will see in Chapter 4 if we can incorporate grammatical relations into CxG or maybe the term construction should be reserved for idiomatic combinations but not for productive syntax.[23]

In conclusion, various theoretical approaches to syntax have pointed out for us the simplest, most basic syntactic constructions involving verbs in English: the core grammatical relations subject–verb, verb–object, and verb–indirect object. As these syntactic relations form the core of clauses in English, we believe that children need to master them at an early stage of syntactic development in order to lay the foundations of syntactic knowledge. In the rest of this monograph, we shall explore the input and output of syntactic development at its earliest stages, concentrating on parental modelling of the three core grammatical relations in child-directed speech and on children's own early productions of these syntactic patterns.

Notes

1 Note that the term of 'construction' as used in Construction Grammar is not identical to its customary use in linguistics. Constructions in traditional grammar are multiword syntactic strings with given structural features and specific grammatical behaviour, as a rule restricted as to the repertoire of verbs that can be used in the pattern (e.g. Hornby, 1945). However, in this tradition there is no claim that a particular verbal pattern imposed an a priori meaning on the participant verbs and their dependents. In traditional grammar, the point of identifying these patterns and the verbs appearing in them was descriptive, drawing attention to the fact that there is a great deal of arbitrariness in syntax, for instance, in which verb can take an object in the form of a to-infinitive and which, a bare infinitive.

2 In several publications, the fixed part of the frame consisted of pronouns and the variable part, of verbs which are in grammatical terms, their Head (e.g. Childers and Tomasello, 2001; Dodson and Tomasello, 1998; Pine *et al.*, 1998). For example, Pine *et al.* proposed that children acquire a pattern consisting of '*I* + X', *I* being the first-person nominative pronoun and X any verb. In a more recent study of this series (Bannard *et al.*, 2009), the patterns were abstracted by a computer program that allowed any number of words in the sentence to be the 'fixed' part of a frame, with any number of 'slots' in between, using a random search algorithm. For example, one of the patterns the program came up with was 'X *want* X *one*'. Neither the pronoun-centred frames nor the computer-derived ones can be justified on linguistic grounds as constituents of sentence structure. Indeed, they merely represent statistical patterns in which some word happened to be relatively more frequent than an adjacent one in a random collection of word-strings. The items making up such frames do not possess some kind of definable grammatical relations between them,

one that could justify the formula on other grounds than relative frequency, nor explain why one element would be a fixed 'pivot' and the other, a variable 'slot-filler'. Indeed, these statistically derived patterns are offsprings of Braine's (1963) 'Pivot Grammar', using the same criteria as their parent theory to classify words in strings into fixed and variable elements of formulae. However, Pivot Grammar was shown to suffer from serious faults as its rules did not fit well the empirical data it aimed to describe (Bowerman, 1973; Brown, 1973, p. 110). The most fundamental flaw resided in the very logic of basing grammatical categorization on the relative-frequency criterion; if applied consistently, this criterion would result in many cases in both members of some word-combination to be classified as its pivot, just because both of the relevant words appeared multiple times with various different associates (see Ninio, 2006, pp. 24–6). For these and similar faults rising from its purely statistical nature, Pivot Grammar was soon abandoned. At present, it is not clear how the slot-and-frame approach overcomes similar problems. We shall return to test some predictions of this approach in Chapter 5.

3 These frequency-derived formulae are also known as 'low-scope patterns', 'formulaic frames', or 'utterance schemas' (e.g. Dabrowska, 2000; Tomasello, 2003). Often, the variable element of such frames lacking linguistic status is defined as a member of some formal part-of-speech category, such as 'V' in the formula 'I wanna + V'. However, it is unlikely that children who consider 'I wanna' as a frozen expression, unrelated to 'You wanna' and so forth, still are able to classify their vocabulary into verbs and other form-classes, and to choose only verbs to fill the variable slot of such formulae.

4 On the convergence between Chomskian linguistics and Dependency Grammars see Carnie (2008), Chametzky (2000, 2003), Collins (2002), Epstein (1999), Epstein et al. (1998), Hudson (1995), and Miller (1999). For a review, see Ninio (2006, pp. 6–10).

5 A longer summary of the concept of valency can also found in chapter 1 of Ninio (2006).

6 Other authors pointing out lexical substitutability, free word order, or inserted elements in idioms are, for instance, Erman and Warren (2000), Fernando (1996), Fillmore et al. (1988), Fraser (1970), Müller (2006), and Sinclair (1991).

7 In the Minimalist Program, there is a generalized Move operation with residual uses, which, however, some theoreticians claim can be covered by Merge (e.g. Cormack and Smith, 2001). Dependency Grammars have no movement although Hudson's Word Grammar acknowledges a syntactic

role he calls 'visitor' which is reserved for items placed in other than their canonical position in the sentence (1990, p. 192).

8 In grammars formally acknowledging the dependency relation, these more detailed grammatical relations are seen as subtypes of dependency. It has been a central tenet of Dependency Grammar that grammatical relations are related to the universal Dependency unification-relation, the latter building up syntactic connectivity between any and all pairs of words. In some systems (e.g. Mel'cuk, 1979, 1988) it is proposed that there is a set of deep syntactic relations, universal and independent of the surface relations existing in a given language. They are used as labels on the deep-syntactic dependency tree; the surface-syntactic tree is labelled by another set of language-specific grammatical relations. In a monostratal system like Word Grammar (Hudson, 1990) they are used to distinguish subtypes of dependents. In linguistic writings not specifically associated with Dependency Grammar (e.g. Keenan, 1976), grammatical relations are discussed as primitives of grammar without tying them to a general Merger or Dependency relation.

9 Grammatical relations are often called syntactic functions, although some authorities (such as Andrews, 1985) make a differentiation between them that we shall not be following in this work. Sometimes, though, the term syntactic function is used for the case role of the noun-phrases filling the roles of the Dependent (for instance, the subject), rather for the relationship holding between the pair Head–Dependent. In this work, the term grammatical relation or syntactic function will be used to refer to the relationship of the syntactic couplet.

10 In a chapter on control and complementation, Bresnan (1982) lays out in the clearest way possible how her theory of grammar sees grammatical relations. It is worth mentioning a short extract from this text:

> [F]irst, grammatical functions are universal primitives of syntax, not derived from phrase structure representations or from semantic notions; second, grammatical functions are lexically encoded predicate argument structures in varying ways; third, constituent structure categories are universally decomposed into features and types, the features being definable in terms of the primitives SUBJ, OBJ; and fourth, grammatical functions are syntactically encoded directly in surface representations of phrase structure, according to structural configurations or morphological features.
>
> Bresnan (1982, p. 282)

11 Some linguistic systems using grammatical relations as atoms of grammar are so-called traditional grammar: Goldenberg (1989); Lexicase (Starosta, 1988); Functional Grammar (Dik, 1978); Arc-Pair Grammar (Johnson and Postal, 1980); Systemic Grammar (Butler, 1985); Generalized Phrase Structure Grammar (Gazdar *et al.*, 1985); various Unification Grammars

(Covington, 1990; Fraser, 1993; Hellwig, 1986; McCord *et al.*, 1992; Pollard and Sag, 1987; Sleator and Temperley, 1991); and see papers in Cole and Sadock (1977).

12 Not all theories consider grammatical relations primitives; in some, they are derived notions, and see a review by Siewierska and Bakker (in press). In addition, some approaches such as Construction Grammar (e.g. Croft, 2001; Fillmore *et al.*, 1988; Goldberg, 1995) reject grammatical relations as named atoms of syntax. Fillmore *et al.*'s (1988) CxG was developed in order to handle cases that intrinsically went beyond the capacity of generative grammar; their solution was to adopt a different set of units. See section 1.5 for a detailed discussion of the Construction Grammar approach.

13 Psycholinguistic evidence also supports this approach, as argument phrases are easier to process than adjunct phrases; for example, arguments are read faster than adjuncts. For a review, see Pylkkänen and McElree (2006).

14 Agreement or crossmarking is a morphological process, although it is conditional on the presence of the relevant syntactic dependent of the marked verb. Strictly speaking, agreement is not 'syntax' but inflectional morphology, as it generates words, not phrases. Morphological processes do not have the same features as syntactic processes and they tend to be much more rigid than rules regulating syntactic combinations (Hudson, 1990, p. 103); for instance, morphology is characterized by rigid and unchangeable order among the morphemes comprising a word, while syntactic ordering is relatively flexible even in languages considered to have a fixed word order, such as English. Despite some efforts to subsume syntax under morphology or morphology under syntax, mainstream linguistics is clear on the distinction between the two, and see the Chomsky citation in Chapter 1.2, Chomsky, 2000, pp. 10–11).

15 For a detailed treatment of different marking devices, see Nichols (1986).

16 Bresnan proposed that the 'raising' of complement clause arguments with verbs such as *seem, believe, strike* and *appear* or with adjectives such as *unlikely* or *certain*, as well as other grammatical patterns related to 'functional control' is in all languages restricted to subjects (Bresnan, 1982). This appears to be the only subject property which is universal.

17 See, for example, the chapters in Plank (1984).

18 Other authorities connecting hierarchy of grammatical relations and order of composition of arguments with the verb are, for example, Dowty

(1982), Hudson (1990), Keenan (1979), Larson (1988), Pollard and Sag (1987); but cf. Lambek (1958), Steedman (1988).

19 See Culicover and Jackendoff (2005, p. 191) on the uneasy treatment of Government-Binding/Principles-and-Parameters theory of indirect objects. They mention that this theory has only two 'structural cases', the nominative and the accusative, and it resorts to complicated measures to deal with the anomaly presented by indirect objects.

20 Some authorities suggest a distinction between primary objects and secondary objects instead of, or in addition to, the direct–indirect object differentiation (e.g. Dryer, 1986). A discussion of this topic is beyond the scope of the present work.

21 It should be mentioned that according to some authorities CxG suffers from as yet unresolved theoretical weaknesses, see Holmes and Hudson (2005), Hudson (2008), Jackendoff (1996, 1997), and Müller (2006) for details.

22 Other developmental studies employing Dependency or Minimalist principles are Green (1997), MacWhinney (1975, 1982), Ninio (1994a, 1996), Powers (2002), Radford (1990), Robinson (1986), and Van Langendonck (1987), among others.

23 Two older theories of development, both nativist in their orientation, made strong claims about children using innate knowledge regarding regular and universal links between syntax and semantics in their acquisition of syntactic knowledge. Gleitman's (1990) syntactic bootstrapping hypothesis and Pinker's (1989) semantic bootstrapping hypothesis both assume that there is in fact a ruleful mapping of syntactic roles to semantic roles and the converse which the child can make use of in acquisition, and, indeed, must make use of, as otherwise the input is too degenerate and the learning task too complicated. It goes without saying that work in linguistics reviewed in this chapter, as well as the present lexicalist theory offered by Chomsky (2000), do not afford the theoretical premises on which these acquisition theories are based. Interestingly, recent studies on children's syntactic development, whether experimental or cross-linguistic, offer quite decisive empirical counter-evidence to these bootstrapping hypotheses (Bowerman and Brown, 2008; Jaakkola and Akhtar, 2000).

Chapter 2

Registers and corpora

According to Roger Brown (1973), syntactic development in children occurs in several well-demarcated stages. The basics of syntactic knowledge are laid down in Stage I, which is devoted to the development of semantic roles and grammatical relations in the simple sentence. In subsequent stages, children will engage in the modulation of meaning, and acquire more complex constructions, embedding, and coordination. In Stage I, though, the focus is on the basics. This stage of development is the subject matter of our present project.

In order to map the input to early syntactic development and its output, we adopted the approach of Corpus Linguistics and build two large corpora, one of 1.5 million running words representing English parental speech to young children, and the other of 200,000 running words, representing Stage I speech by young children acquiring English as their first language. Hand-parsing the corpora for the three core grammatical relations SV, VO, and VI, we obtained a large sample of spontaneous tokens of these three relations, close to 350,000 for parents and 26,000 for children. Samples of this size make it possible to employ the analytic tools of Lexical Statistics (Baayen, 2001; Zipf, 1935/1965) and Statistical Physics (Albert and Barabási, 2002) in order to gain a fresh look at parental and early child core grammar.

2.1 Corpora in a developmental study

In order to compare child-directed English which is the input to learning, to children's productions, we need a good estimate of both. For various historical reasons to be detailed below (see section 2.2), we have only partial and fragmented knowledge on how parents present the core syntax of the English language to young children and how the core syntax children construct, looks like in comparison.

This situation can be rectified as the field as a collective has accumulated all the raw data necessary for the conduction of a respectable corpus-based linguistic project. CHILDES—the Child Language Data Exchange System—is a public domain database for corpora on first and second language acquisition

(MacWhinney and Snow, 1985, 1990). The publicly available, shared archive contains documentation of the speech of more than 500 English-speaking parents addressed to their young children, and almost the same number of records of the early parent-addressed speech of English-speaking children. Although each separate study is by necessity limited in its coverage of the phenomenon, whether because of too scanty sampling of contexts and conversations between parent and child, or because children are usually spoken to by other people as well besides their own mothers or fathers, the different studies pooled together can provide the requisite solid database for generalization.

In order to be able to make a valid generalization about the characteristics of child speech, we built a large and systematically constructed corpus of speech produced, collectively, by the English-speaking children of the CHILDES archive and a parallel corpus of parental child-directed speech based on all English-speaking parents on CHILDES.

The use of pooled corpora of unrelated mothers as a representation of the linguistic input is a relatively conventional move in child language research,[1] and there have also been some studies in which child speech was characterized on the basis of pooled corpora. The pooling of different speakers into a single corpus is usually justified by the fact that the speech of different parents to their young children is quite similar (e.g. Huttenlocher *et al.*, 1991, and see also in section 2.2.1). As we mentioned above, multiple speakers of child-directed speech may provide a good estimate of the total linguistic input to which children are exposed, which includes, besides the speech of the individual mother or father, also the speech of grandparents, aunts and uncles, older siblings and other family members, neighbours, care professionals, and so forth—represented in our corpus by the speech of mothers and fathers unrelated to the individual child. Such a corpus creates a stricter than usual test of the claim that children's productions follow the implicit rules exhibited by the input, because the pooled database represents the *normative* rules of language behaviour exhibited by the community as a whole when addressing young children, rather than the behaviour of the individual mother who may well adopt forms of expression created by her child.

Although there have been previous studies that used pooled corpora, the novelty in the present project is in the size of the corpus: Basically, we have taken sizable samples of the speech of all English-speaking parents and young children on the CHILDES archive, excluding only a few for technical reasons.

This research strategy has its own existence and justification in the field of linguistics where it is known as 'corpus-based linguistics'. This approach has as its goal the empirically-based characterization of languages, dialects, or registers, when large corpora—namely, systematically constructed collections of texts by multiple speakers—are analysed to arrive at an empirically grounded generalization about a language or language registers.[2] In applying such a methodology to a developmental question, we are relying on the evidence detailed below according to which child-directed parental speech is a distinct kind of identifiable language style with characteristics of its own, and so is early child speech.

Corpus-based linguistics is applied in cases when the focus of interest is not an individual speaker (or writer) but a whole variety of language. Large corpora covering the speech of many different English-speaking parents or young children can give an accurate picture of, respectively, child-directed speech and early child speech, averaging out local dialect differences and idiosyncratic speaking habits, and representing the central tendencies of the language variety. Assembling a broad speaker basis should result in more representative results, reflecting the linguistic norms of the speech registers.

Our research strategy is slightly unusual in the study of child language development and worth explicating. Rather than following the course of development of individual children, the focus of our investigation is the features and characteristics of early child utterances in general, which we compare to the characteristics of parental child-directed speech. Given that parental speech is the major input for, as well as the target of acquisition for young children, the comparison tells us to what extent children's early language resembles, or falls short of, the immediate developmental target. Expecting children to eventually reach the level modelled by parental speech, child and parental speech thus represent two developmental periods in syntactic acquisition, an earlier and a later stage. For obvious reasons, we expect early child syntax to be simpler and more restricted than the syntax of parental speech; how the two syntactic systems differ is yet to be established. We are interested in gauging the degree to which children's syntax is similar to parents'; both similarities and differences are considered data for a theory of acquisition.

In addition, this research strategy is also suggested by the principles of Complexity Theory according to which the important aspects of complex systems such as language are the global, macroscale characteristics of the system considered as a whole (Barabási and Albert, 1999; Watts and Strogatz, 1998). Such features are manifest only when the system is measured as an aggregate, which in our case means looking at a corpus pooling many speakers and a large number of the relevant sentences rather than looking at individual utterances produced by individual speakers. In the present chapter (in section 2.4) we shall report on the distribution of the three core grammatical relations in parental and child speech, mapping out the composition of the clausal core as a whole in the two language registers of interest. Similarly, we will ask in Chapter 5 about the shape of the rank-frequency distribution of different verbs serving as the Heads of the three grammatical relations, a central analytic question in the characterization of complex systems. Such global comparisons will help us pinpoint the similarities and differences between the parental input and children's output of early syntax.

In summary, the two corpora will estimate, respectively, the parental register and the child dialect of English. We shall turn now to a more formal definition of these language styles.

2.2 **The parental register**

It is generally believed that there exists a special style or *register* of English language that is used when parents and other caretakers address infants and young children.

A register is a socially defined variety of language, its vocabulary, phonology, prosody, morphology, syntax, and pragmatics all potentially influenced by its context of use (Crystal, 1987). One of the most prominent researchers of this topic, Halliday, pointed out that the concept of registers refers to the fact that speakers possess a large repertoire of language varieties, and they make a choice from among them in different situations (Halliday, 1964, 1978; and see also Biber, 1995). On all criteria, parental speech addressed to young children is a specific register of English. Interaction with infants and young children apparently elicits from caretakers and other adults this distinct style of speech,[3] just like interaction with their bank manager probably elicits from them a relatively formal code of address.

We believe, together with most researchers in the field, that the linguistic input to syntactic learning is not all of the English language but a specific subset of it; for young children, the major input is child-directed caretaker speech.[4] In this study, we use a large sample of parental child-addressed speech, pooled over many different speakers, as our data on this genre of speech. Multiple speakers are thought to represent better the total linguistic input to which children are exposed as compared with the speech of the child's individual mother or father. As we said above, the other parents in the sample are thought to represent the speech of grandparents, aunts and other family members; friends and neighbours; nannies, baby minders, daycare centre professionals, and other child-care providers, and so forth, who also talk to the child. According to the literature, this type of speech possesses some unique features and it is best considered a unique speech register; however, there also exists some variability in individual speakers' use of the same register, and our employment of a corpus pooled over multiple speakers is a way of representing not only the register in general but also the variability inherent to it.

2.2.1 **Previous studies of the parental register**

The existence, features, and possible role in development of a parental child-directed speech register was one of the characteristic preoccupations of empiricist researchers in the mid-twentieth century. Many journal articles as well as edited collections were devoted to the subject, for instance Snow and Ferguson's (1977) *Talking to children* and von Raffler-Engel and Lebrun's (1976) *Baby talk and infant speech*. These publications treated the parental register as representing alterations, modifications, or adjustments that speakers make when interacting with young language-learning children, when the comparison was to speech addressed to adults or older children. The parental register was thought to be different from standard adult-addressed speech in several characteristic ways and these included being syntactically simpler (e.g. Sachs *et al.*, 1976; Snow, 1972).

These researchers maintained that the speech style they are documenting is an established register, namely, a type of language use that is shared by different speakers in the same use situation. For instance, the title of Ferguson's (1977) chapter was 'Baby talk as a simplified register'. This claim was based initially on researchers' intuition that they see familiar kinds of simplifications in different parents' speech. These intuitions were later backed by solid empirical evidence: When researchers began to study the speaking style of largish groups of parents addressing young children and to systematically compare the speech of unrelated parents, they found a considerable degree of similarity (e.g. Huttenlocher *et al.*, 1991; Vihman *et al.*, 1994). The degree of similarity found more than justifies the title 'register'.

2.2.2 **Features of syntax in the parental register**

As our present focus is on the syntax of core grammatical relations, it should be noted that, on this topic, past studies of the parental register are not particularly informative. The studies conducted in the mid-twentieth century concentrated on syntactic features of whole sentences, finding that they contained, on average, fewer words and morphemes, fewer hierarchically embedded units such as subordinate clauses, and fewer conjoined clauses than adult-addressed speech. On the basis of such findings, it was concluded that sentences in parental speech addressed to young children are syntactically simpler than the sentences of adult–adult talk (Furrow *et al.*, 1979; Newport *et al.*, 1977; Phillips, 1973; Snow, 1972, 1977a).

Although these features are characteristic of speech addressed by parents to young children in general, there are interesting age-related differences in their intensity. First, when the children are about two years of age, parental speech slowly starts to converge on adult-addressed speech, increasing in length and variability of vocabulary (Fraser and Roberts, 1975; Furrow and Nelson, 1986; Kaye, 1980; Nelson, 1973; Snow, 1986; Stern *et al.*, 1983). It takes about eight years of gradual change for parental speech to reach an adult level of syntactic complexity (Phillips, 1973). Before children turn two, there are few differences as a function of children's age, including before or after the onset of speech at around 12 months (Henning *et al.*, 2005; Kavanaugh and Jirkovsky, 1982; Nelson *et al.*, 1984; Newport *et al.*, 1977; Snow, 1977b). It is possible that speech to young infants below the age of eight months is actually more complex than at eight months and above (Sherrod *et al.*, 1977; but see Kaye, 1980).

We might summarize with Phillips (1973) that parental speech shows a floor effect and that at no age of the children do parents use simpler sentences than sentences with 4.0 MLU (mean length of utterance measured in morphemes). It appears that for the first two years of their children's lives, parents simplify their speech to a level of minimal complexity needed for communication which is about 4.0 MLU. Given that English is a considerably isolating language with little morphology, this means that parental sentences are, on the average, somewhere between three and four words long during this period. On the basis of such a low MLU, we may expect parental sentences to consist of little more verbal syntax than core grammatical relations.

In a study of the parental input to syntactic development, it is of special interest to establish the size of parents' verb repertoires in the core grammatical relations. Unfortunately, there is practically no information on this issue, leaving it to be explored in the present study. We do know that, in general, parents' vocabulary when addressing young children is less diverse than when they speak to older children or to other adults, including their repertoire of different verbs (Broen, 1972; Hayes and Ahrens, 1988; Phillips, 1973). We cannot estimate on the basis of previous studies how many different verbs adults typically employ when using basic grammar to young children, although we may assume without making a serious mistake that the range is smaller than in other discourse.

As to more recent investigations of the input, Naigles, Hoff, and their colleagues carried out several studies that explored, among other things, grammatical relations in parental speech; however, in these studies a small set of a priori defined verbs were targeted rather than the total verbal repertoire. For example, Naigles and Hoff-Ginsberg (1998) targeted 25 verbs; Naigles and Hoff (2006) targeted 17 verbs in the first study of input in this publication and 30 in the second study; and the recent Naigles *et al.* (2009) study explored 34 verbs in the input. Given that parents probably use over 1000 different verbs when addressing their young children, these numbers represent a very low proportion of the total parental repertoire and this restricts the generality of their findings. For some research questions, the a priori choice of verbs in these studies is rather unfortunate, see section 2.5.2 on the relative frequency of subjects and objects, and section 4.2.2 on the prevalence of light verbs in early child speech.

In present-day Construction Grammar-oriented studies, the constructions studied are, as a rule, rather elaborate multi-element sentential templates rather than the two-element subject–verb, verb–object, or verb–indirect object patterns, although the latter are constructions, too, according to the theory (section 1.5.4). We might, therefore, consider the present exploration of core grammatical relations in the parental register a contribution to CxG's literature on the parental origins of some of the more simple phrasal constructions in children's speech.

2.3 The child dialect

One of the goals of this project was to characterize the syntax of young English-speaking children's speech, in order to compare its features with those of parental speech. Similar to the group of parents, we are treating young children acquiring English as their first language as a homogeneous group, as far as the important characteristics of their syntax is concerned. In this, we are in the tradition of researchers who examine pooled corpora of child speech for various characteristics thought to reflect on the relevant class of child speakers (Radford, 1990; Serratrice *et al.*, 2003).

It is clear that the term register is less appropriate for children's early productions than for parental child-directed speech. One of the ideas behind the notion of registers is that the speaker is in possession of the totality of the language and that in a given type of context or communicative situation, he or she chooses a specific subset of the total repertoire of language forms in order to adapt to the demands of that specific social situation (Halliday, 1977). Young children, however, do not select the forms to employ with their parents out of a larger repertoire that they already possess in that language but rather, they probably use their complete repertoire with them. Therefore, young children's speech is better described as an *age dialect* (Bright, 1997; Chambers, 1995; Wardhaugh, 1992). If a register is a variation in language according to context of use, a dialect is a variation in language according to the users, whether they form a regional or social group (the best-known examples), or whether its speakers are distinguished by some individual characteristic as their gender or age (Biber, 1995). If child speech is similar across different English-speaking children in its major syntactic features, it can be thought of as a proper dialect. This is probably the case, as the restricted syntactic characteristics derive from similar developmental limitations in different children.[5]

As mentioned in Chapter 1, we are focusing on the first period of word-combinations involving verbs, targeting an age group upper bound by three and a half years of age. This period is best known as Brown's (1973) Stage I of English-speaking children's language. In previous investigations of child syntax, this period is often seen as a child dialect with characteristic features of its own, its syntax to some extent dissimilar to adult syntax. We are beyond children's very first word-combinations which were sometimes thought to be generated by production rules quite alien to adult syntax, such as Pivot Grammar (Braine, 1963) or some semantics-based rules (as in Brown's own conceptualization). In fact, it is safe to generalize that in the last two decades there is a quiet consensus in the field that children's verb-related word-combinations are generated by a syntax fundamentally similar to adult syntax, something along the lines of bona fide grammatical relations. Nor is there much dispute regarding the lexical specificity of children's early syntactic combinations. Since the early days of the modern study of child language, researchers such as Maratsos (1983) have repeatedly pointed out the piecemeal, item-specific nature of early grammatical learning, displayed in the lack of uniformity in the morphosyntactic frames in which different verbs appear in the same period.[6] This includes also the two linguistics-based theories contrasted in Chapter 1. As the children we are investigating are almost all three years old or younger (see section 2.4), both a lexicalist theory and a CxG-based one place them in the period of item-specific learning; a lexicalist theory, because for it all learning is item-specific in any case, and a CxG-based theory, because for it this is a pre-constructions period when children are said to acquire verb-specific combinatory patterns. It seems quite settled in the field that, initially, young children learn grammatical rules for specific words in a piecemeal fashion.

Opinions are divided, however, regarding the degree of organization of children's syntactic system in this first period of syntax. For researchers working in the CxG tradition, the period of item-specific word-combinations is a pre-grammatical phase, in which children accumulate an inventory of largely unrelated 'verb-island' constructions. It is thought that there are very few structural relationships among these constructional islands, and, in fact, children do not at this stage possess an 'overarching grammar of their language', in the expression used by Tomasello (2006, p. 263).

On a lexicalist theory, on the other hand, the existence of item-specific syntactic rules stored in the lexicon is the adult norm and not a more primitive level of organization characteristic of pre-grammatical children. Accordingly, item-specific learning, by itself, does not deem children's early period of syntax a phase lacking in overall organization. Evidence such as transfer and mutual facilitation between different lexical-specific combinations at the very start of verb-based combinations (Abbot-Smith and Behrens, 2006; Keren-Portnoy, 2006; Kiekhoefer, 2002; Ninio, 1999a,b, 2003) seems to point to the presence of well-established structural relationships among the different item-based constructions. The accelerating learning curve is just one kind of manifestation of possible connectivity and systematicity in children's developing grammar. Under a lexicalist theory, there should be others, and, in this project, we shall be able to see if they indeed exist.

2.4 **Building the parental and child corpora**

As discussed earlier, we followed the methodology of corpus-based linguistics and built two pooled corpora of transcribed speech, one of English-speaking parents and the other of young children acquiring English as their first language. Both corpora were based on the publicly available English samples transcribed and stored on the CHILDES archive (MacWhinney and Snow, 1985, 1990).

CHILDES is a 45-million-word collection of spoken texts in the public domain. Transcriptions of native English speakers comprise a large part of it. We created a systematic English-language parental corpus and a child corpus, by methodologically sampling the CHILDES archive. Parents and children from different English-speaking countries and dialects were included, from Great Britain as well as the United States. In building our corpora, we followed closely the principles established in linguistics for constructing systematically assembled large corpora (e.g. Francis and Kučera, 1979; Sinclair, 1991; Svartvik, 1990). Details on the construction of the corpora appear in Appendix A to this chapter.

Our analysed corpora consist of close to 1.5 million running words for parents and 200,000 running words for children.[7] The number of participant speakers is 506 in the parents' corpus and 421 in the child corpus.[8] The corpora represents several hundred hours of transcribed speech based on naturalistic observations.

The parental corpus compares well in size with the first-generation of large computerized corpora of English. The Brown Corpus of American English contains almost exactly 1 million running words of text (1,014,312), and the Lancaster–Oslo–Bergen (LOB) British Corpus is also about 1 million words (Francis and Kučera, 1979; Johansson et al., 1978). As many characterizations of these two corpora have been published, we can compare our parental register, of the same magnitude, to both these corpora that are thought to represent adult–adult English language. Such a comparison can give an indication of the relative prevalence of various interesting patterns of English usage, and reveal what, if anything, is special about child-directed speech in those respects.

2.4.1 Building the corpora

We selected projects among the ones available on CHILDES by applying a set of criteria regarding the age of the children in the project and the nature of the interaction recorded, when we only target naturalistic interaction between parents and children, and children below the age of 3;6. The details of the selection process appear in Appendix A to this chapter. This process resulted in the selection of parents and children from 33 research projects in the CHILDES archive: the British projects Belfast, Howe, Korman, Manchester, and Wells, and the American projects Bates, Bernstein-Ratner, Bliss, Bloom 1970 and 1973, Brent, Brown, Clark, Cornell, Demetras, Feldman, Gleason, Harvard Home-School, Higginson, Kuczaj, MacWhinney, McMillan, Morisset, New England, Peters-Wilson, Post, Rollins, Sachs, Suppes, Tardif, Valian, Van Houten, and Warren-Leubecker.

From these projects, we selected 471 observational studies of parent–child dyads involving a target child of the correct age range. In 35 of the studies there were two active parents interacting with the target child, resulting in a parental sample of 506 different parents. Of the 471 children, 50 did not produce utterances with verbal grammar, resulting in a child sample of 421 different children who produced our to-be-analysed child speech corpus. Tables 2.3 and 2.4 in Appendix A to this chapter present the number of parents and children selected, according to the research project in which the data was originally collected.

After deciding which observational studies and which speakers to sample, we applied a set of criteria for the inclusion of utterances in the parental or child corpora, checking the speaker, addressee, and spontaneity of speech, and restricting the individual contribution of each speaker to the corpus to 3000 sentences, as detailed in Appendix A. The utterances selected were addressed by the parents solely to their own (target) child. As for the age of the target child talked to, 93% of the parents in the sample talked to a child between one year and two and a half years of age, in all or the majority of the observations we included. A few parents talked to younger children, some only six weeks old, or to older children, up to three and a half years of age. Thus, although we did not intend this result, the parental corpus mainly represents speech to children in the 1;0–2;6 age range.

The resultant parental corpus contains a total of 1,470,811 running words— almost 1.5 million—of transcribed speech based on naturalistic observations of interaction between parents and their young children.

We built the children's corpus in a similar manner, limiting the age of the children to three and a half years and restricting the contribution of each individual child to 300 multiword sentences (see Appendix A for details of the method of construction). We did not measure the MLUs of children in the corpus and it was not a selection criterion. However, we do have in the corpus utterances of the three children in Roger Brown's original sample, Adam, Eve, and Sarah, which we included in accordance with the criteria employed for all children, namely, the first 300 multiword utterances from the start of observations. For these children, we can establish the resulting MLU based on Brown's own estimates (1973, pp. 74–80). Our sample of Adam's speech is from 27 months, which is within Stage I for this child as, according to Brown, this stage ends for Adam at 28 months; our sample of Eve is between 18 and 18.5 months, which is Stage I for Eve, since Stage I ends at 20 months for this child; and our sample for Sarah is between 27 and 28.5 months, again, within Stage I, which ends at 29 months for Sarah according to Brown's estimates. In other words, taking the first 300 multiword utterances from the start of observations for children below the age of 3 and half years appears to tap into Brown's Stage I speech.

Using the criteria detailed in Appendix A, we built a child corpus of almost 200,000 running words, more precisely 194,359 words. The children's corpus contained 101,064 utterances; this makes the mean MLUs in words 1.92. The mean age of the children was 2;0.29 (namely, almost exactly 2;1) with a standard deviation of 0;4.09.

Although the size and age information of the total corpus is relevant for an evaluation of the results, in actuality these totals are not very informative for our focus of interest which is syntactic expressions of the three core grammatical relations. In particular, young children tend to produce multiword utterances built on other pivots besides verbs, such as '*more X*'; this was true also for our corpus. Hence, the truly relevant statistics come from subsets of the corpora consisting of exemplars of subject–verb, verb–object and verb–dative object relations. We shall turn now to these data.

2.5 Distribution of grammatical relations in the clausal core

2.5.1 Coding for grammatical relations

The corpora were hand-parsed for the three core syntactic relations subject–verb, verb–object, and verb–dative object.[9] Parsing rules were based on the principles of the Minimalist Program (Chomsky, 1995a) and English Word Grammar (Hudson, 1990). For details, we followed rather closely the traditional definitions of these grammatical relations, in particular Allerton (1982), Hornby (1945), and Quirk *et al.* (1985). For methodological details, see Appendix B to this chapter.[10]

2.5.2 Tokens in the clausal core

In the parents' corpus, we identified a total of 338,970 tokens of the three core syntactic relations. In the children's corpus, we found a total of 25,796 tokens. Table 2.1 and Figures 2.1a and 2.1b present the distribution of the tokens by syntactic relation, in the parents' and in the children's corpus. Table 2.1 also gives the number of different verbs used in generating the relevant grammatical relation.

The first thing to notice in Table 2.1 and Figure 2.1 is the amazing similarity in the distribution of the three core grammatical relations in the parents' and the children's corpora. Despite the large difference in the size of the sample on which the estimates are based, and in the number of different verbs used, the relative frequency of subject–verb, verb–object, and verb–dative object is almost identical in the two samples.

The similarity is the more impressive because of the unexpected shape of the distribution: SV tokens take up a majority with close to 60% of the tokens, next comes VO with 40% or more of the tokens, and far behind, VI with a paltry 1–2% of the tokens. The almost-disappearance of verbs with dative objects is not a result we would expect intuitively, as both parents and children surely say things like *gimme*—which we coded as the bona fide *give me* combination, as we did all contractions. However, the corpora cannot be argued with: dative objects are very infrequent.

Just to be sure we are not missing indirect objects only because we excluded prepositional *to*-objects from this study, we coded for them as well. In the parental corpus we found 2482 tokens of prepositional *to*-objects, in the child corpus

Table 2.1 Distribution of syntactic relations in parents' and children's corpora

Syntactic relation	Parents			Children		
	Tokens	Percent	Number of verbs	Tokens	Percent	Number of verbs
SV	195,206	57.6%	601	14,375	55.7%	220
VO	137,756	40.6%	776	11,115	43.1%	238
VI	6,008	1.8%	66	305	1.2%	24
Total core	338,970			25,795		

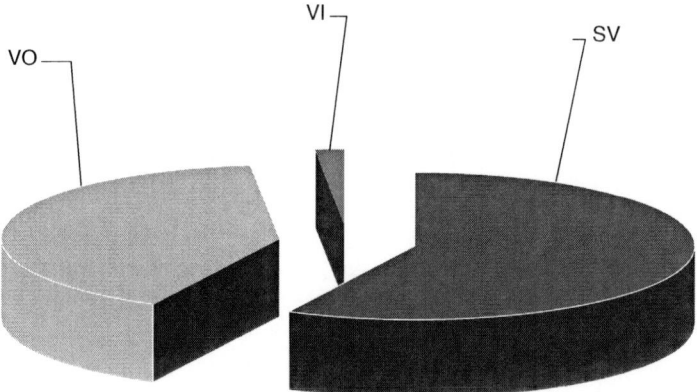

Fig. 2.1a Relative frequency of three basic syntactic relations in corpora: parents.

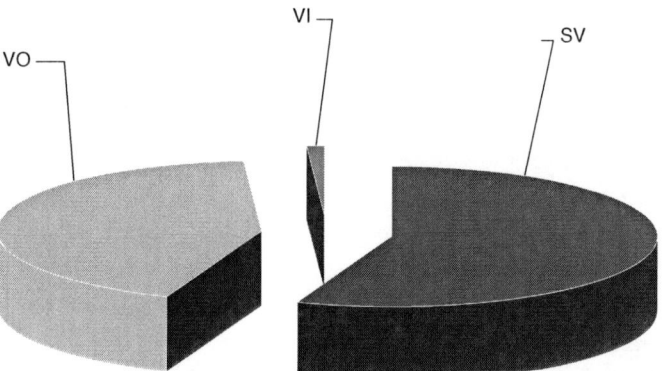

Fig. 2.1b Relative frequency of three basic syntactic relations in corpora: children.

we found 58 tokens. Thus, even if we combine the two forms of expression of indirect objects, VI is still very infrequent in these speech registers, relative to subjects and direct objects. In fact, the prepositional indirect objects are much less frequent than the dative objects in both parental and child speech. In the case of children, a prepositional object puts them at a disadvantage because the combination with the verb requires three words at the minimum while the subject–verb, verb–object and verb–dative object combinations require only two. However, prepositional indirect objects are disfavoured even by adult speakers who probably do not have a problem with adding another word to the length of a clause.

The finding that children produce more expressed subjects than objects was unexpected in view of a recent publication (Naigles *et al.*, 2009) that concluded that young children of a quite similar age range as our sample, produce more VO tokens than SV tokens at this developmental period:

> [...] only 32% (SD = 22%) of the verb tokens were produced with overt subjects. Overt direct objects were more common, produced with an average of 46% of the tokens (SD = 25%). [...] Similar findings obtained when calculations were performed by verb [...] On average, then, the children more frequently produced verbs with direct objects than with subjects.
>
> Naigles *et al.* (2009, p. 35)

The contradictory findings are worrisome until we realize that while our results are based on corpus data that covers the complete verb repertoire of young children, Naigles *et al.* base their analysis on just 34 chosen verbs. Inspection of the verbs included in the Naigles *et al.* study reveals the reason for the conflicting results: the verb *be* was not included among the 34 common verbs they studied, so, unfortunately, the study misses the one most frequently occurring verb in the SV pattern. As we shall see in Chapter 4, this verb accounts for no less than 60% of all tokens with a subject, hence its exclusion severely depressed the estimate of how many subjects were expressed by children. As Tomasello and Brandt (2009) pointed out, some frequent transitive verbs were also not included by Naigles *et al.* in their study, such as *make, do,* and *have*. These verbs, however, do not appear in child speech nearly as frequently with a direct object as *be* does with a subject (their combined share of tokens is about 16%), thus their exclusion does not counterbalance that of *be* in the overall estimate of subjects and objects in that study. In general, a corpus is more accurate than a sample of verbs for overall estimates of token frequencies, as a sample is biased by inclusion and exclusion criteria. Hence, it is probably the correct generalization that young children in the Stage I period express about 30% more overt subjects with verbs than direct objects, as we can observe in Table 2.1.

2.5.3 Age at production

Figure 2.2 presents the distribution of children's ages when producing word-combinations expressing the core syntactic relations SV, VO, or VI, in categories of 6 months.

Figure 2.2 show that we built a corpus of early syntax in child speech in which child ages distribute in an approximately normal, bell-shaped function around the modal category 2;0–2;6. The shape of the distribution and the concrete statistics demonstrate that in actuality the corpus represents the syntax of children three years old and younger, as 98.6% of all syntactic word-combinations in the corpus were produced by children at this age range and only a very small proportion of the data, merely 1.4%, was produced by children who were over three years of age. Moving down one age category, it is

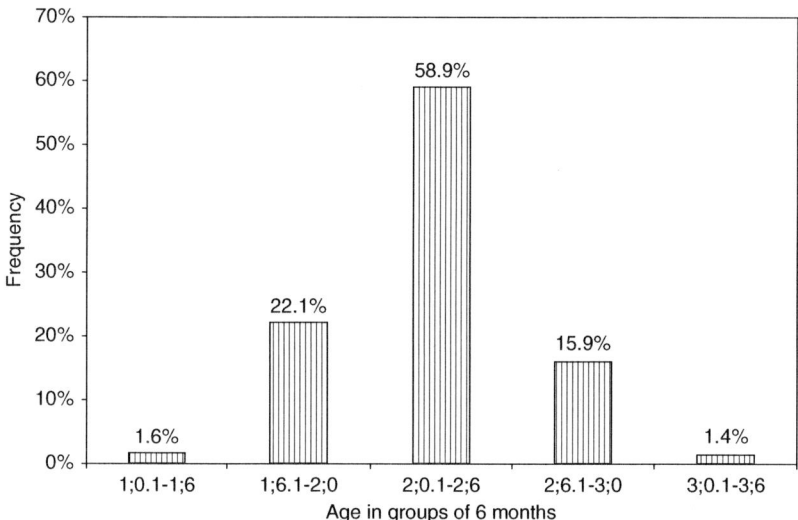

Fig. 2.2 Distribution of child age in months in the corpus of three grammatical relations.

evident that in fact the great majority of exemplars were provided by children under two and a half years of age, more precisely, 82.7%.

As we saw in the previous section, children did not produce exemplars of SV, VO, and VI in equal numbers. We now consider the possibility that the observed differences in use frequency in children's speech reflect the order of acquisition, so that the relatively infrequently used grammatical relations occur infrequently because they begin to be generated at a later age than the relatively frequent ones. Given the upper limit on the age of the children in the corpus, a late-emerging syntactic construction has less chance to be produced during the period sampled by the corpus, hence even if the relevant construction were equally popular in use (once acquired), it would show up as an infrequent one in the total corpus. Such an age effect would not account for the frequency differential in parental speech, although if an age effect were found, it might also influence parental speech by 'fine tuning'. Table 2.2 presents the mean and standard deviations of the age of the children producing tokens of the three core grammatical relations in the corpus.

The results are clear: there is no difference between the ages of the children producing the three grammatical relations in the corpus. All three patterns average at two years, three and a half months in the sample, with four months' standard deviation. It seems the frequency differential is not a result of differences in the age of emergence of the SV, VO, and VI patterns for young children.

Table 2.2 Age of children producing tokens of the three core grammatical relations in the corpus

Grammatical relation	Tokens	Mean age	Standard deviation
SV	14,375	2;3.20	0;4.0
VO	11,115	2;3.12	0;4.3
VI	305	2;3.13	0;4.6
All 3 grammatical relations	25,795	2;3.17	0;4.1

Recall that in the total corpus (including also non-verbal sentences) the mean age was 2;1 (also with a four months' SD), namely, we apparently managed to catch the children a little before the production of verb-based word-combinations started. This promises that if there were a true difference in order of emergence, we would have indeed seen it in the means and standard deviations. The absence of such an age effect demonstrates that the relative frequency of some syntactic combination in the corpus does not necessarily reflect the age of emergence of that pattern—we tend to assume it does. In any case, when it comes to the frequency differential observed in the use frequency of the three core grammatical relations, we should consider other effects and not a staggered order of acquisition.

2.6 Conclusions: children recreate parents' clausal core

2.6.1 Recreating the Accessibility Hierarchy

Interestingly, it seems parents as well as young children use core grammatical relations in their speech in proportions reflecting the hierarchy of verbal dependents, or the Accessibility Hierarchy of linguistics (see section 1.4.1). The higher a dependent of the verb is on the hierarchy, the more it is used in parental and child registers. The highest dependent, namely, the subject, is the most frequently used, then the second-highest which is the direct object, and the least frequent of the three is the dative object which takes third place on the hierarchy. We can also add the prepositional indirect object as being on the fourth position on the hierarchy, and our frequency estimates place it as even less frequent in use than the dative-object form. In addition, the first two positions on the hierarchy—namely, the subject and the direct object—are indisputably in the clausal core, whereas the dative/indirect object, as we mentioned in section 1.4.1, is of questionable core status. Quite unexpectedly, the linguistic constructs of clausal core versus periphery, as well as the Accessibility Hierarchy, translate to relative frequency of use, and this is in two speech regimes where the clause is maximally simplified. Apparently, being in the core indeed means the element is necessary for the clause, and the higher on the hierarchy within the core, the more likely that the dependent will be syntactically expressed, at least in child-directed speech and in children's own early speech.[11] I must admit I could not find another empirical study making such a connection.[12]

Although the relative frequency of the three core relations averages over different kinds of sentences types, some of which, such as imperatives, do not usually have an expressed subject, it seemed possible that the higher use frequency of subject over the other two relations may be related to English making the overt expression of subjects obligatory in declarative and interrogative clauses. To check this possibility, we computed the relative frequency of the three core grammatical relations in a Hebrew-language maternal corpus (Ninio, 2009). Hebrew is a nominative/accusative language with an SVO word order like English, but, having a richer verbal agreement system, first- and second-person subjects are omitted in the past and future. Despite the difference in obligatoriness, in Hebrew, too, there were more SV than VO relations expressed in the corpus, and the least frequent were VI relations. Of a total of 43,310 exemplars, the proportion of SV combinations was 48.1%, while that of VO and VI was only 33.4% and 18.5%, respectively. It seems that despite the partial pro-drop character of Hebrew, SV combinations are still the most frequent syntactic combinations in the core, and no less so than in English. Although obligatoriness of subjects in English in declarative and interrogative clauses may contribute to the frequency of subjects, this factor obviously does not fully account for the ordering of the three core relations.

The constructs of clausal core and the Accessibility Hierarchy are backed up by a set of grammatical behaviours in the language, and, in general terms, they summarize central organizational features of a particular language. It is not immediately obvious how these features—e.g. order of unification, semantic tailoring, possibility of topicalization—add up to the relative importance of verbal dependents for speakers who are motivated to say the most with the simplest verbal means. But, add up they do, opening up a new direction of inquiry into what makes certain clausal elements but not others, important for conveying communicative messages with a minimum of investment.

2.6.2 **A global similarity**

The most surprising finding of this chapter is, undoubtedly, the close similarity of children's use pattern of the three core grammatical relations to the parents' proportions of use. Whatever is the reason for parents' distribution of the subject–verb, verb–object, and verb–dative object relations in their speech, children recreate the same distribution, although they use a much smaller repertoire of verbs than do parents. There are obvious quantitative differences between child speech and parental speech, and, as we discussed earlier (section 2.3), children probably need to continue to accumulate item-specific syntactic knowledge for quite a while until they catch up with the parental verbal lexicon. Regardless of the quantitative gap between child speech and parental register, children's speech appears to have already caught up |with parental speech at the least with respect to this global feature. It appears that young children's dialect may differ from the parental register in concrete, local characteristics, for instance, parents may use some verb or other which children never yet use; but still, children's core syntactic system could already be rather similar to the parental system in its various global features. This is our first hint that children are not qualitatively different in their syntactic system from parents, even at this early stage. Given the global similarity in the distribution of the three core relations, it is likely that the dynamics generating it is similar in parents and children. Namely, whatever causes the relative weights of the three core grammatical relations to be as they are, operates similarly in parental and child speech. This is an exciting possibility and we shall try to substantiate it throughout the rest of the book.

Appendix A: **Building the parental and child corpora**

A modern professional language corpus is a collection of written or spoken texts which has been compiled so that it has maximum representativeness for the language variety it aims to sample. This means that the corpus is designed and constructed systematically, based on a set of clearly defined criteria. We observed these principles and applied clear criteria in the construction of the pooled corpora of this project, to be described in the following sections.

A.1 **Selecting speech samples for inclusion**

We aimed to sample the speech of normally developing young children and their parents, native speakers of English, produced in the context of naturalistic, dyadic parent–child interaction. Each parent and child was selected individually, so that from the same research project involving the same target child, we included either the mother, or the father, or both parents as separate speakers, as long as either or both passed the criteria for inclusion.

A.2 **Criteria for including projects, parents and children**

The CHILDES archive contains the transcribed texts of several hundred studies, but not all of them could be included in the two corpora of English we compiled. The formal criteria for including (and excluding) projects were the following:

Project Criterion 1: **English**: All parents and children we included were native English speakers, from the USA and from the UK, including England, Wales, and Ireland.

Project Criterion 2: **Normal development**: All children included were normally developing, with no diagnosed hearing or speech problems. This means we included the control participants for a study of Specific Language Impairment by Bliss—but not the experimental subsample of the same study.

Project Criterion 3: **Parent–child interaction**: The projects involved parents and children engaged in dyadic interaction. This excluded projects involving groups of children interacting with adults or each other in a school context, for example the Gathercole-Burns project in which groups of children were observed during a structured play session, or the Garvey study of school dialogues between two children with no adult present.

Project Criterion 4: **Other-addressed speech**: The projects involved parent–child interaction rather than recorded monologues by the child, as in the Nelson study consisting, mostly, of a child's crib monologues.

Project Criterion 5: **Parent main partner**: The projects had a parent interacting with a child on most of the observational period, rather than investigators, grandparents, other adults, or other children. For example, we did not include Morisset's child number 395 as the sole adult interacting with the child is the grandmother, nor the Fletcher study in which an investigator rather than a parent interacted with the child. We also excluded the Bohannon study as most of the interaction was between a child and students; apart from the mother there were 10 or 17 students present and interacting with the observed children.

Project Criterion 6: **Child age**: The projects involved children whose age was below 3;6 at least on part of the observations. This excluded studies such as the ones by Hall, by Carterette and Jones, and by Evans, all involving children over 4;6. If the project contained observations below and above the critical age, we only included the sessions involving the younger age range. We included also observations where the child was an infant, imposing no minimal age requirement on the child addressed. In this decision we relied on the findings in the literature that parental speech retains some minimal level of complexity even when the child spoken to is a young infant, and that speech to very young infants is in fact quite similar in its syntactic complexity to speech to children up to the age of four or so (Fraser and Roberts, 1975; Phillips, 1973, see section 2.2.2). At the conclusion of the corpus building stage, it is possible to summarize that the parental corpus consists of the speech of parents addressing children most of whom are under 3;0. Only seven of the 506 parents of the corpus had any sentences addressed to children past the age of 3;0. Similarly, the child corpus was restricted to the speech of children below age 3;6. Because of the way the child sentences were sampled—a maximum of 300 for each child from the beginning of multi-word speech—the children included were almost all three years of age or less; 98.6% of all grammatical relations analysed in this study were generated by children up to 3;0. Thus although the formal restriction was an age limit of 3;6, the two corpora involved in actuality almost exclusively children under three years of age.

Project Criterion 7: **Size of transcript**: The size of the unanalysed transcript for a particular parent approached at least 100 turns at speech. An example of an excluded parent is from the observations on Sean in the Wells project, where both mother and father were present at all the home observations but the father only sporadically spoke to the child, and hence was not sampled for the parental corpus.

A.3 Parents and children in the corpora

After applying the criteria listed above, we arrived at 471 different families in which naturalistic interaction of parents with infants and young children was observed. In 436 families only one parent passed the criteria, while in 35 families two parents from the same family were included in the corpus, making the total number of different parents in the corpus 506.

Of the 471 families, all of which contained an infant or child we designated the target child, 50 had children whose speech we checked but could not include in the child pooled corpus as they were not producing syntactic word-combinations. Thus, the children's corpus contained a total of 421 children.

Table 2.3 presents the number of parents included in the corpus from each observational project selected.

Table 2.4 presents the number of children included in the corpus from each observational project selected.

A.4 Selecting utterances to be included in the pooled corpus

After deciding which observational studies and which speakers to sample, we applied a set of criteria for the inclusion of utterances in the parental or child corpora.

Table 2.3 Number of parents included in the corpus from each observational project selected

Investigator/project	Number of parents included	References
Bates	31	Bates *et al.* (1988) Carlson-Luden (1979)
Belfast	4	Wilson and Henry (1998)
Bernstein-Ratner	9	Bernstein (1982) Bernstein-Ratner (1984)
Bliss	1	Bliss (1988)
Bloom 1970	3	Bloom (1970)
Bloom 1973	1	Bloom (1973)
Brent	14	Brent and Siskind (2001)
Brown	5	Brown (1973)
Clark	2	Clark (1978)
Cornell	7	Hayes (2000)
Demetras	5	Demetras (1989a,b)
Feldman	2	Feldman (1998)
Gleason	13	Bellinger and Gleason (1982)
Higginson	3	Higginson (1985)
Howe	14	Howe (1981)
Korman	7	Korman (1984)
Kuczaj	2	Kuczaj (1976)
MacWhinney	2	MacWhinney (2000)
Manchester	12	Theakston *et al.* (2001)
McMillan	2	McMillan in CHILDES
Morisset	88	Morisset (1991)
New England	51	Snow *et al.* (1996)
Peters–Wilson	2	Wilson and Peters (1988)
Post	3	Post (1992)
Rollins	3	Rollins (2003)
Sachs	2	Sachs (1983)
Suppes	1	Suppes (1974)
Tardif	25	Tardif *et al.* (1999)
Valian	23	Valian (1991)
Van Houten	21	Van Houten (1986)
Warren-Leubecker	18	Warren-Leubecker (1982) Warren-Leubecker and Bohannon (1984)
Wells	30	Wells (1981)
Total	506	

Table 2.4 Number of children included in the corpus from each observational project selected

Investigator/project	Number of children included
Bates	30
Belfast	4
Bernstein-Ratner	2
Bloom 1970	2
Bloom 1973	1
Brown	3
Clark	1
Cornell	5
Demetras	3
Feldman	1
Gleason	7
Higginson	2
Howe	14
Kuczaj	1
MacWhinney	1
Manchester	11
McMillan	2
Morisset	185
New England	44
Peters-Wilson	1
Post	3
Sachs	1
Suppes	1
Tardif	23
Valian	21
Van Houten	17
Warren-Leubecker	9
Wells	26
Total	421

A.5 Criteria for utterances to be included in the pooled corpus

Examination of utterances for inclusion in each corpus was done by hand, and involved systematic selection by speaker, addressee, and spontaneity.

The transcribed dialogue was read by the research staff—including the action and other contextual comments—in order to ascertain that the utterance passed the criteria, and that we actually included only spontaneous utterances from target parent to target child or vice versa.

The criteria for inclusion of utterances were the following:

Utterances Criterion 1. **Specific target speaker.** We included in the parental corpus only the speech of individually selected parents but not of investigators or other family members. Similarly, we included in the child corpus only the speech of individually selected children but not their siblings or visitors.

We used for coding the transcripts of the CHILDES basic-format ASCII text files, deleting the morphological and syntactic 'tiers' (lines) (see Appendix B to this chapter for the reasons). As the transcripts in the CHILDES archive, including in the basic-format files, are marked for the content of each 'tier', including an explicit marker for the speaker of transcribed utterances, we did not have to code for speaker. However, a first run-through revealed that there were mistaken speaker attributions in the transcripts, therefore we hand-checked the files in order to ascertain the correctness of the 'tier' labels and the speaker codes. For each utterance marked as one uttered by the child, we checked the context to made certain that the line was speech, and if so, that the speaker was indeed the child.

First, there were lines marked as child utterances but in fact they were action descriptions, for example, the examples in Table 2.5 from the Bates corpus.

Second, there were lines marked as child utterances but in all probability they were said by the parent or some other adult, according to their content, length, or level of complexity that did not match the child's contributions at the same time.

For example, in the observations on child number 06 in the Valian project the sentences in (1) are attributed to the child, but, according to the conversation before and after, the speaker is the mother:

(1) child 06 (Valian) at 2;3.15:
    a. who gave you baby Laura?

Table 2.5 Examples of action descriptions marked as child utterances in the Bates corpus

Child	Age	Text of line
Ivy	2;4	picks up two nesting cups.
Ivy	2;4	puts one nesting cup to stack.
Doug	2;4	puts man at bottom of ladder and then walks him up one step at a time.
Frank	1;8	puts nesting cups in stack.

b. do you remember?

Similarly, Peter in the Bloom sample at 1;9.08 was credited with the utterance (2).

(2) let's see if this little cow would like to ride the seesaw.

when this sentence was more likely to have been emitted by Patsy, an adult present at the observation. Peter's other contributions to this conversation were utterances like 'seesaw # seesaw' or 'mm'.

In the transcriptions of Oliver in the Howe project there were a considerable number of utterances by the mother mistakenly attributed to the child, for instance those at (3).

(3) Oliver (Howe) at 1;7:
   a. he's never seen Dougal on television so this is completely new to him.
   b. do you think that's Humpty Dumpty?
   c. oh # have you seen that # Oliver?
   d. come on # up you get.
   e. oh # that's a nice one # isn't it?
   f. are you driving?
   g. that's a door # yes.
   h. oh Oliver # how lovely darling.
   i. there # is Oliver going to have a cup to tea.

At the time, Oliver's utterances were like the ones in (4):

(4) Oliver (Howe) at 1;7:
   a. baby.
   b. dog.
   c. not baby.
   d. that.
   e. look.
   f. lorry.
   g. train.

and similar. It is clear from the transcript that the sentences at (3) were not produced by the child but by the mother and we excluded them and similar utterances from the child corpus and added them to the maternal corpus.

Utterances Criterion 2. **Specific target addressee:** The utterances included were speech by the parent addressing an individually selected target child, not some older child, other family members, or the investigator.

In most observations, there were participants present other than the target parent and the target child, including the investigators, the other parent, grandparents, other children, cameramen, and guests. We excluded from the corpus all utterances where the parent spoke to someone other than the target child. Exceptions were rare occasions where the parent was ostensively speaking to another person present but, reading the dialogue, it was obvious that the child was the intended audience and the child did take up the thread.

In some observational sessions there were a considerable number of utterances not addressed to the child. For instance, in the transcript of the Rachel observation of the Belfast sample there were a total of 2194 maternal lines. Of these, 1300 (59%) were addressed to the child and 894 (41%) were addressed to the investigator. These lines are very easy to identify by reading the dialogue. For example, (5) is a few turns of conversation between the mother (MOT) and the investigator (INV) in this observation:

(5) Rachel (Belfast) observation:
　　*INV: you're nice and handy here aren't you?
　　*MOT: I know ach it is it is although next year we're hoping to move
　　　down to Bangor so we are.
　　*INV: oh are you # do you have connections down there?
　　*MOT: no not really # we were just having a look through the property
　　　papers and seen that you got really good value for money and then the
　　　idea sort of developed from there # I've got one friend who lives down
　　　there and she loves it.

Other examples of utterances addressed at the investigator or another adult are presented in Table 2.6.

We decided to exclude all utterances from the parents' corpus that were addressed at another person except at the target child of the sample as these utterances had an unknown degree of higher complexity in vocabulary and grammar relative to child-addressed utterances.

The criterion of addressee selection was not applied to child speech. Although we were mainly interested in speech addressed by the target child at the child's parents, some utterances of the child included in the corpus may have been addressed at others rather than at his or her parents. We made sure this will be a marginal phenomenon in the corpus by selecting only observations in which the parents were the child's main interactants. If the interaction in the observational period mainly involved other people rather than the parents, that observation was not sampled in the first place (see Criterion 5 for the selection of projects).

Utterances Criterion 3. **Spontaneous speech**: The utterance contained the parent's or child's spontaneous speech, not texts read from books, or nursery rhymes recited or sang. Utterances were included if they were not quotes, thus, verbatim reading of the text of books was excluded, but a paraphrase of them was included.

Table 2.6 Examples of utterances addressed by a parent at the investigator or another adult (M=mother, F=father)

Child	Project	M/F	Utterance
Abigail	Wells	M	I am very much a person who needs somebody else #3.
Abigail	Wells	M	Harry had this stall in the antique market.
Abigail	Wells	M	I just spoke to the person on the phone that if I let you in at least you could be getting on.
Abigail	Wells	M	Becky insists she's eaten at school.
Alice	Bernstein-Ratner	M	that (i)s an interesting toy, but it scared her last time, so I (a)m gonna kind of # go easy on it # it might be kind of interesting to see what happens now, yeah, you (a)re right +...
Alice	Bernstein-Ratner	M	she's really into books right now.
Alice	Bernstein-Ratner	M	because I [/] I don't feel very much like talking to her today, I have not talked to her a lot today, and we've been on each other's nerves today, so +...
Alice	Bernstein-Ratner	M	try to # get her to talk or just kind of # be as natural as possible?
Brandon	Cornell	F	Barb, Barbara_Salomon stopped by.
Brandon	Cornell	F	and she just left her name and number, and suggested that sometimes, if you guys are going stir+crazy in the cold weather that you get together and form a little social support group.
Brandon	Cornell	F	he might not feel as much competition xxx.
Brandon	Cornell	F	and there seems to be an awful lot less competition between them today.
Brandon	Cornell	F	you've got to realize that you're dealing with a symme-try freak here .
Brandon	Cornell	F	Brendon has nudged Joshua once, in the last hour and a half, and that's it.
c10	Valian	M	you know when you're around your children all the time, you get used to the way they talk.
c12	Valian	M	she knows we usually rewind our tapes before we play them, so she's used to tapes.
Gail	Bernstein-Ratner	M	and if he doesn't get used to sleeping in there in the daytime.

Utterances Criterion 4. **No immediate imitation:** The child's utterance was spontaneous, not an immediate imitation of any of the previous three utterances by the parent or any other speaker.

A.6 Correcting for continuation of speech lines

After deciding that certain lines of the raw transcription were to be included in the pooled corpora, we hand-checked the file to ensure that all the text of a particular turn was on a single line of the file. When a turn at speech continued into a second and further lines, we cut and pasted the continuations onto the appropriate position on the first line, creating one line per turn at speech. This made it possible ultimately to sort the file containing the texts for the observation, speaker, or child age, and for other codes inserted during coding, without losing parts of the utterance.

A.7 Size of individual samples' contribution to corpus

Individual parents' contribution to the pooled corpus was restricted to 3000 unanalysed utterances each, taken from the beginning of observations in the respective research project. Namely, we checked the child's age and ordered the observations by chronological ordering, starting when the target child was the youngest. If some archived corpus was longer, it was trimmed. Parents with fewer than 100 utterances were not included in the corpus, with two exceptions where the number almost reached this minimum. This measure was taken in order to equalize as much as possible the weight of each individual speaker in the pooled corpus. In the CHILDES archive there are transcripts of some longitudinal observations continuing for several years besides single-shot cross-sectional observations, and if we did not set the maximum and minimum contribution of particular parents, the pooled corpus would have represented mostly the speech of the parents of longitudinal studies. The range of 100–3000 unanalysed utterances we allowed represented a compromise between wishing to maximize the number of different parents included in the corpus and the wish to equalize their respective contributions.

It should be noted that the limits on the number of unanalysed lines puts some constraint on, but does not determine how many tokens of word-couples expressing the grammatical relations of the subject–verb, verb–object, and verb–dative object each parent will actually contribute to the pooled corpus. Hypothetically, it is possible that in some parent's talk, a large part of the raw unanalysed 3000 utterances are single-word utterances without any syntactic relations expressed, while another parent uses long and elaborate sentences with many different syntactic relations expressed in each. We used a limit on the maximum number of unanalysed utterances rather than on the number of one or more of the syntactic relations ultimately coded in order to equate a potential for syntactic expression among the different speakers, including, possibly, of other patterns than the three basic relations we were planning on coding in this project.

In the children's corpus, we limited the size of sample from an individual child to 300 unanalysed lines containing multiple words, but set no minimum limit, so that effectively we allowed a range of 1–300 lines per child. We used as a criterion the number of multiword lines and not the raw number of all child utterances because, at the relevant developmental stage, there was a possibility that the great majority of children's utterances will be of a single word, hence not containing even potentially words in a syntactic relation. As in the case of parental speech samples, the allowed ratio of minimum to maximum per speaker was 300-to-1, not a puny range but a constraint on inequality nevertheless. Thus, individual children contributed up to 300 utterances each from the start of their production of multiword-combinations, potentially but not certainly containing one or more of the core grammatical relations we were to code for.

The sampling from the start of each observational project was a similar move to the constraints on maximum age and maximum contribution of utterances, aimed at reducing the variability in the ages of the children speaking or spoken to by the parents. As we were utilizing a collection of research projects each conducted for its own purposes, our degrees of freedom were restricted to choosing which project to include and which to exclude from the constructed pooled corpora. As mentioned before, we restricted the children's age to 3;6, but did not set a minimal age limit. Sampling systematically from the earliest observations of each study meant that we aimed at the youngest age possible, restricting variability in ages as much as possible. When it concerns parental speech to children, this characterizes the input speech as aimed at infants and at young children at the start of producing word-combinations. When it is applied to children's corpus, it means that we are covering the earliest period of children generating the relevant basic grammatical word-combinations, regardless of their chronological age, as long as it does not pass 3;6.

Appendix B: **Coding for grammatical relations**

In order to code two large corpora by hand in the fastest way possible, much use was made of automatic search programs, co-sorting of uncoded and coded lines, and other computer functions and macros that offered first approximations to the hand-coders.

B.1 **Definition of verbs for this study**

As we intended to code only for grammatical relations of verbs, the first task was to define the class of stems we consider verbs for this study. Most of this decision was obvious, but two issues are worth noting. First, we included all auxiliary verbs such as *be, have, do, can, must,* and *may,* and made no distinction between them and other verbs. In general, we only had a universal category of verbs with no subdivisions, nor did we prepare an a priori subcategorization into intransitive, transitive, and ditransitive verbs or any other subclasses. Second, we separated all contracted forms into their component parts for coding purposes and for identifying the verb stem, so that *wanna* was treated as *want to* and *I'll* as *I will*.[13]

B.2 Lemmatization of verbs in the corpora

Lemmatization is the grouping of related verb forms (or other words) found in texts that share the same stem and differ only in inflection or spelling (Francis and Kučera, 1982). We lemmatized all verbs in the texts into their respective stem-groups for frequency analysis. For example, *eat, eats, ate, eaten*, and *eating* were all grouped into the stem-group or lemma of *eat*. Suppleted forms for irregular verbs such as *am* and *was* of *be* were also included in the lemma of the relevant stem, regardless of their altered form. This process neutralizes differences in morphological shape irrelevant for the syntactic behaviour of verbs we were interested in, nullifying differences of tense, aspect, person, and so on. Lemmatization was also carried out to neutralize spelling differences and undo the fusional effect of contractions that could otherwise disguise the identity of verbs. This process is especially important in dealing with spoken corpora like the observations in CHILDES which are sometimes transcribed in partially phonetic transcription.

We encountered in the corpora 1779 text-strings of verb forms which we classified into 807 verb stems. Once this list of strings-and-stems was compiled, we ran the list over the whole corpus (using the 'vlook' function of Excel) and obtained suggested lemmas for each verb-like string in the text. In the computational linguistics literature this method is said to be 'brute force stemming' as it employs a lookup table which contains matched inflected and root forms. As usual in this project, the automatically obtained verb stems were treated as suggestions only and they were hand-checked and corrected for each utterance in the corpus. The text-strings identified as verbs were, potentially, inflected forms of verbs, but this was only probabilistic, as they could be nouns (as in the case of *ring, shout*, or *walk*) or members of other form classes such as adjectives or adverbs. English possesses a large degree of zero-derivation and it is extremely risky to use automated part-of-speech annotation without hand-checking it.

We used this list of verbal text-strings and associated verb stems in several procedures besides lemmatization, such as the reduction of the raw corpus into lists of to-be-coded utterances versus utterances unlikely to contain verbs. In all cases, the automatic process was just a guideline, and each utterance was hand-checked for all decisions.

B.3 **Parsing for grammatical relations**

Parsing was done by five graduate students at Hebrew University with training in linguistics. We checked for reliability by having three pairs of coders blindly recode 1200 utterances produced by four different parents. A checking of all reliability codes showed that the accuracy of each coder was above 98%, based on codes actually given by the relevant pair of coders. If we count the match between coders on the basis of all codes that were potentially possible (five SV, five VO, and three VI relations to be identified per utterance), the accuracy climbs to close to 100%.

Throughout coding, all problem cases were discussed and resolved, and the relevant coding rules added to the coding book and the syntactic dictionary. Ultimately each coded utterance was double-checked by another coder and then by myself.

The speech samples were organized into Excel files, which could accommodate a maximum of 65,000 lines, each of which contained one sentence. As the first run-through, these raw files were searched by computer macros for single-word utterances and for utterances apparently not containing verbs, which were then separated from the lines potentially containing a verb in a multiword utterance. Single-word utterances were then double-checked by the string-stem program to retrieve contractions to be added to the multi-word set.

Parsing rules were based on the principles of the Minimalist Program (Chomsky, 1995a) and English Word Grammar (Hudson, 1990), with details based on Allerton (1982), Hornby (1945), and Quirk *et al.* (1985), consulted in this order. For some particularly thorny problems, we relied on further linguistic texts such as Huddleston (1980). We prepared a detailed coding book with definitions of the grammatical relations and principles of coding. We also prepared a syntactic dictionary listing the direct and dative object patterns for each verb, using example sentences from the linguistics sources we used and from our own corpus. Coders used both of these to guide their decisions. In addition, parsing was aided by a collection of already-coded examples—ultimately containing 60,000 fully coded sentences—to serve as models during coding. The solved examples were sorted together with the yet uncoded sentences by verb stem and text, scaffolding coding decisions for similar sentences.

We coded each sentence at one go, listing the verbs appearing in SV, VO, and VI constructions in that sentence. At a later stage, the sentences were separated into three files each containing only the exemplars of one grammatical relation, when each different word-pair in a particular relation gets a separate line for further analysis.

B.3.1 Difference between our system and the automatic syntactic parser of the CHILDES

A short while ago, an automatic syntactic parser MEGRASP was added to the programs available to CHILDES users, updating the previous version called GRASP. This program, developed by Kenji Sagae (see Sagae *et al.*, 2010; and also Sagae *et al.* 2004a,b for the previous version) uses information on the morphological tier of the CHILDES files to generate labelled syntactic dependencies. On the face of it, this is a parser in the tradition of Dependency Grammar that provides precisely the kind of information we were interested in. However, we could not use the automatic parser because of significant differences in the details of the grammatical analysis. The major discrepancy between the linguistic approaches adopted by us and by Sagae *et al.* concerns the status of auxiliary verbs. In particular, Sagae *et al.* code uninflected non-finite verbs as receiving subjects, rather than the inflected and finite auxiliary verbs of the relevant sentences. For example, in the sentence '*The fish are swimming*', the syntax-parsing line presently in CHILDES identifies *swimming* as the word getting the subject, not the word *are*. In our coding system, the head of the subject is the auxiliary verb *be* (in this case, *are*), and not the non-finite verb *swimming*. In this we rely on a wide consensus in linguistic texts according to which it is a universal rule of syntax that only finite, inflected verbs and auxiliary verbs get subjects, not non-finite participles, infinitives, or gerunds (Hudson, 1998, p. 53; Noonan, 1985, pp. 49–91). According to Noonan, the most frequent device for marking secondary-predicate status, and one that characterizes complementation phenomena across languages, is the loss of the capacity of complement-predicates to have an overt or syntactic subject. This is also true for English, according to all published linguistic sources we consulted. There are other differences between the grammatical relations we derived from Hudson (1990), Quirk *et al.* (1985), and the other linguistic texts we mentioned earlier and the system used by the Sagae *et al.* parser, but the difference regarding the head of subjects is the most prominent one in terms of the present study. Auxiliary verbs are very frequent in the corpus and it is a nontrivial matter whether or not we treat them as heads of subjects. The various publications describing the Sagae *et al.* parser do not mention the linguistic texts it is based on, and we could not weight the arguments for this treatment and for any other in which they diverge from the syntactic analysis we derived from linguistic texts. Our decision therefore was to follow the linguistic consensus and not to use the Sagae *et al.* parser. The decision made our system of dependency coding correspond to the linguistic conventions used in the Conference on Computational Natural Language Learning (CoNLL) Shared Task for 2007,

2008, and 2009, and in particular the tool used to build dependency tree-banks, namely, the converter constructed by Johansson and Nugues (2008). This made possible the comparison of our results with some results of the syntactic analysis of adult English texts mentioned in the main text of this chapter.

A second reason for opting for hand-coding from scratch instead of using the automatic morphosyntactic analysis of CHILDES is because we wanted a higher level of accuracy than an automatic parser provides. It is well known in corpus work that automatic parsers in general do not yet reach a high level of accuracy, and hand-coding or at least correction is necessary to avoid their limitations, and see, for example, the discussion of this issue in a recent article by Roland *et al.* (2007). As we started processing the CHILDES transcripts, we realized that the transcripts needed much hand-checking and a fully automatic process would be inaccurate to an unknown degree. As mentioned in Appendix A to this chapter, there were mistakes in speaker identification and addressee identification in the transcripts and unless hand-checked, automatic parsing would include sentences in the incorrect class, for example, some action descriptions and maternal utterances as if they were child sentences. Other problems concern morphological annotation and spelling. Unfortunately, the morphological tagging program of CHILDES is not yet sufficiently accurate,

Table 2.7 Mothers' utterances with typos, by target child and project

Child	Project	Transcription with mistake	correction
Benjamin	Wells	even when its off you musn't touch it.	*its* should be *it's*
Benjamin	Wells	ill make you some in a minute lovey.	*ill* should be *I'll*
Benjamin	Wells	and well make it all pretty colors shall we?	*well* should be *we'll*
Benjamin	Wells	better go up the school put your name down for school wont I?	*wont* should be *won't*
Cristopher	Korman	well that's what your trying to get hold of.	*your* should be *you're*
Cristopher	Korman	I hope your not going to carry on like this all day.	*your* should be *you're*
David	Rollins	look you wanna where the hat.	*where* should be *wear*
David	Rollins	oh I here a fun noisy toy in there.	*here* should be *hear*
David	Rollins	what to bunnies <do>?	*to* should be *do*
David	Demetras	wed [: red] better put that back together.	*wed* should be *we'd*
Gillian	Korman	mum's just going to get you're pants.	*you're* should be *your*

and there are quite a number of mistakes in the annotations. These carry over to the automatic syntactic parsing and cause further mistakes (see Laakso, 2005; Sagae *et al.*, 2004a,b).

In addition, there were quite a few typographical errors in the transcripts that an automatic morphosyntactic parser could not be expected to detect or correct. Table 2.7 brings some examples of mis-spelled words in maternal utterances.

Although all the mistakes mentioned above—typos, speaker and addressee identification, action descriptions marked as speech, morphological misclassification—can be detected and corrected by hand, this seemed to us a labour-intensive task and one prone to errors. For this reason and because of the divergence in the linguistic categories from the ones we wanted to use, we decided we cannot use the existing automatic parsing and will parse the corpora by hand. Obviously, research using the Sagae *et al.* automatic parser will have different results than our study.

Notes

1 For examples of developmental studies using pooled corpora see Cameron-Faulkner *et al.* (2003), Goodman *et al.* (2008), Huttenlocher *et al.* (1991), Lee and Naigles (2005), Naigles and Hoff-Ginsberg (1998), Ninio (1985, 1992, 2006), Pine *et al.* (1998), Serratrice *et al.* (2003), Tomasello (2003), Zamuner (2009), and Zamuner *et al.* (2005).

2 For the principles of corpus-based linguistics see Biber *et al.* (1998), McEnery and Wilson (1996), Sinclair (1991), and Svartvik (1992).

3 For some time, it was thought that the simplifying parental register is universal. Subsequently it was found that the register is probably only found in Westernized cultures with nuclear families, not in traditional cultures with different child-rearing arrangements (e.g. Ochs, 1982). In any case, the parental register is probably shared in its main features by parents in the industrialized English-speaking countries sampled in our corpus.

4 Akhtar *et al.* (2001) show that children can also learn words from overheard speech. In the observational sessions serving as the data basis for the present corpus, the speech children could overhear was almost always addressed to an adult (e.g. the investigator or the other parent). In contrast to the study by Akhtar *et al.*, the topics discussed in the children's hearing were often outside the children's life experience. Some examples can be seen in Appendix A to this chapter. It is not clear that children can indeed learn from this type of overheard speech. As one example, the utterances Akhtar *et al.* made the children in their experiments overhear

were descriptions of some visible object or action, whereas the utterances exchanged by parents and other adults in real life are almost never are; they tend to be about errands to run, past events, parenting decisions, or other abstract or non-present subjects.

5 The high degree of overlap existing in the productive vocabularies and basic syntax of young children makes possible the construction of developmental checklists comprising of a priori items, in such instruments as the MacArthur Communicative Development Inventory (CDI; Fenson *et al.*, 1994) and the Language Development Survey (LDS; Rescorla *et al.*, 2001).

6 The issue of item-specific syntactic development was a central topic in the 1970s and the 1980s; the syntactic patterns for which this phenomenon was documented include wh-question constructions (Bloom *et al.*, 1982; Forner, 1979; Klima and Bellugi-Klima, 1966; Kuczaj and Brannick, 1979); constructions with complement-taking matrix verbs getting *to* infinitives and other connectives (Bloom *et al.*, 1983, 1989); argument structures and syntactic multiword constructions (Baker, 1979; Bates and MacWhinney, 1987; Bowerman, 1976; Braine, 1963; Clark, 1978; Gropen *et al.*, 1989; Maratsos, 1983; Ninio, 1988; Pinker, 1984; Slobin, 1985). Later studies (e.g. Allen, 1998; Clark, 1996; Goldberg *et al.*, 2003; Lieven *et al.*, 1997; Pine and Lieven, 1997; Pine and Martindale, 1996; Tomasello, 1992) also reported the same developmental picture.

7 Counting words followed the protocol of the Brown corpus manual (Francis and Kučera, 1979). The major feature is that the statistics excludes all punctuation marks.

8 Most professional corpora are like Brown and LOB, and have a fixed size. So do the present corpora: we stopped the addition of more data at some point, after including all up-to-then available and suitable corpora in the CHILDES archive. However, the present corpora are potentially able to become so-called monitor corpora, namely, open-ended, as CHILDES continues to receive donations of observations and in principle it could be possible to add more samples to this corpus and increase it in size.

9 We also coded for indirect object with the preposition *to-*, but decided not to include it in the core. For more details see section 2.5.2.

10 These corpora compare well in size with parsed professional English corpora, e.g. the hand-coded COMLEX (COMmon LEXicon; Grishman *et al.*, 1994) consisting of 38,000 words, or with the Penn Treebank

corpora which were automatically parsed but hand-corrected
(Marcus *et al.*, 1993).

11 Liu Haitao (personal communication) computed for this project the
token frequencies of the three core grammatical relations SV, VO, and VI
in the dependency-grammar coded part of *The Wall Street Journal* in the
Penn Treebank project. In the Penn Treebank project, 2499 different news
articles from three years of *The Wall Street Journal* were syntactically
annotated. The original constituent-structure annotation was then
converted into a dependency-grammatical annotation using the
algorithms described in Johansson and Nugues (2008).

The analysed part of *The Wall Street Journal* consists of a total of
446,573 running words. It contained a total of 67,070 core syntactic
relations. Of these, 35,033 or 52.2% were SV, 30,177 or 45.0% were VO,
and 1860 or 2.8% were VI syntactic relations. Given that there may be
some differences in grammatical analysis between our coding system and
the dependency annotation of the Penn Treebank, the results are
strikingly similar to the ones we reported on in this chapter.

We did a further comparison analysis, using a not very systematic
collection of adult-addressed utterances produced by the parents of the
corpus. These sentences were said to the other parent, to a grandparent,
or to the investigator during the observational session, and they were
transcribed in the CHILDES files. We analysed a corpus consisting of 6343
running words, and the results, again, closely resemble the findings based
on the parental child-directed speech. The corpus contained a total of
1570 core syntactic relations. Of these, 964 or 61.4% were SV
combinations, 562 or 35.8% were VO combinations, and 44 or 2.8% were
VI syntactic relations. Again, the distributions are very similar to parents'
child-addressed speech. Apparently, child-directed speech does not
diverge from adult-addressed speech and written English on this feature.

12 In the future we plan also to code the corpus for adverbial adjuncts, even
lower on the hierarchy than indirect objects, to test the prediction arising
from these data that adjuncts are truly infrequent in these two registers.

13 The decision to treat contractions such as *I'll* as the combination of a
pronoun and a verb is thus different from the treatment in a recent
project also using the CHILDES database to estimate the language
environment of the child, namely, the study by Christiansen and
Monaghan (2006). In this study, 'contractions were classified according to
the syntactic category of their first element, so *you're* was classified as

pronoun, *could've* was classified as verb, and *what's* as wh-word' (p. 100). We found in our work that in CHILDES transcripts, *be* and *have* appear cliticized to pronouns in a considerable proportion of the time, so that the methodological choice made by Christiansen and Monaghan is unfortunate, in particular in view of the goal of the study which was the definition of the syntactic class of verbs.

Chapter 3

Verbs

In the last chapter (Chapter 2) we reported on the distribution of the three core grammatical relations in parental and child registers, and commented that the two distributions were almost identical, despite a considerable difference in the size of the verbal repertoire used to generate them in the two samples. In this chapter, we shall focus on the verb repertoires themselves, when our goal is to understand better the choice of verbs by parents and children to generate tokens of core grammar. We shall start by estimating the relative size of parents' and children's total syntactic verbal lexicon, correcting for the difference in sample size in the present study. Then, we shall search for the dimension of choice that may be responsible for the selective reduction of the vocabulary in the parental register, testing two candidate features—which are soon seen to be nearly identical—first, native origin; second, morphophonemic or articulatory simplicity. Lastly, we shall ask if the same factors operate in children's choice of verbs, relative to the linguistic input.

3.1 **Size of syntactic verb repertoires**

We saw in Chapter 2 that the size of parental and child verbal repertoires used to generate core grammatical relations are considerably different. To remind us, parents use 601 different verbs in the SV relation, 776 in the VO relation, and 66 in the VI relation. The children use 220, 238, and 24 verbs, respectively, in the three relations. The values for parents and children cannot be compared directly as the samples on which they are based are of a different magnitude. To be able to compare them, we need to base the comparison on equal sample sizes.

As a first step, we reduced the three estimates, each for a different grammatical relation, to just one global measure of syntactic vocabulary size. We estimated the total verbal vocabulary used by the parents and by the children in generating the clausal core, counting verbs used in at least one of the three core syntactic relations. Interestingly, the degree of flexibility in using the same verb for more than one core syntactic relation was not at all different in the two samples, when parents used each verb in an average of 1.62 syntactic contexts and children, in 1.65 contexts. The total verb vocabulary of parents was 892, and of children, 292; namely, parents used three times as many verbs as children for core grammar. We might check back to Table 2.1 and see that this 3-to-1 ratio is apparent also when each syntactic relation is considered separately.

It is appropriate to refer to these numbers when we want to underscore the impression of how similar the relative token frequency is of the three relations in parents' and children's speech, despite the large difference in the absolute number of types and tokens in the two corpora. However, when we want to ask how children compare to parents in size of verb vocabulary, using the raw numbers becomes unfair, as the estimates are based on a considerably larger sample size for parents. It is well known that number of types or repertoire size is a function of sample size; the larger the sample, the bigger the estimated type size (Baayen, 2001).[1] In order to get a more realistic comparison of parental and child repertoires of verbs in the three core grammatical relations, we need to compare them on identical-sized samples.

As we were reluctant to assume without more information that children would linearly increase their vocabulary size had we sampled their speech in the order of magnitude of the parental corpus—which was 338,970 syntactic tokens strong as compared to the children's total of 25,796 tokens—we preferred instead to play safe by artificially reducing the parents' corpus to the size of the children's. In a move often used in statistical physics,[2] we generated ten virtual corpora of parental syntax, equal in size to the children's sample, by randomly sampling the large parental corpus. In order to equate the comparison samples to the children's one as closely as possible, we included SV, VO, and VI tokens according to how many there were in the child corpus, namely, we sampled ten times 14,375 SV tokens, 11,116 VO tokens, and 305 VI tokens from the large parental corpus. In the ten comparison samples, the totals were in each case 25,796 syntactic tokens, with an internal distribution equal to the children's. This technique overcomes the artefactual inflation of parental verb types due to our originally sampling a larger sample of parental speech than child speech. Table 3.1 presents the results.

As we can see in Table 3.1, in a sample identical in size to the child corpus we arrived at a halved estimate of total parental verb vocabulary, which is 412.3 different verbs used in at least one of the core grammatical relations. Although we considerably diminished the size differential with children, the parental verb repertoire is still about 40% larger than children's total verb vocabulary of 292 (the exact ratio is 1.41). That is, children at this early stage of development indeed use significantly fewer verbs in basic syntactic combinations than parents, using each verb for a larger number of tokens on average. In the usual terminology, their type-token ratio is smaller than that of parents.

Table 3.1 Size of verb repertoires of parents, children, and ten parental samples of equal size to children's corpus, used in core grammatical relations

Corpus	Tokens	Verb repertoire
Parent's full corpus	338,970	892
Sample 1 parents	25,796	410
Sample 2 parents	25,796	414
Sample 3 parents	25,796	405
Sample 4 parents	25,796	407
Sample 5 parents	25,796	419
Sample 6 parents	25,796	411
Sample 7 parents	25,796	409
Sample 8 parents	25,796	419
Sample 9 parents	25,796	422
Sample 10 parents	25,796	407
Mean of parental samples (SD)	25,796	412.3 (5.9)
Children	25,796	292

This is the place to point out that the difference in repertoire size between the children's corpus and the equal-sized parental sample is a strong counter-argument to the possible claim that children's distribution of the three core grammatical relations is similar to that of parents because children copy some sample of parents' utterances. A genuine statistical sample of the parental corpus (which by definition recreates the token distribution of the three core grammatical relations in the origin), the size of the children's corpus, contains a much larger number of different verbs than the children's corpus. We created ten random samples and children's verbal repertoire size does not fall into the range defined by these samples, it is consistently smaller for the same number of tokens. There is, in other words, some qualitative differences between the collection of utterances from children's speech and a sample of parental speech. The repertoire size shows one difference, which is that children manage to recreate the global distribution of the parental corpus with a much smaller number of verbs than parents would use if they only said this many sentences, the children over-using the ones they know, relative to parents. This is interesting by itself, but at the moment we would just like to summarize that children's global token distribution manages to be very similar to that of parents not because children copy a statistically random selection of utterances parents say, but because they generate a set of utterances of their own which, differing in some features, nevertheless, distribute similarly to the parents' large speech corpus.

In the following analyses, the equal-size random samples of parental speech will serve us as a well-controlled comparison group for the children's sample. It is possible that sample size influences not only type size but also the various breakdowns of the vocabulary we are interested in; we want to avoid the artefact of confounding sample size with type effects.

The researchers of the older wave of studies of the parental register (Broen, 1972; Hayes and Ahrens, 1988; Phillips, 1973) were quite accurate when they claimed that parents use a reduced vocabulary when addressing young children. Even with the maximalist estimate of 892 verbs, the verbal lexicon of the parental register seems quite small relative to the complete English verb vocabulary which contains at least 10,000 verbs. We know that, in general, parents simplify their speech when taking to young children, but we don't know if this also applies to the selection of verbs. In the following, we search for the dimension of simplification that may be responsible for the selective reduction of the vocabulary in the parental register, testing two candidate features, first, native origin; second, morphophonemic or articulatory simplicity.

3.2 Origin of English verbs

The first question we ask concerns the historical origin of the verbs children hear and produce in core grammatical relations. English is a hybrid language, built of two historical strata that differ in their typological characteristics.

3.2.1 English is a mixture

English is a blend of the Germanic and Latinate subfamilies of the Indo-European family of languages. The native stratum is Anglo-Saxon, the later borrowing is the Norman French and the Latin vocabulary. Anglo-Saxon was a dialect of West Germanic, closely related to Old Low German and Dutch.

Even before the Norman conquest of Britain and the imposition of French as a higher-status language of the ruling classes, the Anglo-Saxon native stratum had began to change in character. In Edward Sapir's term, the originally highly inflected Germanic language underwent a serious 'analytic drift', losing most of its verbal inflections and derivational morphology (Sapir, 1921, chapter 7). This trend intensified as a consequence of the meeting with Norman French, and it continues to this day. We might say that Present Day English is a blend of an isolating[3] language made of native stems and a more morphologically rich language made of Latinate stems.

The native verbal vocabulary is a closed class, by definition. It is, as we said, the remnant of an ancient Germanic language that has undergone local changes, and which is not identical in its features to present-day German or Dutch, having lost most of the inflectional morphology characteristic of Germanic languages. The Latinate verb vocabulary is an open class one, as any day it is possible to borrow yet another French, Italian, Latin, or Spanish verb.[4]

The 'analytic drift' thus created a two-part vocabulary for English, differing in its morphophonology: the morphologically simple—even isolating—Germanic vocabulary is made of short words, the Latinate vocabulary, of longer ones. In particular, native verb stems are short, most are one syllable long. Most Latinate verbs are multi-syllabic, but some are monosyllabic, and there is evidence that as to their grammar, the latter get assimilated into the Germanic lexical subdomain (Grimshaw and Prince, 1986; Zwicky and Pullum, 1986). We will ask if origin and length, either or both, play a role in the shaping of parental speech and in acquisition.

3.2.1.1 Composition of the vocabulary

Finkenstaedt and Wolff (1973) summarized the etymology of about 80,000 words in the third edition of the *Shorter Oxford Dictionary*. On this basis, they estimated that about 25% of present-day English words originate in Old and Middle English and other Germanic sources such as German, Old Norse, and Dutch. About 62% originated in Latin languages, including Old and Modern French, and Latin, including also about 5% words of Greek origin (which we shall adjoin to Latin words for simplification's sake). All other languages contributed less than 1%, about 3% are derived from proper names, and of 4% there was no etymology given in the dictionary. Similar estimates have been arrived at by Green (1990), Skeat (1917), Williams (1975), and others.

Despite the fact that native Anglo-Saxon or Germanic words are a minority in the lexicon, they are very frequent in use. Slocum and Lehmann (2009) state that more than 80% of the thousand most common words in modern English come from Old English. A similar statistic was compiled by Jones and Wepman (1966) who claim that 88% of the 200 most commonly used words are Anglo-Saxon (including Old Norse) in origin. In the verb lexicon, the native and frequent vocabulary includes all irregular verbs and all auxiliary verbs (Bybee, 1985; Greenberg, 1966; Lieberman *et al.*, 2007).

Native words tend to predominate in informal speech registers, whereas the Latinate vocabulary is usually reserved for more formal uses such as legal and scientific texts (Quirk, 1974, p. 138). This is true also for the verbal lexicon (e.g. Autret, 1945). The two streams are different enough so that from time to time they are likened to two different languages. For instance, Autret says English speakers are bilingual:

> One may correctly state that [...] the native speakers of English, are too often unaware that they are bilingual, or diglots, in the sense that the English language avails itself of the wealth of two languages, one Anglo-Saxon, and the other Latin, that comes to us through one of its modern forms, French. This "diglottism" becomes more apparent when one compares the written language with that of the unguarded every-day conversation, and even more so if one compares it with accepted slang.
>
> Autret (1945, p. 350)

For this reason, it is expected that parent–child discourse—an intimate speech register—will tend heavily to the Anglo-Saxon vocabulary. Indeed, Phillips (1973) reported that the speech of mothers to young children has a higher percentage of native Anglo-Saxon verb tokens than speech addressed to adults (Phillips, 1973). Phillips' exact proportions are problematic to consider as she based her statistics on merely 40 tokens of verbs per speaker; nevertheless, it is interesting that she found that, in maternal speech, 38 of 40 verb tokens were of native origin, whereas in adult-addressed speech, only 36 were.[5] The 40 tokens represented between 7 and 10 different verbs; Phillips does not give a breakdown of their origin but, given the token statistics, over 90% of the verb types were of native origin.

Similarly, it has been shown that Latinate vocabulary is in general a later acquisition in children than the native Anglo-Saxon one (Anglin, 1993; Clark, 1993). Although previous studies did not treat children's syntactic verbal lexicon in particular, we expect that the generalization will also be true of the verbs used to generate basic syntactic word-combinations in children in Stage I of their grammar. The question, how exactly does child vocabulary relate to the parental one, remains as yet open, and we shall attempt to answer it in this chapter.

3.3 Articulatory complexity

Historical origin is a somewhat perilous construct in psycholinguistics. If taken literally, it appears to imply that speakers—whether adults or young children—are actually aware of the etymology of words they use, and make choices among them based on some preference or bias for words of some origin over others. Although it is possible that adult speakers of English are aware of the native or Latinate category membership of many words, feeling that the latter are more 'fancy' or 'learned', it is unlikely that either parents or children have actual knowledge of the etymology of all individual verbs. Still, native stems could have special features that make them more attractive to be employed in the parental register and child speech, such as their simplicity, semantic generality, or the basic concepts they encode, as the literature often claims (e.g. Pinker, 1989, p. 121). Here we shall consider an objective, easily quantifiable feature that distinguishes most native stems from Latinate ones and that is their phonemic or articulatory simplicity.

3.3.1 Anglo-Saxon verbs are shorter

The most visible effect of the 'analytic drift' described by Sapir (1921) is the shortening of vocabulary items undergoing it (see section 3.2.1). Native stems are short, many or most monosyllabic. The ones longer than a single syllable tend to be two syllables long, with stress on the first syllable. As Zwicky and Pullum (1986, p. 96) summarize it, '[in] the Anglo-Saxon stratum of the vocabulary, [...] virtually all the root morphemes are monosyllables or initially stressed bisyllables'. By contrast, Latinate stems tend to be multisyllabic, and, moreover, stressed on the last or penultimate syllable.

Short words are easier to process and produce (e.g. Bock, 1982; Keren-Portnoy et al., in press); it is not surprising that parents' speech has been found in several studies to contain a large proportion of short words. There have been no studies that specifically focused on verbs used in core grammar, but the results regarding the total verb repertoire of parents indicate that the parental input may contain a high proportion of short verbs.

For an analysis of child-directed speech, Cassidy and Kelly (1991) used the sample of ten mothers speaking to 15-month-old children, recorded by Landau and Gleitman (1985). The mean number of utterances spoken by the mothers was 485. They found that the mean number of syllables of verb types (lemmas) was 1.07 (SD 0.02), and the mean of verb tokens was 1.01 (SD 0.03) syllables, namely, above 90% of different verb types and verb tokens must have been monosyllabic. For a comparison with adult-directed texts, they analysed the most frequent 750 verb lemmas in Francis and Kučera's (1982) word frequency table, based on a corpus of written American English (the Brown Corpus). They found that verbs in this set had a mean of 1.68 syllables, that is, in adult language there was a much lower proportion of monosyllabic verb types.[6]

Vihman, Kay, de Boysson-Bardies, Durand, and Sundberg (1994) arrived at a quite similar estimate of the length of verbs in child-directed speech as did Cassidy and Kelly (1991). They reported on the speech of five mothers talking to 12-month-old children, and found that of 621 (inflected) verb tokens produced by the mothers, 86% were monosyllabic. Vihman et al. do not report length statistics on verb types or lemmas in addition to tokens of inflected verbs, but their token statistics is close enough to the other study to count as a replication.[7]

Somewhat different estimates than the two above are provided by a recent, large corpus-based study by Monaghan, Chater, and Christiansen (2005).

These researchers analysed the transcribed speech of all English-speaking adults from the CHILDES archive.[8] They selected the 5000 most frequent different orthographic forms in the corpus, categorized them for the most probable grammatical form-class they belong to, getting 1139 verbs. The mean syllable length of the verbs was 1.53; they report that 53.5% of the verb forms were monosyllabic. Thus, their estimate of how many verb forms are monosyllabic in child-directed speech is considerably lower than the estimates of either Cassidy and Kelly (1991) or of Vihman *et al.* (1994), and compares in magnitude to the estimate of adult texts for the most frequent 750 verb types, made by Cassidy and Kelly.

The conflicting estimates could be a result of differences in unit of analysis (text words, lemmas, types, and tokens), sample size, how many frequent and infrequent verbs enter the sample, as well as the identity of the speakers and the addressees. Whatever the reason, past studies do not provide an unequivocal estimate of how much of the verb repertoire of child-directed speech is monosyllabic.

As for length of verbs in child speech, we do not really have an estimate based on past studies. Some indirect indication is provided by a recent study by Storkel (2004) who studied the age of acquisition of nouns by word length, and found that early acquired words are shorter in length than late acquired words. In all probability, we shall find such an age effect also with respect to the syntactic verb vocabulary, meaning that children's verb are expected to be shorter than older speakers', on average.

We now turn to our corpus study. In this chapter, we ask the two questions discussed earlier: first, what is the historical origin of English verb lexemes used in parental and child speech, in core grammatical relations? Second, what is the length in syllables of verb lexemes used in core grammar? Our goal is to find out what part of the English lexicon the parental register uses for core grammar, namely, what is the composition of input with respect to origin and length; and, second, how children compare to parents. Along the way, we will attempt to clarify if articulatory simplicity indeed accounts for the preference for native words or perhaps operates as a separate factor.

3.4 Historical origin of verbs in core grammar

The first analysis concerns the historical origin of verb stems in core grammar.

3.4.1 Coding for origin

We mentioned in Chapter 2 that as part of the preparation of the basic statistics of our corpora, we lemmatized the verb stems of all verbs appearing in the three core grammatical relations (see Appendix B in Chapter 2). For this chapter's statistics, we classified all verb lexemes according to their historical origin, based on the *Online Etymological Dictionary* which is based on several different printed etymological dictionaries and on the *Oxford English Dictionary*. Three categories were used: (1) Native or Anglo-Saxon (including words whose origin is Old Germanic, Old Norwegian, or other Scandinavian languages; if the origin was unknown, also words that first appeared in Old or Middle English; also words borrowed from modern Germanic languages); (2) Latinate (including, except for words of Norman French origin, also words borrowed from Latin and modern Latin languages, and, for simplification's sake, also words borrowed from Ancient Greek, so that it is in fact the category of Graeco-Latin vocabulary, see Quirk, 1974); and (3) other or unknown.

3.4.2 The origin of verbs used for core syntax

Table 3.2 presents the distribution of verb types and tokens by origin in the three corpora, namely, in the complete parental corpus, in the reduced-size parental samples equal in size to the child corpus, and in children's corpus.

In order to see more easily how the three corpora compare, Figure 3.1 presents the distribution of verb types by origin, in the parental full corpus, in the equated-size parental samples, and in the children's corpus.

Table 3.2 Distribution of syntactic verb vocabulary by origin in three corpora

Verb origin	Types	Percent types	Tokens	Percent tokens
Parental full-sized corpus				
Anglo-Saxon	539	60.43%	324,718	95.80%
Latinate	333	37.33%	14,152	4.18%
Other	20	2.24%	100	0.03%
Total verbs	892		338,970	
Reduced-sized parental samples, mean value of 10 samples				
Anglo-Saxon	281.2	68.21%	24,676	95.66%
Latinate	125.6	30.46%	1,111.1	4.31%
Other	5.5	1.33%	8.9	0.03%
Total verbs	412.3		25,796	
Children's corpus				
Anglo-Saxon	227	77.74%	24,624	95.46%
Latinate	62	21.23%	1,166	4.52%
Other	3	1.03%	6	0.02%
Total verbs	292		25,796	

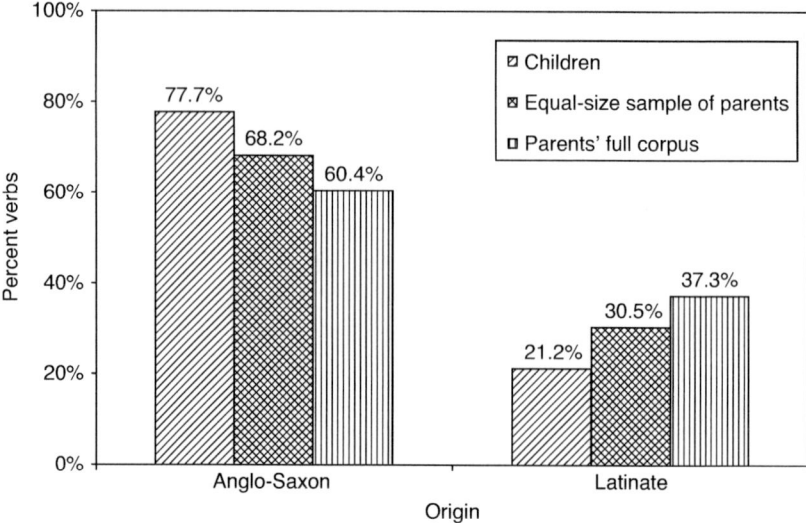

Fig. 3.1 Proportion of Anglo-Saxon and Latinate verbs in parents' full corpus, in ten random parental samples equal size to the child corpus, and in children's corpus.

Table 3.2 and Figure 3.1 make it clear that the actual distribution of verb types used in core grammar is much less biased for native origin than we expected, and indeed contains a considerable proportion of Latinate stems as well. The three samples give us different estimates of this diversity. The large-size full parental corpus, with its close to 900 different verb types, has the largest dispersion of origins; there are close to 40% verbs of Latinate origin. In the reduced-size random samples of parental speech containing about 420 verb types, the percentage of Latinate stems drops to about 30%, demonstrating that sample size affects this estimate as well as the number of types (see section 3.1). This effect explains why our estimate of diversity of origin is so much higher than that based on Phillip's (1973) very small parental sample reviewed earlier in section 3.2. Lastly, in the child corpus the proportion of Latinate verb types drops to about 20%, which is only two-thirds of their proportion in the equal-size parental corpus. However, even in children's speech there are about a fifth of verb stems of non-native origin, showing that the verb vocabulary is much more diverse in composition than the impression we got from the literature review.

As for tokens, Figure 3.2 presents distribution of tokens of core grammar produced by Anglo-Saxon and Latinate verbs, in the parental full corpus, in the equated-size parental samples, and in children's corpus.

Here and in the previous tables we can clearly observe the repetition of the phenomenon observed in Chapter 2 for the distribution of the three core grammatical relations: although the number of types is different, the global

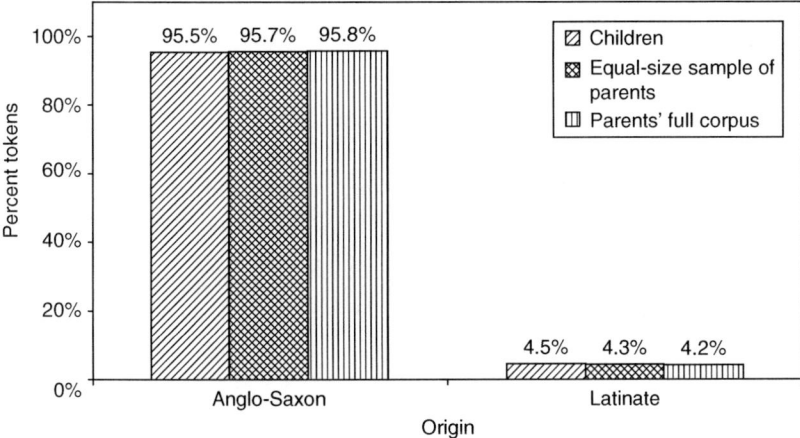

Fig. 3.2 Proportion of tokens generated by Anglo-Saxon and Latinate verbs in parents' full corpus, in ten random parental samples equal size to the child corpus, and in children's corpus.

distribution of the tokens is almost identical in the parental and child corpora, and stands on about 96% of all tokens in all three samples. As with all relative frequency statistics, the reduction in size of the parental corpus by itself makes no difference; however, the child corpus is not merely smaller but also built of barely 300 different verbs as compared to the parents' 900. Our conclusion is a repetition of the one reached regarding the distribution of the three relations in the clausal core: the generation of all but a few percent of all tokens with native verbs must answer to some functional need of parental and child registers—and maybe also of other informal and intimate speech registers for just this parameter and no other. The generation of a constant 96% of tokens built on native stems, regardless of how large the percentage of such verbs in the complete repertoire used, is in effect a rather complicated achievement, from a statistical point of view. In a corpus where 40% of the verbs are Latinate, they must be used much more rarely in order to end up accounting for the same 4% of the total tokens as in a corpus where only 20% of the verbs are Latinate. Truly, this is an amazing phenomenon of global self-organization to a constant critical value, and we shall continue to try and understand the processes by which such overall similarity between children and parents is achieved.

In addition, these results add support to the notion that the native\Latinate dichotomy in historical origins is a psychologically real feature influencing verb choice in both input and output languages. We shall ask in the following section whether we can explain away this variable by the more objective feature correlated with origin, namely, phonological length.

3.5 **Length of verbs in syllables**

3.5.1 **Coding for length**

The second analysis we did was to categorize verbs by their length. Again, we used as our unit verb lemmas, namely, uninflected stems, rather than text words. We checked the length of verb lexemes in syllables. We used the Wordsmyth online English dictionary (Parks, 1999), and complemented the analysis for a few verbs by hand. Two categories only were used: monosyllabic and polysyllabic.

3.5.2 **Length of verbs in the core**

Table 3.3 presents the distribution of the core verb vocabulary by syllable length in the three corpora.

Figure 3.3 presents distribution of types of verbs by length in the parental full corpus, in the equated-size parental samples, and in the children's corpus.

Figure 3.4 presents the distribution of tokens of core grammar produced by monosyllabic and polysyllabic verbs in the parental full corpus, in the equated-size parental samples, and in the children's corpus.

Inspection of Figures 3.3 and 3.4 as well as Table 3.3 reveals that syllable length is a powerful variable affecting verb choice in parents and children. How much the bias is towards monosyllabic verbs depends on how we measure it. As with historical origin, there is a contrast between verb types and tokens: whereas the percent of monosyllabic verb types in the repertoire is

Table 3.3 Distribution of syntactic verb vocabulary by syllable length in three corpora

Length	Types	Percent types	Tokens	Percent tokens
	Parental full-sized corpus			
Monosyllable	573	64.24%	332,767	98.17%
Polysyllable	319	35.76%	6,203	1.83%
Total verbs	892		338,970	
	Reduced-sized parental samples, mean values for 10 samples			
Monosyllable	313.0	75.92%	25,313.8	98.13%
Polysyllable	99.3	24.08%	482.2	1.87%
Total verbs	412.3		25,796	
	Children's corpus			
Monosyllable	258	88.36%	25,342	98.24%
Polysyllable	34	11.64%	454	1.76%
Total verbs	292		25,796	

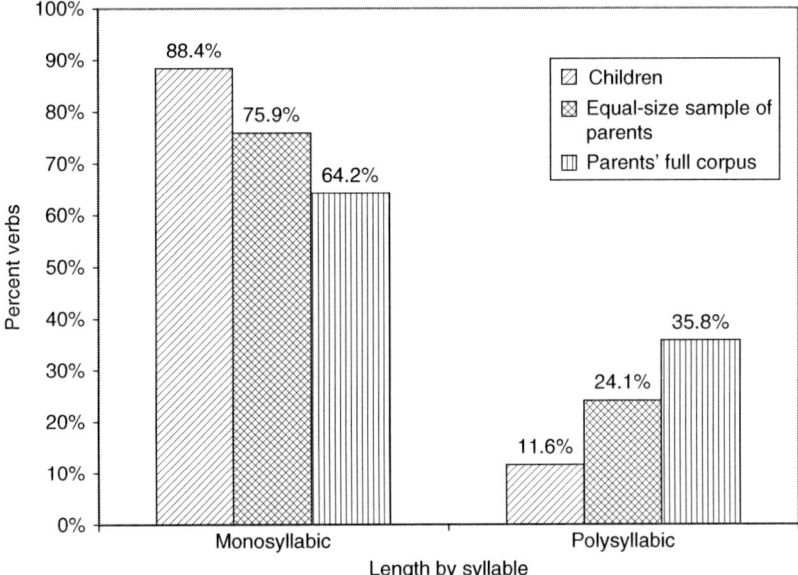

Fig. 3.3 Proportion of monosyllabic and polysyllabic verbs in the core grammatical verb repertoire of children and of parents in the full corpus, and of parents in ten samples the size of the child corpus.

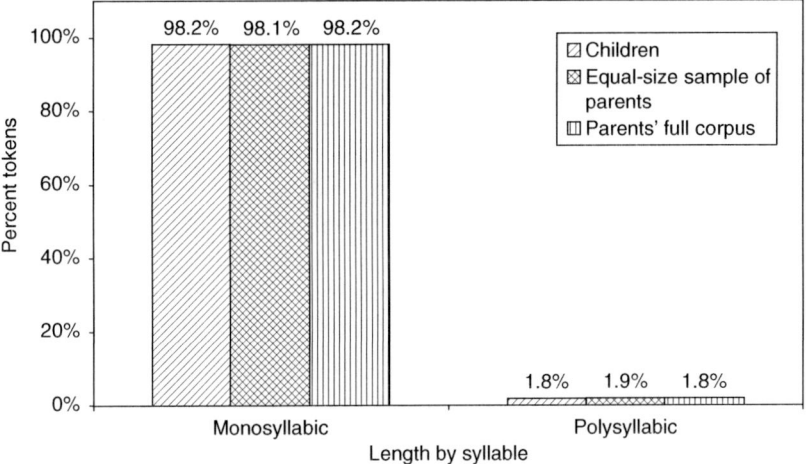

Fig. 3.4 Proportion of tokens generated by monosyllabic and polysyllabic verbs in children's corpus, in parents' full corpus, and in ten parental samples the size of the child corpus.

strongly influenced by sample size and register, and varies between about 65% in the full parental corpus, 75% in the reduced-size parental samples, and almost 90% in the child corpus, the percent of tokens stays at the constant value of just over 98%, regardless of sample size or identity of speakers. We seemed to have uncovered another constant of the informal registers of the English language: the vast majority of grammatical relations in the clausal core are built with monosyllabic verbs; and a bare minimum of 2% contains polysyllabic ones. Interestingly, the small slice of polysyllabic tokens contains a serious variety of different verb stems that changes in magnitude as a function of register: parents actually use many polysyllabic verbs, but with very low type-token ratio, whereas children use just a few, but these still account for the same volume of tokens as the parents' many polysyllabic verbs.

We repeat, thus, the conclusions we arrived at regarding historical origin: there is a quite a diversity of verb lengths in parental verb repertoires that gets reduced in child speech; if, however, we observe the global distribution of this variable over all tokens of core grammar, we get an identity of child and parental registers. It appears that regardless of the difference in the size and composition of their verb repertoires, children and parents both self-organize to reach a constant of 98% token volume of monosyllabic verbs in their speech.

3.6 The interaction of origin and length

Based on the two analyses we have just presented, it appears as if core grammar in parental and child regimes follows two different regulatory principles: it aims to reach a constant of 96% tokens built on native Anglo-Saxon verb stems, and it also aims to reach a constant of tokens built on 98% of monosyllabic verbs. We know, however, that the two factors are not independent, but, rather, native stems tend to be monosyllabic and monosyllabic stems tend to be native. Indeed, it is possible that on closer inspection, the two phenomena reduce to just one, most likely to a bias for the more objective articulatory simplicity. In order to test the mutual relationship of the two factors, we performed a cross-categorizing of the verbs to both historical origin and length. Appendix A presents the verb repertoires of parents and children, in the resulting six categories (Anglo-Saxon, Latinate, or Other X monosyllabic or polysyllabic). Table 3.4 presents the distribution of verb types and tokens in the full parental corpus, in the reduced-size parental samples, and in the children's corpus.

Figure 3.5 presents the distribution of types of verbs in the four categories by length and origin, in the vocabulary serving the core grammar. We dropped the category 'Other' from the graphs as there were too few items for a meaningful presentation.

Table 3.4 Distribution of verbs by origin and length, in the three corpora

Verb category	Types	Percent types	Tokens	Percent tokens
Parental full-sized corpus				
Anglo-Saxon, monosyllable	430	48.21%	321,799	94.93%
Anglo-Saxon, polysyllable	109	12.22%	2,919	0.86%
Latinate, monosyllable	132	14.80%	10,892	3.21%
Latinate, polysyllable	201	22.53%	3,260	0.96%
Other, monosyllable	11	1.23%	76	0.02%
Other, polysyllable	9	1.01%	24	0.01%
Total verbs	892		338,970	
Reduced-sized parental samples, mean values for 10 samples				
Anglo-Saxon, monosyllable	241.2	58.50%	24,449.4	94.78%
Anglo-Saxon, polysyllable	40.0	9.70%	226.6	0.88%
Latinate, monosyllable	68.2	16.54%	857.5	3.32%
Latinate, polysyllable	57.4	13.92%	253.6	0.98%
Other, monosyllable	3.6	0.87%	6.9	0.03%
Other, polysyllable	1.9	0.46%	2.2	0.01%
Total verbs	412.3		25,796	
Children's corpus				
Anglo-Saxon, monosyllable	206	70.55%	24,281	94.13%
Anglo-Saxon, polysyllable	21	7.19%	343	1.33%
Latinate, monosyllable	49	16.78%	1,055	4.09%
Latinate, polysyllable	13	4.45%	111	0.43%
Other, monosyllable	3	1.03%	6	0.02%
Other, polysyllable	0	0.00%	0	0.00%
Total verbs	292		25,796	

Figures 3.6a and 3.6b present the distribution of tokens of core grammar produced by monosyllabic and polysyllabic verbs in four categories by length and origin, in parents' and children's speech.

It is clear that the category 'Anglo-Saxon monosyllabic' dominates both type and token distributions of verbs in the core. When we look at types in the vocabulary, these verbs account for the majority but there are certainly other kinds of verbs as well. As expected, parents use less of these native monosyllabic verbs and children use more; however, the proportion of tokens is constant at 94% of all tokens in both parental and child speech. It appears that the

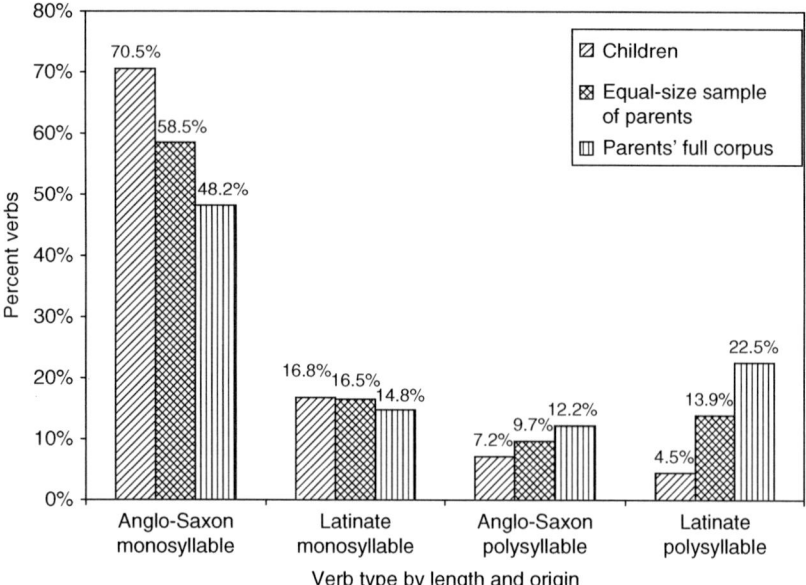

Fig. 3.5 Distribution of verbs (types) by origin and length in three corpora.

major process by which speakers arrive at such a large proportion of both native origin and short length is by making use of the lexical subdomain of monosyllabic Anglo-Saxon verbs. Hence, self-organization into constants of global proportions translates—at least in part—to a bias for very specific vocabulary items.

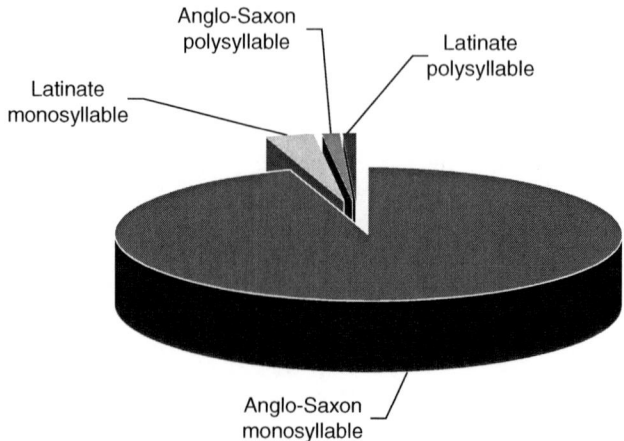

Fig. 3.6a Distribution of core grammar tokens by origin and length of verbs in parents' full corpus.

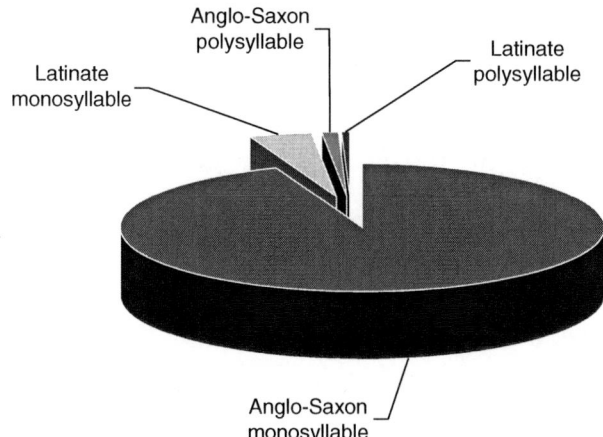

Fig. 3.6b Distribution of core grammar tokens by origin and length of verbs in children's corpus.

3.6.1 Missing verbs in child repertoire by origin and length

In order to test the hypothesis that the two factors of origin and length may reduce to just one that effectively accounts for the results, we performed yet another analysis. We know that children use fewer different verbs to build core grammatical relations than parents. Overall, they are missing about 40% different verbs in order to reach the verb diversity of parental speech even in a sample of identical size.

To find out which kinds of verbs children already mostly master and which they still need to learn, we compared the number of verbs in each of the four main categories by length and origin, namely, Anglo-Saxon monosyllabic, Anglo-Saxon polysyllabic, Latinate monosyllabic, and Latinate polysyllabic in children's verb repertoire relative to the equal-sized samples of parents (again, dropping 'Other' from analysis). The difference between the two samples shows us how many verbs are still missing from children's productive repertoire of each type of verb, comparing to a parental speech sample of the same number of tokens. If the two factors reduce to just length, origin should not play a part in determining the difference between parents and children, only length should. The results are presented in Table 3.5. We can get a feel for the actual verbs involved from Appendix A that presents in separate lists verbs said by children and verbs said by parents but not by children, in each category of verbs by length and origin.

We can observe in Table 3.5 that not only verb length but also its origin has a serious effect on how many of parents' modelled verbs children will take up

Table 3.5 Percent of verbs missing from children's repertoire relative to equal-sized samples of parents, by verb origin and length

Verb type origin X length	Number of verbs		Percent of verbs missing in child corpus
	Mean of 10 samples of parents	Children	
Anglo-Saxon monosyllable	241.2	206	14.6%
Latinate monosyllable	68.2	49	28.2%
Anglo-Saxon polysyllable	40.0	21	47.5%
Latinate polysyllable	57.4	13	77.4%
Total (including 'Other')	412.3	292	

in their own speech. For each category of length (namely, mono- and polysyllabic), almost twice as many Latinate verbs are missing as yet from children's repertoires than Anglo-Saxon verbs. If only length were the factor influencing uptake, we would expect children to use the same percentage of parental verbs in each pair of categories for the same length regardless of historical origin of the stems.

It appears that children selectively simplify their own output relative to the forms modelled for them in the input. Shorter words are obviously simpler to produce than longer ones; apparently Anglo-Saxon verbs are simpler than Latinate verbs on some other dimension, perhaps the basicness of the concepts encoded or semantic generality. We shall return to this question in Chapter 4. In addition, in Chapter 5 we shall examine the possible effect or non-effect of input frequency on children's uptake of forms modelled in the input; we shall also check if children's selective adoption of native and monosyllabic verbs is caused by a relatively higher token frequency of the relevant verbs in the input.

It is worth remarking that children appear to have mastered almost all Anglo-Saxon monosyllabic verbs in the parental register (the comparison corrected for sample size, as the true parental repertoire is much larger), barely needing to complete the learning of another 15% of verbs. By contrast, both added length and Latinate origin increase the proportion of 'missing' verbs, in quite a linear fashion. In fact, the results seem to be derived from two independently working variables, additively affecting the learning of syntactically productive verbs from the input: one being syllable length, the other, historical origin.

Despite the strong bias in token distribution that favours monosyllabic native verbs, these young children at the start of the acquisition of syntax already use longer and Latinate verbs as well. We are dealing here with biases and not absolute constraints; the factors of syllable length and historical origin operate to shape the specifics of distribution within an inherently diverse verb repertoire, both in parents and in children.

Articulatory simplicity is a factor not often examined in the context of syntactic development. Our corpus study shows that when it comes to the early production of core grammar, verbs' length is quite a crucial variable in determining what children selectively pick out from the input. Given that we found a constant of both parental and child speech according to which 98% of all tokens in core grammar are built on monosyllabic verbs, morphophonetic simplicity of verbs appears to be a general parameter of this mode of discourse in parents as well. We seem to support Zipf's (1949/1972) dictum that speakers opt for short words because they reduce the cost of producing speech;[9] it remains to be seen how hearers pay for speakers' convenience in terms of the added difficulty of interpretation presented by short words—also pointed out by Zipf.

As for the historical origin of verbs, it is, of course, up to us to translate the linguistic construct of origin to some proximal factor that in actuality affects children's choices in acquisition. We shall try to answer this question in the next chapter (Chapter 4) where we deal with features of English grammar that differentially apply to Anglo-Saxon and Latinate verb stems. Judging from the composition of their vocabulary, it certainly seems young children are acquiring a native or Anglo-Saxon English, with its specific syntax.

3.7 Conclusions: children learn an Anglo-Saxon verb vocabulary

We discussed in this chapter some new information about the relationship between parental input and child output, with regard to the verbs used to produce the clausal core. First, we found that the parental verb repertoire is about 40% larger than children's total verb vocabulary, even when we measure the parental vocabulary conservatively in an equal-sized sample. That is, children at this early stage of development indeed use significantly fewer verbs in basic syntactic combinations than parents, using each verb for a larger number of tokens on average.

Second, English is a blend of words from a native Germanic and a borrowed Latinate origin; words of the former stream tend to be shorter. We found that parents as well as children use more native verbs and monosyllabic verbs than other kinds, but not exclusively so—there is considerable diversity of verb types by origin and length in both registers, although it is more pronounced in parents' speech.

Third, children learn more native verbs and more monosyllabic verbs out of the available input than other types, and these two factors appear to influence their verb choice separately, in an additive linear manner.

Lastly, the most surprising finding of this chapter is a repetition of the phenomenon observed in Chapter 2 for the distribution of the three core grammatical relations, this time with respect to the distribution of verbs by origin and length. That is, the phenomenon of global similarity despite local differences, between parental speech and child speech. Although the number of verb types is different, the global distribution of tokens is identical in the parental and child corpora, and stands on about 96% of all tokens for native origin and 98% for monosyllabic verbs. It seems we have uncovered two constants of informal speech in English, to do with a preferred and highly biased equilibrium between the volume of native and Latinate verbs and between monosyllabic and polysyllabic verbs, in the clausal core. The significance of these tendencies is that 94% of all core grammatical tokens used by parents and by children are built on native monosyllabic verbs; English-speaking parents thus model and children learn to produce native, Anglo-Saxon core grammar. The significance of this finding will be explored in the following chapters.

Appendix A: **Verbs used by children and parents, by origin and length**

A.1 **Anglo-Saxon, monosyllabic**

A.1.1 Used by children and parents

Ask, bake, bang, bark, bash, bath, be, beat, beg, bet, bite, bless, blow, bounce, break, bring, build, bump, burn, burp, buy, call, can, clap, clean, click, climb, comb, come, cool, cough, crack, crash, crawl, cross, cut, do, draw, drink, drive, drop, dry, dump, dunk, eat, fall, feed, feel, fetch, fill, find, fit, fly, fold, get, give, go, grab, guess, hand, hang, have, hear, help, hide, hit, hold, hook, hop, hug, keep, kick, kiss, knock, know, laugh, lay, leave, let, lick, lie, lift, like, live, load, lock, look, lose, love, make, mark, match, may, mean, meet, melt, mind, miss, must, name, nap, need, own, pack, park, pat, peck, peek, pet, pick, play, plug, poke, pop, pull, put, race, rain, rake, rap, reach, read, ride, ring, rip, rock, rub, run, salt, say, scare, scoot, scratch, see, send, set, shake, share, shoot, shout, show, shut, sing, sit, ski, sleep, slide, slip, smack, smell, smile, smoosh, smooth, snap, speak, spill, spin, spit, splash, spray, squeeze, stack, stand, start, steal, step, stick, sting, stop, swap, sweep, swim, swing, swish, switch, take, talk, tape, tear, tell, thank, think, throw, tie, tip, tuck, twist, wake, walk, want, wash, watch, wave, wear, wet, whip, win, wind, wing, wipe, wish, work, write, yell.

A.1.2 Used only by parents

Back, bag, ball, bead, bend, bleach, blend, block, blot, boo, boss, braid, breathe, bruise, bug, burst, bust, care, carve, chip, choke, choose, clam, cling, clip, crank, creep, crunch, curl, dab, dare, die, dip, dive, drag, dream, drill, drip, duck, dust, earn, end, eye, fan, fart, fight, fish, flap, flash, flick, flip, float, flop, freeze, fudge, fun, fuss, goad, goof, grind, grow, grunt, hatch, hate, heat, hitch, hoard, hog, hole, hope, horn, hum, hunt, hush, ice, inch, iron, itch, jog, kid, kill, knead, kneel, knit, land, last, latch, lead, leak, lean, learn, lend, light, list, loan, loop, man, mash, meow, milk, moan, mow, muck, mush, nag, nip, nod, ooh, ought, owe, peep, pin, plunk, poop, pound, pout, prop, Quack, raid, raise, rest, roar, round, row, sack, sail, saw, scalp, scoop, scorch, score, scrape, scream, scrub, scrunch, seat, seem, sell, sew, shade, shave, shine, shove, shred, sift, sip, skin, skip, slap, sling, slob, slop, slow, slurp, smash, smear, smoke, smush, snatch, sneak, sneeze, snow, soak, soap, sock, spank, spare, spell, split, splodge, spoon, spot, spread, squirm, squirt, stab, stain, stamp, stash, steam, steer, stink, stir, stitch, stomp, stretch, string, stroke, stroll, stub, stunt, suck, swear, swipe, tan, teach, tease, thread, thump, tick, tide, tilt, tire, toot, top, toss, trade, trash, tread, trim, trip, trust, tug, tweak, twirl, wag, wang, warm, warn, weed, weep, weigh, weight, whack, wheel, wrap, wreck, wring, yank.

A.2 Anglo-Saxon, polysyllabic

A.2.1 Used by children and parents

Answer, believe, belong, borrow, bother, cuddle, dig, empty, forget, hammer, happen, hurry, listen, open, settle, squeak, swallow, tickle, undo, unlock.

A.2.2 Used only by parents

Afford, babysit, become, begin, behave, blob, bubble, bully, bury, butter, bye-bye, chatter, cornmeal, crumble, defrost, dirty, doggone, download, dribble, dry-clean, fasten, fiddle, follow, forbid, forgive, frighten, gather, gobble, handle, head-butt, holler, jingle, loosen, mumble, nibble, outtalk, overcome, paddle, peekaboo, poopoo, rattle, recall, reckon, redo, reload, remind, repot, retie, rewind, scatter, shadow, sharpen, shatter, shovel, smother, sniff, sparkle, straighten, struggle, stumble, tackle, threaten, tidy, tighten, tumble, turtle, understand, unload, unplug, unsnap, unstick, unthread, untie, unwind, unwrap, uppie, upset, waddle, waken, water, welcome, whisper, whistle, wiggle, wobble, wonder, worry, wriggle, wrinkle.

A.2.3 Used only by children

Bobble.

A.3 Latinate, monosyllabic

A.3.1 Used by children and parents

Brush, catch, cause, change, chase, check, close, cook, count, cry, dance, dress, fix, guard, hurt, jump, mend, mix, move, paint, part, pass, pay, pee, peel, pinch, post, pour, press, push, quit, roll, save, screw, sound, spoil, squash, squish, stay, taste, touch, trick, try, turn, type, use, visit, wait, waste.

A.3.2 Used only by parents

Act, add, ah, aim, blame, boil, calm, camp, cave, charge, chop, chuck, clear, cost, crush, curse, damn, darn, dish, doubt, face, fail, fence, flush, fool, force, fry, gain, glue, grade, grate, grease, growl, gum, haul, joke, page, pant, paste, phone, pile, pipe, plan, plant, please, point, pounce, praise, print, prompt, prove, pry, punch, quote, rhyme, rinse, rush, seal, serve, shock, sign, slice, soil, sort, spend, spy, strap, stuff, style, suit, tap, tempt, tend, test, toast, trace, treat.

A.4 Latinate, polysyllabic

A.4.1 Used by children and parents

Buckle, carry, colour, cover, dial, excuse, finish, juggle, pardon, pretend, remember, suppose, unbuckle.

A.4.2 Used only by parents

Abandon, absorb, accept, accuse, adjust, admit, adore, afraid, agree, allow, announce, annoy, apologize, apply, appreciate, arrange, arrive, assert, assume, assure, attach, attack, balance, bandage, button, circle, collect, combine, comfort, complain, conduct, confirm, confuse, connect, consider, contain, contemplate, continue, control, cooperate, coordinate, copy, correct, corrupt, crayon, debate, decide, decorate, defy, deliver, deny, depend, deposit, deprive, describe, deserve, destine, destroy, detect, determine, digest, dilute, direct, disappear, discover, discuss, dismantle, displease, disrupt, distort, distract, disturb, electrocute, enclose, encourage, enjoy, entertain, entice, erase, escape, establish, evade, excite, exhaust, exist, expect, explain, explore, express, fancy, fascinate, figure, flatten, guzzle, hasten, identify, ignore, imagine, imitate, improvise, insist, insult, intend, interest, interfere, interpret, interrupt, introduce, invent, invite, involve, irritate, jiggle, join, manage, marry, matter, measure, mention, merit, misjudge, mistreat, neglect, notice, offer, operate, order, pedal, perform, persuade, picture, plaster, polish, practice, prefer, prepare, prevent, produce, profile, promise, propose, protect, protest, provide, punish, realize, rearrange, recognize, recommend, reconsider, reconstruct, record, regret, relax, remedy, remove, repeat, replace, require, rescue, respect, return, rotate, ruin, separate, strangle, study, suffer, suggest, support, surprise, sustain, telephone, torture, unbutton, uncover, undress, unpack, unpeel, unscrew, unstrap, vacuum, vanish, vibrate, volunteer, wallop.

A.5 Other origin, monosyllabic

A.5.1 Used by children and parents

Bonk, zip.

A.5.2 Used only by parents

Beep, bop, chug, clunk, foo, honk, swoosh, zap, zoom.

A.5.3 Used only by children

Brrmm.

A.6 Other origin, polysyllabic

A.6.1 Parents only

Buggle, clobber, hoover, menorah, mummy, shampoo, teetee, unzip, zuggle.

Notes

1 The correlation of number of types with sample size is familiar in corpus studies, as it constitutes a problem for deriving type-token ratios as estimates of lexical diversity of different sized speech samples (e.g. Corkum and Dunham, 1996, and see also Sichel, 1986).

2 This technique is seldom used in developmental psycholinguistics. An exception is Rowland and Fletcher (2006) who, in a study of biases stemming from small sample sizes of child speech, employed a similar randomized-sampling method to construct simulated samples of various sizes on the basis of diary data.

3 An isolating language is one in which words have no internal structure but consist of a single form which does not change in different uses. For instance, an isolating language such as Mandarin Chinese does not inflect verbs for number or tense, whereas a morphologically rich language such as French uses systematically alternating forms according to these nuances of meaning. Formally, words in an isolating language consist of a single morpheme whereas words in morphologically rich languages are polymorphemic. For a central treatment of the morphological typology of languages, see Sapir (1921).

4 Dutch, too, has a hybrid vocabulary, with simplex Dutch verbs consisting almost exclusively of Germanic verbs; Latinate verbs in this language are derived and contain a verbalizing suffix (De Schutter and Gillis, 1990).

5 Phillips (1973) excluded auxiliary verbs from her statistics on 'verb forms', cited above; had she included them, the proportion of tokens generated by native stems would be even higher.

6 Cassidy and Kelly (1991) also checked the date of entry into English (in centuries) of different verbs into the language and correlated it with syllable length, getting significant increase of length with recency of entry. Although they did not cross-classify the words by historical origin, it is likely that some of the correlation reflects the length difference between modern verbs of Anglo-Saxon and Latinate sources we discussed in section 3.2, when the presently short Anglo-Saxon verbs are of an earlier 'date of entry' than Latinate verbs.

7 In a recent study, Roark and Demuth (2000) analysed approximately 80,000 words produced by nine English-speaking parents from the CHILDES archive. Their results do not break the statistics by word-class, but provide only the distribution of the total vocabulary. Analysing inflected text-words rather than stems, as did Vihman *et al.* (1994), they found that monosyllabic and disyllabic words with initial stress accounted for about 90% of the tokens produced by the parents. As these statistics refer to all vocabulary items, it is somehow difficult to estimate from them the distribution of verbs by length. We know that monosyllabic closed-class function words such as *of, and, to, in, that,* and *it* are among the most frequently used words (Johansson and Hofland, 1989), and a large part of monosyllabic word tokens will consists of these. On the other hand, the words analysed include nouns as well as other open-class words besides verbs, and the former are on average longer than verbs, both in adult written prose and in parental speech (Cassidy and Kelly, 1991), raising the relative proportion of longer words. Thus, the mean estimate in Roark and Demuth is suggestive but not specific enough to provide a clear picture of the relative proportion of short verbs in the input.

8 Although there are some parents among those whose utterances are transcribed in CHILDES who address quite a few of their utterances to an adult present during observations (see Appendix A to Chapter 2), in most probability the majority of this collection truly consists of child-directed utterances.

9 Longer words take up more of the speakers' resources than short words; they take longer to pronounce, take up more space in working memory (Baddeley, 1999), and are more difficult to retrieve from long-term memory than short words (Bock, 1982).

Chapter 4

Input and output

4.1 The special syntax of Anglo-Saxon verbs

The results of Chapter 3 showed that, on the whole, parents model and children learn a native verb vocabulary for generating core grammatical combinations. More precisely, parents demonstrate and children concentrate on learning the morphophonetically simplest Anglo-Saxon verb vocabulary, to which they add monosyllabic verbs of Latinate and other (onomatopoeic) origin.

We shall begin this chapter with descriptions of the special syntax of Anglo-Saxon verbs in linguistic texts; then, we shall ask how characteristic this kind of usage is in the parental register and the child dialect. We know from the results of Chapter 3 that these varieties of speech employ the Anglo-Saxon verbal vocabulary for core grammar, but the question is, do they use the special multiword verbal patterns unique to this vocabulary? As we shall see, the answer is positive, with important consequences for acquisition.

A note on the native verbal lexicon and its grammatical behaviour. As we emphasize in this chapter, the syntactic features of Present Day English fit rather well the description of an analytic language that got shaped in the still ongoing synthetic-to-analytic 'drift'. The features we focus on are distinct and specific to the Anglo-Saxon vocabulary; they are not shared (except by assimilation) with the Latinate part of the English lexicon.[1] In section 3.3.1 we mentioned that native verb stems are short, most are monosyllabic, and if bisyllabic, have stress on the first syllable. Latinate words tend to be polysyllabic and to have stress on the last or penultimate syllable. However, some Latinate verbs are short and have a stress pattern typical of Germanic verbs—and these tend to be assimilated into the Anglo-Saxon verb vocabulary in terms of their grammatical behaviour (Green, 1974). When we discuss the special grammatical features of native verbs, we include also the assimilated short Latinate verbs.

4.1.1 **Grammatical verbs**

4.1.1.1 Auxiliaries

Modern English, as the result of the 'analytic drift' (Sapir, 1921)[2] mentioned in the last chapter, became an analytic language. The original Anglo-Saxon dialects were synthetic languages, with rich morphology. Present Day English is almost completely devoid of inflectional morphology. Much of its tense, aspect, and modal specifications are done with the help of auxiliary verbs. It uses a host of other functional verbs such as a copula and other semi-copular 'raising verbs'; semi-auxiliary and quasi-auxiliary modal verbs; vector verbs; a dummy verb for questioning and negation, and so forth. That is, much of the language's grammatical modulations or functions for tense, aspect, mode, and so forth, are expressed by periphrastic combinations involving an inflected, finite auxiliary verb and an uninflected, non-finite verb or other predicate. We might look on these constructions as a composite verb, with the non-finite predicate providing the content and the finite auxiliary providing the grammatical meaning which in synthetic languages is provided by bound morphemes on the lexical verb.[3]

For us, the most interesting fact regarding the set of verbs serving such grammatical functions is that, almost without exception, they belong to the Anglo-Saxon stratum of the lexicon. The copula is the verb *be*; the dummy verb is *do*; the auxiliary verbs are *be* and *have*, the modal auxiliaries are *can, may, must, need, ought*, and *have*; all are native verbs. In addition, English also has hybrid verbs with partial auxiliary features variously called semi-lexical verbs (e.g. *get, go, come, make, let*, and possibly *want* and *say*; Emonds, 1985, p. 169; 2000, chapter 3), quasi-auxiliaries, or vector verbs (Hopper and Traugott, 1993, pp. 108–9); *want* as well as *have* are said to be semi-modal (Biber *et al.* 1999; Mindt, 2000; Palmer, 1990), and *want to* or *wanna*—an incipient modal auxiliary (Verplaetse, 2003).[4] Whatever the terminology, verbs with such grammatical uses are Anglo-Saxon verbs (Gneuss, 1991, p. 23).[5]

It need not be said that grammatical verbs get subjects in ways formally indistinguishable from any other verb, namely, the verbs are crossmarked for person and number of the subject and not of the object; the subject term is in the nominative case and positioned preverbally, and so forth. On any formal coding criterion, grammatical verbs receive core grammatical complements and thus belong to the clausal core. The anomaly is in the semantics of the subject: the inflected auxiliary verb and copula do not possess a thematic role for the subject; in terms of meaning, the subject is a logical/semantic argument of the non-finite predicate which is another dependent of the auxiliary or copula. Thus, in the sentence '*I am hungry*', the copula *to be* is the inflected main verb getting the subject, but the semantic role and interpretation of the subject is given by the adjective *hungry*. The formal syntactic Head of the subject has no meaning for it; the predicate having a semantic role for it, does not get it formally as its own syntactic dependent. This complexity is shared with all patterns employing auxiliary verbs, so that in the sentences '*He was running fast*', '*He has written several letters*', or '*He was invited to the meeting*', the participles contribute the semantics but the auxiliaries get the syntactic subject. The set of verbs which make such grammatical contribution to the syntax and semantics of grammatical relations they participate in, are *grammatical verbs*, *functional verbs*, or *functor predicates* as contrasted with *content verbs* or *lexical verbs* (Emonds, 1985; Lehmann, 1991; Lyons, 1968; Quirk *et al.*, 1985; Ritter and Rosen, 1993).

The effect of these facts of English on the grammar presented by parents to young children is that some proportion of their SV combinations—which we know are mostly with the native set of verbs—will consist of grammatical verbs getting a formal subject rather than of content verbs getting a semantically meaningful subject. We shall see later (section 4.2.1) how large this proportion is, and will discuss the significance of this phenomenon at that point.

4.1.1.2 Complex predicates, multiword verbs

Except for periphrastic combinations for tense, aspect, mode, and so forth, which are grammatical functions affecting English in general, there is another kind of special use of Anglo-Saxon verbs, this time in constructions unique to this vocabulary. Once again, we are talking about analytic patterns in which a multi-word syntactic pattern is used to generate a composite meaning, but, in this case, the meaning is totally lexical and not a combination of grammatical tense, aspect or mode and lexical meaning. I refer to so-called multiword verbs, phrasal verbs, complex predicates, and so forth—all involving a verb and some complement which can be verbal, nominal, or non-finite predicative such as adjective, adverb, and so on. These constructions are in evidence already in Old English (e.g. Nickel, 1968) but, as part of the 'analytic drift', their frequency sharply increased in Middle English and has been continuing to increase in use to this day (Bacchielli, 1993; and see chapters in Brinton and Akimoto, 1999). The majority of these constructions use native verbs (Hiltunen, 1999). There are a considerable number of different constructions of this kind, all of which represent multiword lexemes.[6] As in this book we are exploring grammatical relations in the clausal core, the only pattern relevant for us at the moment is the one in which the verb receives a direct object with such an idiomatic feature, namely, the verb–nominal or Light-Verb Construction (LVC).[7]

A good source to learn about LVCs is Butt (2003), who gives the following definition:

> Jespersen (1965, Volume VI:117) is generally credited with first coining the term *light verb*, which he applied to English V+NP constructions as in (1).
>
> (1) *have* a rest, a read, a cry, a think
> *take* a sneak, a drive, a walk, a plunge
> *give* a sigh, a shout, a shiver, a pull, a ring
>
> The intuition behind the term "light" is that although these constructions respect the standard verb complement scheme in English, the verbs *take, give*, etc. cannot be said to be predicating fully. That is, one does not actually physically "take" a "plunge" but rather one "plunges". The verbs therefore seem to be more of a verbal licenser for nouns. However, the verbs are clearly not entirely devoid of semantic predicative power either: there is a clear difference between *take a bath* and *give a bath*. The verbs thus seem to be neither at their full semantic power, nor at a completely depleted stage. Rather, they appear to be semantically *light* in the sense that they are contributing something to the joint predication. However, exactly what this component is is relatively difficult to characterize.
>
> Butt (2003, p. 1)

Canonical light verbs are *do, give, have, make,* and *take* (Algeo, 1995, Kearns, 1998; and see chapters in Brinton and Akimoto, 1999). Other verbs participating in this construction are *put, come, go, pick,* and so on.

The noun serving as the complement of the light verb is special, too: it is in all cases an eventive noun; that is, a noun that carries the eventive meaning usually carried by the verb (Allerton, 2001).[8]

Not all researchers define the LVC identically; there are more restrictive and broader definitions. Interestingly, the verbs are always the same set of verbs; the definitions hang on the complement allowed. The LVC is in fact a family of similar constructions, differentiated by the features of the nominal. The most strict definition requires that—as in Butt's examples, above—the nominal will be a 'verb-stem noun'; namely, a noun that relates to an existing verb by zero-derivation.[9] In these cases, the noun is identical in form to the simple verb synonymous to the whole LVC; to have a bath is, in one word, to bathe. A slightly broader definition allows deverbal nouns, derived from a verb stem by some nominalizing suffix such as *-ent, -ion,* or the gerund's *-ing*. An example may be '*to have a discussion*', which can be replaced by the simple verb '*to discuss*'. Algeo (1995) and Allerton (2001) employ such a definition. Finally, the broadest definition (employed, for instance, by Matsumoto, 1999) also allows nouns which are not derived from a simplex verb, resulting in LVCs which do not have simple verb synonyms with a cognate verb, such as '*take heart*'. The issue of definitions will become relevant presently, when we describe the methodology of our corpus study of LVCs in parental and child speech and compare our results with those of Algeo.

As with subjects of copulae and auxiliary verbs, the direct object of LVCs is a formal object identical in its coding features to all other objects: the object term is in the accusative case and its canonical position is postverbal. The problem is, as before, with the semantics of the object vis-à-vis the verb.[10]

LVCs appear to be a rather complicated subtype of verb–object combination. In the first place, the combination is an idiomatic collocation, and in most cases its meaning cannot be compositionally derived from the simplex meanings of the verb and the object (Givón, 1979; Sapir, 1931). Traugott (1999) argues that LVCs undergo lexicalization, meaning freezing of form and meaning, as well as idiomatization, as part of the process of their historical derivation. The morphological form of the noun is mostly fixed and cannot be flexibly altered; this is in contrast to the freedom characterizing nouns serving as canonical direct objects. LVCs also have various odd syntactic behaviours, including restrictions on the determination, attribution, and pronomization of the complement noun (Brinton, 2005; Butt, 2003; Macfarland, 1995; Kearns, 1988). The verb, as we said, is weakened, the noun is eventive and predicative, and the combination of the two has unusual and often unpredictable semantics.

The outcome of a LVC is a complex multiword verb, whose meaning needs to be lexically stored, rather than a canonical verb–object combination whose meaning is derived ad hoc from the a priori valency of the verb and the semantics of the noun complement. Indeed, according to some theoretical analyses the weakened and 'bleached' verb does not contribute much or any meaning to the construction (Cattell, 1984; Jespersen, 1965), nor does it possess more than a skeletal argument structure; the thematic roles are of the object nominal and it donates them to the verb in a process of complex predicate composition (e.g. Grimshaw and Mester, 1988; Kearns, 1988; Rosen, 1990; Szabolcsi, 1986). This process turns upside down the usual roles of verbs and their objects, as in the case of 'heavy' or main verbs it is the verb that defines the thematic role of the object argument, and the job of the nominal expression is merely to specify what entity fills the relevant semantic role vis-à-vis the verb.

To add to the complication, there is no such thing as a designated light verb. Instead, Light-Verb Constructions exist side by side with 'heavy' uses of the same verbs. That is, the verbs participating in LVCs—the light verbs—are merely light versions of verbs concurrently used in the language in full or 'heavy' versions.[11] This appears to be a cross-linguistic fact (Butt, 2003), and it certainly is perfectly true of English. Butt proposes that light verbs and their form-identical main verbs share a single lexical entry, and the difference between them is merely the syntactic context of their various uses. This is not the only opinion there is; there are linguists who thinks that the verb serving as light verb is a polysemous and polyvalent lexeme with several listable lexical entries, rather than a monosemous, vague, and underspecified verb that can be used in various different contexts, including the heavily 'bleached' use in a LVC (Newman, 1996; Pustejovsky, 1995).

Whatever the outcome of this theoretical debate, the fact remains that the verbs of LVCs are functionally polysemous and polyvalent, and as such, they potentially violate the desirability principle that each linguistic form has a single meaning, mapped to it on a one-to-one basis. If parents indeed follow some simplifying strategy such as only using each lexeme in one meaning context, they might reduce the use of LVCs to a very minimum or eliminate them completely, to spare the polysemy and the complicated idiomatic meaning of the phrasal predicates from the young child. Proposals such as this have been made on related phenomena, for instance, Pinker (1987) suggested that maternal speech has very few deverbal nouns (citing the results of an unpublished study by Hochberg and Pinker from 1987 on p. 405) because mothers tend to avoid these zero-derived (aka converted) heterosemous forms so as not to complicate children's task of associating nouns with the semantic content of objects and not with that of actions. As the majority of LVCs use deverbal nouns as the nominals of the construction, if mothers indeed avoid them or restrict their use, this should also considerably reduce the frequency of LVCs in their speech. Apparently, English-speaking parents do not completely drop LVCs from their speech as previous studies of parental speech found that parents do use them with young children, including children in Stage I of grammar (Barner, 2001; Macnamara, 1982; Nelson et al., 1993; Oshima-Takane et al., 2001). The magnitude of their use is unknown, and if Pinker is right, it should be quite minimal.

In any case, it is not obvious that such combinations are within young children's capacity to comprehend, and even less, within their power to learn to produce. There is not much data on the question, but at least one study found that children in Stage I do not produce LVCs, and these begin to be produced only in Stage II or III of development. Barner (2001) analysed the speech of nine children taken from CHILDES[12] for their use of five verbs *do, get, give, have,* and *take,* and did not find any LVCs in Stage I speech of the children. If the pattern is a rare one, however, he might have missed it because his sample is so small. Nevertheless, previous findings strengthen the impression that these patterns may be difficult for children. In a study of an English-speaking child's first 20 verb–object combinations with different verbs, there were no LVCs among these early sentences (Ninio, 1999a).[13] At a slightly later stage, the same child, Travis, began to generate SVO combinations; but there was no LVCs among her first 20 SVO-sentences with different verbs, either (Ninio, 2003). The very first sentence with a new verb in some pattern is not the best estimate of its total uses within the same stage of development; it is possible that after the first combination with some complement (typically a pronoun, for Travis), a child might expand the use to other complements, including eventive nouns.

Thus, it appears possible that LVCs are not a very early pattern in young English-speaking children's speech, but the issue is far from settled. There is a study on the acquisition of Dutch—a very similar language to the native core of English—that at first glance appears to support such a conclusion, but with further scrutiny, raises some questions. Hollebrandse and van Hout (1994) studied four Dutch children's verb combinations. Three of the children were slightly older, between 2;4 and 3;10; they also had an MLU of about 2.30 at the relevant period and thus were beyond Stage I that ends at MLU of 2.0 (Brown, 1973). These children produced many Light-Verb Constructions, such as the Dutch equivalent of 'give a kiss' or 'make photo'; they in fact seemed to prefer these verbal collocations to their full verb variants, e.g. 'make a drawing' was preferred over 'draw' (p. 83). The fourth child who was much younger (1;9.18–2;2.18), and at an earlier developmental stage than the rest, with an MLU of 1.42, and who probably just generated her first VO combinations, produced very few LVCs, similar to Travis at the very earliest stage of multiword speech. The problem with the generality of this study is that the three children who produced many LVCs were not typically developing children; two were said to be disfluent and the third, a slow starter. Thus, it is possible that their speech at Stage II in fact represents more fluent children's Stage I pattern. These previous findings leave it an open question if normally developing Stage I children—such as the ones in our corpus—do or do not use LVCs in any numbers at this stage of development.

In the next section, we shall examine the parental and child corpora for patterns of use of auxiliary verbs in SV relation and of light-verbs constructions in the VO relation. If parents' speech demonstrates these constructions for the Anglo-Saxon verbs we know they use, we can go on and ask, can children master the complexities involved? In particular, we expect difficulties in formal-grammatical rather than content-full uses of subjects; in semantically bleached uses of verbs in the verb–object constructions; and in the parallel employment of verbs in more than one type of construction, in both grammatical relations. This question is rather important for English-speaking children as the complicated analytic constructions we are investigating are central for English; in Hiltunen's (1999) phrase, they are among the core resources of the English language today (p. 132).

4.1.2 **Developmental considerations**

For developmental theorizing, it might come as unwelcome news that the fundamentals of English syntax are presented to young children using the Anglo-Saxon, monosyllabic verb vocabulary. This sub-lexicon is an odd vehicle to carry the didactic burden of modelling for beginning speakers the simplest, most fundamental constructions of their native language. As we have seen, Anglo-Saxon (and short Latinate) verbs have some unique syntactic behaviours not shared by the rest of the verbal lexicon, and, at first glance, these special patterns appear to make syntax more complicated to learn.[14] The native verb lexicon participates in various periphrastic, analytical constructions in which verbs often do not have a semantic slot for their subject or object. In addition, the Anglo-Saxon verbal vocabulary is notorious for its polysemy and heterosemy;[15] and each verb appears to be unique and not quite like any other (Stubbs, 1986).

The fact that the three core grammatical relations in the input language use the native Anglo-Saxon verb vocabulary, makes it somehow less likely that parents' most frequent verbs in these basic constructions will be able to serve as models for the prototypical semantics of these constructions. To remind ourselves (see section 1.5.4), grammatical relations are treated by Construction Grammar as meaningful Argument-Structure Constructions possessing a prototypical semantics (e.g. Croft, 2001). Goldberg (1995, 2005) has offered a theory according to which the prototypical meaning of a construction develops out of parents' most frequently modelled verbs (see also Kay, 1996). However, as I shall show below, the special syntactic features of the Anglo-Saxon vocabulary as employed in the core grammatical relations appear not to fit well with the predictions of Goldberg's theory, in particular as it is well-known that frequent verbs exaggerate the analytic features of the native verb lexicon.[16]

First, in this stream of the English language, core items in the three basic grammatical relations may not have prototypical semantics. According to authorities, the prototypical semantics for the subject in the SV relation is 'agent of action'; the prototypical semantics for the direct object term in VO is 'effected object of agent's action', and the prototypical semantics for indirect object in VI is 'recipient in transfer of possession of object' (Croft, 1990; Goldberg, 1995; Hopper and Thompson, 1980; Lakoff, 1977; Pinker, 1989; Taylor, 1989, 1998). For instance, Taylor gives the following definition:

> The transitive prototype involves an agent (encoded by the subject nominal), which intentionally acts on a patient (the direct object nominal), so as to effect a change-of-state in the patient.
>
> Taylor (1998, p. 187)

If the core verbs happen not to be actions in SV and VO, or deal with transfer of possession in VI, the grammatical construction will not have prototypical semantics. This could be the case because the core verbs in the clause may not have lexical semantics at all; they could be semi-lexical, grammatical, or functional verbs, lacking pure semantics (Emonds, 1985).

Second, core items may be different from non-core items in both semantics and syntax, with the result that other verbs cannot model themselves on them. As Dixon (1991) showed, the most frequent and most central, nuclear items in a group of verbs of similar meaning will be unlike the more peripheral items in that the former will have a wider semantic range and more varied syntactic possibilities, not shared with other items. As an example, Dixon uses the verb *give* that has a more polysemous range of meaning than other verbs, and can participate in various analytic constructions while more specific verbs cannot (p. 125). This is a general problem with the most frequent basic vocabulary items when they are picked as sources of semantic prototypes, as such verbs tend to be syntactically atypical; see Croft (1990, p. 15; 2009) and Borg and Comrie (1984, p. 123) on this topic. This implies that the core verbs of the native stream of English may not be good prototypes for the form-class as a whole.[17]

As these claims refer to English in general and not to parental speech in particular, we shall have to ask of the data how child-directed speech fares on these potentially complicating features. That is, we can ask of the data, how it fits with Construction Grammar's concept of meaningful Argument-Structure Constructions and with Goldberg's theory of how the prototypical meaning of a construction develops out of parents' most frequently modelled verbs. We hope that our large corpora will shed light on these central unsolved questions in acquisition theory. If the description above is true of the way parents talk to young children, and the kind of core syntax young children acquire, we will need to rethink the role of meaningfulness in syntactic development, at least as Construction Grammar and prototype theory visualize it. We will also have to revise our conceptions of what is simple and what is difficult in acquisition, as the Anglo-Saxon type of grammar appears to pose quite a challenge for young children.

4.2 Core grammar in parental and child speech

The section of this chapter devoted to reporting on the parental input and child output of core syntax is organized by grammatical relations, starting with subject–verb and continuing with verb–object and verb–indirect object relations. With each syntactic pattern, we focus on the data most relevant to the issues we are interested in, leaving some other results for an appendix.

4.2.1 **Subject–verb combinations: auxiliaries and content verbs**

4.2.1.1 Grammatical and content uses of the SV combination

There are in all 195,206 tokens of subject–verb (SV) combinations in parents' speech, generated by 601 different verbs. The four most frequent verbs generating SV combinations are the auxiliary verbs *be, do, can,* and *have.* The most frequent verb is *be* which generated 102,700 tokens of SV, accounting for 52.6% of the total. Next comes the verb *do* with 28,360 tokens (14.5%), then *can* with 12,155 tokens (6.2%), and last of the four comes *have* with 9284 tokens (4.8% of the total SV).

Although *be, do, can,* and *have* are the four full auxiliaries of English, not all uses of these verbs is a grammatical use, as *do* and *have* also have content uses. Moreover, there are other verbs that perform grammatical and not content functions, the most prominent being *may, must,* and *ought,* namely, the modal auxiliaries. In order to make a minimal estimate of the grammatical uses of SV, we added up the grammatical uses of these seven verbs, separating out the content uses of *do* and *have.* The results are presented in Table 4.1. There are other grammatical patterns we did not cover in this estimate, such as rarer 'raising verbs' that also do not have a thematic role for their subjects, e.g. *seem* and *appear,* thus the statistics underestimate the proportion of grammatical subjects. The same table also presents the breakdown into the two types of language functions in children's speech.

The distribution of different verbs in children's speech was similar but not identical to that in parents' corpus. Children produced a total of 14,375 tokens of SV, using 220 different verbs. Their four most frequent verbs in SV were *be* (6012 tokens), *want* (1629), *do* (1268), and *go* (951 tokens). The content verbs *want* and *go* pushed the other main auxiliary verbs to fifth and sixth place, *can* with 544 tokens, and *have* with 469 tokens. Also, they produced very few tokens of the modal auxiliaries *may, must,* and *ought,* just 29 tokens for all three. By comparison, in parents' speech there were 833 tokens of these modal auxiliaries, making 0.43% of the total, against 0.20% in children's speech. Although children's pattern is not radically dissimilar, the differences listed above show up as a considerable overall disparity in the percent of grammatical uses in parental and child speech, as we can see in Table 4.1.

In parents, three-quarters of SV tokens are for grammatical uses. Namely, the great majority of subjects in parental speech are formal subjects, not ones filling some semantic role versus the verb that possesses them as its subject.

Interestingly, we found that this is also true of Stage I child speech, a period when children are expected to have 'telegraphic speech' (Brown and Fraser, 1963); here, too, the majority of subjects fill formal and not semantic-thematic slots defined by

Table 4.1 Grammatical and content uses of the subject–verb combination in parents' and children's speech

	Parents		Children	
	Tokens	**Percent**	**Tokens**	**Percent**
Grammatical uses	149,235	76.45%	7,523	52.33%
Content uses	45,971	23.55%	6,852	47.67%
Total SV	195,206		14,375	

their Head verbs, even if in a less extreme manner than in parental speech. Our results thus join those of several recent studies (Becker, 2004; Schutze, 2002) in showing that this stage does not involve the complete avoidance of copulas and auxiliary verbs, as is sometimes the interpretation of the results from Brown and Fraser's study. 'Telegraphic speech' is thus better conceptualized as a reduction in copula and auxiliary use, as evidenced in the lesser proportion of grammatical uses relative to parents. This is in fact a rather significant effect: children use twice as large a proportion of their SV for content verbs than parents do. Children make less use of the dummy verb *do* for negation, questioning, and emphasis; they also employ fewer auxiliaries, copula, and modal auxiliaries in their sentences.

Despite these differences, the most frequent verb in SV in children's speech is still *be*, and in particular, used as a copula. One explanation why this use is not avoided by young children is because copular *be* is often a contraction, and does not add to the length of the sentence in words. Some examples of early SV combinations with a contracted copular *be* are in (1):

(1) Contracted copulae in children's sentences:
Here's ball.
It's a chair.
It's broken.
That's alright.
That's hat.
That's a shirt.
That's a doggie.
That's right.
What's that?

In summary, this children's corpus shows that above half of their subjects are for auxiliary and modal verbs, and these are not semantically loaded uses but purely formal grammatical ones. Thus, even if the details differ, the global pattern of a majority of formal-grammatical subjects is similar to that of parents, albeit in a less extreme version.

4.2.1.2 Polyvalency and polysemy of frequent verbs in SV combination

As mentioned in sections 1.1 and 4.1.1, the verb *be* has more than one syntactic use and its meaning changes accordingly (Quirk *et al.*, 1985). First, it is used as an aspectual auxiliary, followed by a present participle (Verb-*ing*), namely, by a non-finite verb in the progressive participle form and the phrase it heads (as in '*Are you running away from me/looking at the camera/dreaming/sulking?*'). Second, it is used as a copula, in which case it is followed by a predicate complement which is a noun, adjective or adverb and the phrases they head (as in '*Are you hungry/my little boy/there/under the bed?*'). In addition, *be* also serves as a passive auxiliary, followed by the past participle (as in '*You are invited to the table*'). Semantically, the major dividing line is between the use of *be* as an aspectual auxiliary, when the verb merely serves to structure the construction, and its use as a copula, when it contributes some kind of existential or identificational meaning. The passive auxiliary use is closer to the copular one and frequently it is difficult to discriminate between a passive participle and an adjective (e.g. *tired*) as the same form can serve both uses.

Table 4.2 presents the uses of *be* in the parental and child corpora, distinguishing between the aspectual auxiliary and the copular uses (the latter assimilating also passive auxiliaries).

As Table 4.2 shows, parents as well as children use *be* in the two formal grammatical patterns, with the majority of uses in both cases as a copula, and a minority (larger in parents' case) as an aspectual auxiliary verb.

As in the children's corpus both uses of *be* exist, according to the spirit of Corpus Linguistics this demonstrates that the idealized 'child speaker' uses *be* both as an aspectual auxiliary and as a copula. To strengthen the claim that individual children (and not only the pooled sample) indeed use *be* in both kinds of syntactic contexts, we checked the individual data. Given that in the children's speech the auxiliary uses of *be* occur only in 12% of the total cases, we needed a relatively large number of total tokens per child in order to find the

Table 4.2 Uses of *be* in the subject–verb pattern, in parental and child corpora

Total use		Aspectual auxiliary		Copula	
Corpus	Tokens	Tokens	Percent	Tokens	Percent
Parents	102,700	21,706	21.13%	80,994	78.87%
Children	6,012	759	12.62%	5,253	87.38%

rare use. For this reason, we took the 30 children with the most tokens of *be* in the subject-verb pattern, each of whom produced above 45 tokens of this kind, as the sample on whom to test the various uses of *be*. Of this group of children, 28, namely 93.3%, used *be* both as a copula and as an aspectual auxiliary, and only two children, namely 6.7%, used *be* only as a copula. These findings support the conclusion reached on the basis of the corpus data according to which children do not find it especially difficult to use the same verb in two different grammatical uses, and this within the early period of syntax we call Stage I.

Similarly to *be*, the verbs *do* and *have* also have multiple uses, but this time one kind of use is grammatical, and the other, a use like a regular content-verb. The grammatical uses of *do* include being the dummy verb in questioning and negation, while the content-use is in sentences referring to actual actions, even if somehow vaguely. Some examples of sentences produced by children in our sample are given in (2):

(2)a: grammatical uses of *do*
      Because I don't want to.
      Do you have company?
      But I didn't see them.
      Did one get out?
      Did that come?
(2)b: content uses of *do*
      You do it yourself.
      You do more.
      You do that.
      You do that for me.
      You do that Mom.
      You do that one Mama.

Have is a multi-use auxiliary verb and it also serves as a semi-auxiliary modal verb signifying necessity; its content uses include signifying possession. Some examples from the children's corpus are given in (3):

(3)a: grammatical uses of *have*
      I have to put this in motor jeep.
      We have to wait for my chicken to cool off.
      First I have to get another colour.
      I've got toys.
      It's got a coat on.
(3)b: content uses of *have*
      This have a tail.
      She has hair.

Me have that cookie.
I have toys.
I have two.

Table 4.3 presents these two verbs and the proportions of their grammatical and content uses in the parents' and the children's corpora.

As we did regarding the verb *be,* here, too, we checked the use pattern of individual children in order to be certain that the same children use *do* (or *have*) in both kinds of uses, and that the picture we get from the pooled corpus, of multiple uses of the same verb, is not merely an artefact of using a pooled sample.

Regarding *do,* there were 27 children in the complete sample who produced at least ten tokens in the SV pattern; of these, 24 (89.0%) children had both grammatical and content uses of this verb, and a minority of three (11%) had only grammatical uses.

Regarding *have,* there were only ten children who produced at least ten tokens of this verb in the SV pattern. Of this small sample, nine children (90%) used the verb both for grammatical and for content uses; one child only (10%) used the verb only as a content-verb.

We may summarize that the picture of multiple use of these hybrid verbs is not an artefact, and the great majority of children in Stage I indeed use the same verbs both as grammatical verbs and as content verbs.

Although children are similar to parents in that they, too, use *have* and *do* for multiple purposes, the details show pronounced differences between parents and children: Parents use these verbs with a subject mostly as grammatical verbs, while children use them much more frequently as content verbs. As for *do,* parents almost never use it with a subject as a content verb while children

Table 4.3 Content and grammatical uses of *do* and *have* in parental and child speech, tokens, and percentage of total use (in parenthesis)

	Parents	**Children**
	do	
Content uses	1,570 (5.54%).	480 (37.85%)
Grammatical uses	26,790 (94.46%)	788 (62.15%)
Total use	28,360	1,268
	have	
Content uses	2,527 (27.22%)	319 (68.02%)
Grammatical uses	6,757 (72.78%)	150 (31.98%)
Total use	9,284	469

do so over a third of the time. Similarly, children are twice as more likely to use the verb *have* with a subject to signify possession than to employ it for a grammatical function; in parents, the relative frequencies are biased the other way round. We see here in concrete terms how children relatively disfavour semantically meaningless, formal syntactic dependents. Nevertheless, they do produce them, and, for the relation of subject as a whole (see Table 4.1), such formal uses are the majority.

4.2.2 Verb–object combinations: main verbs and light verbs

4.2.2.1 The most frequent verb in the VO combination and its semantics

Parents produced a total of 137,756 tokens of the verb–object (VO) combination; children produced 11,115. The most frequent verb in parents as well as children in VO is *want*; there were 14,259 tokens in parents' speech (10.4% of the total), and 2331 tokens (21.0% of the total) in children's speech. In the literature there are claims that *want* is a type of semi-lexical, semi-auxiliary verb, and its version with a *to* infinitive, *want to* or *wanna*, is an incipient modal auxiliary (Biber *et al.*, 1999; Verplaetse, 2003; and see section 4.1.1). There are other frequent verbs getting a direct object in these corpora which are said to be semi-modals such as *let*, *have*, and so on. However, in contrast to the SV combination, *want* (and the other verbs in VO) do have semantic content and they define a thematic role for their objects. Take note, though, that the direct object of *want* is the object of desire, not a theme object or affected object as, for example, the object of *cut*; the direct object of *let* is a person permitted to act, and of *have*, a possessed object. We shall discuss the implications of this finding in a later section (4.3). Another fact about *want* worth remarking is that this verb is seriously polysemic and polyvalent; see Krug (2000) for a detailed analysis of its various syntactic patterns.

Among the most frequent verbs getting a direct object in parental speech, there are a group of verbs such as *have, get, do, give, make, take, hold*, and *put* which are known, in adult speech, to possess a semantically bleached 'light' version with which they participate in the so-called Light-Verb Construction (Koskenniemi, 1977). These verbs are not auxiliary verbs or even semi-auxiliaries, but, in their 'light' version they are thought to function as 'transitive copulas' (Curme, 1935, p. 69; Koskenniemi 1977, p. 80). This pattern is rather analogous to the periphrastic analytical constructions in which, as we found, the most frequent verbs in the SV pattern participate. It is therefore the next task to find out if parental speech indeed contains such constructions.

4.2.2.2 Weak verbs in VO combinations

In adult English, the verb–object grammatical relation is host to the analytical Light-Verb Construction (LVC), a construction typically employing native verbs and generating complex multiword predicates. We described this pattern in detail in section 4.1.1, and summarized that the existing literature does not provide a definitive description of the use of this construction in parental input and child speech. The question we are asking now is, does the LVC pattern occur in child-directed speech in significant amounts and if so, do children in Stage I produce them, too?

In order to answer the quantitative question, we capitalize on the existence of published adult English data prepared by Algeo (1995), and immediately compare parental usage statistics to his estimates. Algeo analysed two first-generation large computerized corpora of English for LVCs, the Brown Corpus of American English that contains almost exactly 1 million running words of text (1,014,312), and the Lancaster–Oslo–Bergen (LOB) British Corpus, also about 1 million words (Francis and Kučera, 1979; Johansson *et al.*, 1978). Both corpora contain written texts, over a wide variety of different genres. Algeo prepared statistics of the number of tokens of LVCs involving the five most frequent verbs with such combinations, namely, *do, give, have, make*, and *take*, and we will follow suit. To make the comparison with Algeo's data possible, we employed his definition of LVCs, including verb-stem nouns which are identical-form with a verb as well as nominalized forms with a morphological affix. We also required that the LVC have an approximately synonymous meaning to the verb cognate to the predicative noun, a very strict criterion that possibly we did not need to adopt. This meant that we included a combination such as *give a bite* if it meant 'to bite' but not if it meant 'to share food'. Algeo did not actually publish his criteria and definitions but his examples were all this type, and if we are mistaken in adopting a stricter definition than he did, we shall at the most underestimate the rate of LVCs in parental speech relative to the adult language.

Another adjustment was that for this analysis, we used only part of our parental corpus, to match the size of the two corpora analysed by Algeo. We took the parents in the order we originally hand-parsed the files, stopping when we reached about a million running words (966,233). Given that size of sample has an unknown effect on rate of LVCs in the corpus, it was felt to be more accurate to actually analyse an approximately same-sized corpus instead of relying on relative frequency from a different total.

Appendix A presents the token frequency of the five verbs in the light-verb combination, by the nominals that serve as the objects of the verb, in parents and children's speech. Some actual examples from the parental corpus are given in (4):

(4)a: LVCs with *give* in parental speech:
   I am going to give you a bath now.
   Give them a brush.
   Give him a cuddle.
   Are you giving her a kiss?
(4)b: LVCs with *have* in parental speech:
   Have a drink.
   You've just had a big lunch.
   We'll have a snack later.
   Have you had a long sleep?
   Have a good kick.
(4)c: LVCs with *take* in parental speech:
   Do you want to take a bath?
   Are you gonna take a nap?
   Take a little break.
   Take a look inside the house.
(4)d: LVCs with *do* in parental speech:
   You doing a little dance?
   Don't you want to do your exercises?
   Oh, we're gonna do a big bear hug.
   Mummy's doing the ironing.
(4)e: LVCs with *make* in parental speech:
   Oh, I made a mess.
   Let's make a pile.
   It makes a big noise.

Table 4.4 presents tokens of LVCs in about 1 million running words in the parental register and in two adult language corpora, the American Brown Corpus and the British LOB Corpus, the latter two estimates taken from the

Table 4.4 Light-verb combinations: tokens in parental register compared to adult-directed language, in about 1 million running words (Brown = American corpus, LOB = British corpus, based on Algeo, 1995)

Verb	Parents	Brown	LOB
do	159	4	0
give	311	40	40
have	470	55	100
make	365	59	67
take	300	41	38
Total	1,605	199	245

Appendix of Algeo (1995, p. 214). We are using both adult corpora as controls because our parental corpus includes both American and British speakers, and there are, as Algeo points out, some dialect differences in the verbs used for LVCs. As we are interested only in the sheer volume of such combinations in parental speech, the dialect differences are irrelevant for us, except for wishing to avoid underestimation of the rate of LVCs for particular verbs due to picking the wrong dialect as control.

The token data in Table 4.4 are clear-cut: parents use many more LVCs in speech addressed to young children than the rate of such patterns in the written sources of the adult-addressed language covered by the Brown and LOB collections. The higher frequency of LVCs in spoken language is not by itself surprising as it is a well-documented pragmatic effect that the native vocabulary and its idiomatic, analytic patterns occur mostly in informal, spoken language (Autret, 1945). However, it is somewhat unexpected that parental speech to young children would have such a very high rate of these speech patterns: parents use LVCs when addressing young children seven to eight times more than their rate in adult language.

4.2.2.3 Light-verb combinations in child speech

We searched the children's corpus for LVCs with the same five canonical verbs we analysed for parents. Unexpectedly, we did find quite a few exemplars of this construction,[18] although our speech sample is much smaller than the million running words of the three corpora we compared in Table 4.4. To get an estimate of the extent of use, in Table 4.5 we compare the proportion of LVCs out of all VO combinations with each of the relevant five verbs, in children's and in parents' corpora.

It is, unfortunately, inappropriate to use a Chi-square test with a pair of pooled samples such as our corpora, as some of the subjects are not independent but matched (in cases where the sentences were produced by parents and

Table 4.5 Comparison of parents and young children in use of Light-Verb Constructions as a percentage of verb–direct object combinations

Verb	Parents			Children		
	Total VO tokens	Number of LVC tokens	Percent LVC	Total VO tokens	Number of LVC tokens	Percent LVC
do	5,533	158	2.86%	753	21	2.79%
have	6,001	470	7.83%	673	50	7.43%
make	2,404	365	15.18%	286	29	10.14%
take	1,682	300	17.84%	215	30	13.95%
give	1,195	311	26.03%	124	10	8.06%

children of the same family), and in other cases, the parents and children are independent. For this reason, we shall have to do without a formal test of significance. Nevertheless, informal inspection of the results in Table 4.5 reveals that the proportion of LVCs out of all VO combinations with two of these verbs—*do* and *have*—is approximately the same in children's speech as it is in parents' speech. These are the two verbs with the lowest rate of LVCs in both samples. In the next two verbs by relative rank of use in the parental corpus—*make* and *take*—children use less LVCs than parents, but the differences are not very pronounced. Parents use LVCs in about 16% of all VO combinations with these verbs while children use them only in 12% of all VO. The magnitude of use is not much different with these verbs, either.

The last verb—*give*—has a very high rate of use of LVCs in parental speech, taking up no less than a quarter of all VO combinations with this verb. Here children are far behind parents, producing LVCs only in 8% of their VO combinations. The constructions they are missing out on involve a very specific interpersonal content. Checking the sentences, it appears that the difference is not so much because children cannot say the combinations parents use but because they use some of them much less frequently for a pragmatic reason: many of the LV combinations parents produce with *give* ask for hugs, kisses, and other signs of affection (i.e. '*Give me a kiss*'); there are some sentences with the same meaning in children's speech but their number is infinitesimal relative to that of parents. Parent say '*give a kiss/hug/cuddle/smile*' 231 times out of a total of 1195 sentences with *give* in a VO combination; that is, 19.33% of all VO with *give* are devoted to requesting signs of affection from the children. Children produced only four tokens of this kind out of a total of 124, namely, only 3.23% of all their VO with *give* encodes this type of meaning. Other researchers before me commented on this phenomenon, especially Nelson (1995), and as she analysed the data of different parents and children than we did, the relevant pragmatic difference between parents and children appears to be quite general in English-speaking families. In any case, it is obvious that children do not blindly copy all that parents say to them; if some communicative act is not one they wish to express, this will affect also the rate of syntactic constructions devoted to expressing the relevant message.

Beyond the differences in details, it is quite surprising that young children not only produce LVCs in Stage I but actually use them approximately to the same extent as parents. If we total just these five verbs, parents use 9.54% of all their VO tokens as LVCs, while children use 6.83% of their VOs as LVCs. This is not a very serious difference in rate of use, and we might summarize that children are close to matching parents' rate of LVC use of the five most frequent verbs in this construction.

We did one more analysis to clarify the extent of parents' use of LVCs with young children. In Table 4.4 we compared parents' LVC use to written adult-addressed language and found that they use LVCs much more frequently than the construction's appearance in written texts. We can make another comparison, this time to spoken language. As mentioned earlier (Note 11, Chapter 2), we have analysed a small sample of speech by part of the parents in our corpus in which they address adults (the other parent, a grandparent, or the experimental observer). The size of this small corpus is 6343 running words, and it has just 134 VO combinations with the five canonical LVC verbs we analysed above. We did the same analysis on these sentences as we did on child-directed speech and found that they included 13 LVCs, making it an overall rate of 9.70% of all VO tokens with the five verbs. This is, of course, identical to the rate of LVCs in parental speech to young children (9.55%). Given that the speech sample is small, this is just a rough approximation, but if it is close to the true rate, what we appear to have discovered is that parents speaking to young children show the same readiness to employ LVCs as they do in speaking to adult addressees in informal conversations. As we saw, children are not far behind, even in Stage I of development.

4.2.3 **The verb–dative object construction**

4.2.3.1 **The most frequent verb in the VI construction and its semantics**

Parents produced a total of 6008 tokens of the verb–indirect object (VI) combination, using 66 different verbs; children produced 305 tokens using 24 different verbs. Remember that we included in this analysis only those indirect objects that had the form of a preposition-less, direct object.

Table 4.6 Parents' ten most frequent verbs in the VI construction (N=6,008)

Verb	Tokens	Percent
tell	1,670	27.80%
give	1,539	25.62%
show	870	14.48%
get	354	5.89%
ask	242	4.03%
feed	185	3.08%
excuse	180	3.00%
make	134	2.23%
bring	133	2.21%
read	121	2.01%

The most frequent verb in parental speech with an indirect object was *tell*, which had 1670 tokens, accounting for 27.8% of the total. The next most frequent verb was *give*, with 1539 tokens (25.6%). Table 4.6 presents parents' ten most frequent verbs in the VI construction.

The thematic role *tell* defines for its indirect object 'addressee of a communication'. This type of semantics is also shared by the indirect objects of other frequent verbs such as *show* and *ask*. The three together account for 46.3% of all tokens. The semantics that is considered prototypical of indirect objects, namely that of a 'recipient of transfer of possession', was potentially represented by the indirect objects of the frequent verbs *give*, *get*, and *bring*, accounting together for 33.7% of all tokens. These two kinds of semantics, with just three verbs each, made up about 80% of all tokens of indirect object in parents' speech, with the meaning of 'addressee' outnumbering that of 'recipient'. Other verbs had a less direct connection to one of these major semantic categories, so that, for example, *feed* could be seen as a kind of transfer of possession while *read* as a kind of speech act. Even if we classified by thematic role all the different verbs in this construction, the proportions would have stayed biased to the content of 'addressee' rather than 'recipient'.

The identification of the verb *give* with the prototypical thematic role of 'recipient of transfer of possession' is not quite accurate and I think we should reduce the share of this kind of meaning in the total. As we know from the analysis of VO combinations, *give* generated quite a number of Light-Verb Constructions; checking the sentences with an indirect object, it appeared that there were many with idiomatic, deverbal objects, such as *give you a bath* and *give him a ride*, where the semantics of the indirect object is not the prototypical 'recipient of transfer of possession'. Obviously, eventive nouns do not refer to objects but to events, hence they cannot be transferred from one possessor to another. Thus, the share of the 'recipient of transfer' semantics is probably closer to 20% of all parental VIs than the percentage previously estimated. The semantics of 'addressee' thus outnumbers 'recipient' two to one.

Against this background, it is interesting to note that in children's speech, the favoured semantics changes. The most frequent verb is *give*, with 139 tokens, namely, 45.57% of all tokens. Table 4.7 presents the distribution of the ten most frequent verbs in the VI pattern in children's speech.

In children's speech, the thematic role of 'recipient of transfer of possession' is more frequent than that of 'addressee'. The verbs *give*, *get*, and *bring* together account for 51.80%, while *tell*, *show*, and *ask* together accounted for just 25.58% of all tokens. There are a few eventive direct objects in children's speech as well with the verb *give*, but their proportion is very low, so we can stay with this estimate as an approximation. The bias in children usage is for indirect objects to express a 'recipient' rather than an 'addressee of a communication',

Table 4.7 Children's ten most frequent verbs in the VI construction (N=305)

Verb	Tokens	Percent
give	139	45.57%
show	37	12.13%
tell	25	8.20%
get	17	5.57%
ask	16	5.25%
excuse	16	5.25%
make	14	4.59%
feed	7	2.30%
pardon	5	1.64%
write	4	1.31%

two to one. This pattern does not replicate the parental distribution of different semantics for the VI combination; children do not match the details of parents' use of this grammatical relation as for the relative frequency of different verbs taking the complement, nor from the point of view of the semantics of the complement. The reasons are probably pragmatic, yet again; in Ninio and Snow (1996) we documented that parents engage much more than children in speech acts attempting to elicit verbalizations from the addressee (pp. 88–9). The pragmatic difference directly exhibits itself in the divergent semantics of the relevant grammatical relation.

4.3 Conclusions: children learn a formal syntax

In Chapter 3 we saw that parents model and children learn a mostly native, monosyllabic verb vocabulary for generating core grammatical relations. In adult English, this vocabulary is notorious for heading periphrastic combinations and phrasal verbs, for which it employs the regular syntactic functions of the phrasal core. We asked if parents model for children the full complexity of the native syntax, or whether they perhaps simplify their speech when addressing young children and generate simpler sentences in which the analytic constructions are avoided, thus making children's chore of acquisition a less complicated one.

Our examination of parental speech revealed that parents do employ the typical analytic constructions of the Anglo-Saxon verbal vocabulary when talking to young children. For the subject–verb grammatical relation, this involves the use of the copula *be*; the dummy verb *do*; the auxiliary verbs *be* and *have*, and the modal auxiliaries *can, may, must, need, ought,* and *have* as the inflected main verbs of the clause, serving as the syntactic heads of subjects. We found that a staggering 76.5% of all parental subjects were the syntactic dependents of verbs used for these grammatical purposes. Namely, the great majority of subjects in parental speech were formal subjects, not ones filling a semantic role versus the verb that possesses them as its subject.

In the verb–object relation, the native pattern relevant to our concerns is the LVC, a pattern of complex predicate formation by the combination of a semantically 'bleached' finite verb with an eventive noun when the latter carries the majority of the eventive semantics of the combination. We searched the parental corpus for the five most frequent verbs in this pattern, namely *do, give, have, make,* and *take,* and compared their use with young children to the rate of employment in two other registers: written adult-addressed English taken by Algeo (1995) from the Brown Corpus of American English and the Lancaster–Oslo–Bergen British Corpus, and to a sample of speech by part of the parents in our corpus, addressed to adults (the other parent, a grandparent, or the experimental observer). We found that parents when addressing young children use more LVCs than the rate of these constructions in written adult language; there was no difference between their use in child-directed speech and in adult-directed spoken informal speech.

A second feature of native English syntax, characteristic of analytic languages, is the multiple use of the same verbs for various different grammatical purposes, without a morphological marker of their altered status (see section 4.1.1). English has some special cases in which a given verb appears in the same grammatical relation with several different syntactic functions and semantics. In the three grammatical relations making up the clausal core, we traced several central examples of this phenomenon and found that parents do not avoid using the same verbs with different semantics in the syntactic context of the same grammatical relation, although this generates unavoidable ambiguity. The examples we traced were when the verb *be* was used by parents both as a copula and as an aspectual auxiliary; the verbs *do* and *have* both as content verbs and as auxiliaries, and the verbs *do, give, have, make,* and *take,* both as 'light' verbs heading the idiomatic Light-Verb Construction and as 'heavy' or full verbs heading regular VO combinations. Such multiple uses are well-documented cross-linguistically (Butt, 2003), and they are usually connected to the phenomenon of grammaticalization, in which a main verb is gradually emptied of its semantics in some but not all its uses, while it gains various grammatical functions.[19]

We might summarize that parents freely employ the analytic constructions characteristic of the native English verbal vocabulary, and they do not simplify their speech by avoiding such relatively complex and formal uses in their core grammatical relations.

When we checked children's uptake of these features of parental speech, we found that they use the native analytical patterns in their speech even at this early stage of multiword speech. As for the subject–verb construction, children, similar to parents, had the majority of their syntactically expressed subjects—52.3%—dependent on inflected finite verbs in grammatical uses. This rate of grammatical use in the SV relation is lower than in parents; thus, we did find evidence for what is called 'telegraphic speech' (Brown and Fraser, 1963) in these Stage I children; relatively to parents, they disfavour periphrastic combinations and in particular the use of auxiliary verbs. The reason could well be a difficulty of producing long utterances, as children are much less prone to avoiding contracted copulae than fully pronounced auxiliaries. That is, 'telegraphic speech' does not mean a complete avoidance of closed-class auxiliary and copular verbs, just a reduction in their rate of use.

When we checked children's use of Light-Verb Constructions, namely, the constructions using bleached 'light' verbs with an eventive noun, we found that children, too, use these at a higher rate than they are used in written adult English. However, relative to parents, children use LVCs slightly less often. Again, the analytic pattern involving a semantically reduced verb with an atypical predicative noun–object does exist in children's speech, but at a somewhat reduced rate relative to the input.

Lastly, children did not avoid multiple uses of the same verb with different semantics, following parental modelling even if not always with precisely the same proportion between various uses.

Summarizing out impression of the clausal core in input and output languages, it appears that parents model, and children are on the way to master, an undiluted, valid version of English core syntax, dominated by what Emonds (1985) labelled semi-lexical verbs, namely, auxiliaries, semi-auxiliaries, modals, and so forth. As these verbs lack what Emonds called 'pure semantics', a high proportion of the core grammatical relations are purely formal rather than meaningful, whether because the verbs define a periphrastic copular or auxiliary combination with a non-finite predicate or because they are part of an idiomatic combination generating a complex predicate.

It does not come as a surprise, then, that our corpus-based study did not find support for Goldberg's (1999, 2005) theory of how constructions gain their prototypical semantics. As we noted in section 1.5.4, Goldberg proposed that parents' most frequently modelled verbs in each construction stamp their specific meaning on the construction and this becomes the prototypical meaning of a construction for children learning it (and, probably, also for adult speakers).

In this chapter we examined the most frequent items in each of the three core grammatical relations in parental speech but did not find that they present young children with the embodied prototypical semantics of the construction as it is usually defined on independent grounds.

If the prototypical semantics for the subject in the SV relation is 'agent of action', the prototypical semantics for the direct object term in VO is 'effected object of agent's action', and the prototypical semantics for indirect-object in VI is 'recipient in a transfer of possession of an object' (e.g. Goldberg, 1999; Pinker, 1989; Taylor, 1989), the most frequent verbs in parental speech do not possess such semantics. In the SV construction the most frequent verb by far is *be*; as we know, this is a grammatical verb that serves as a copula and auxiliary; as a rule it does not provide thematic roles of the semantic kind for its subject and certainly its subject is not an agent of action.

In the VO construction the most frequent verb in parental speech is *want*; its direct object is, semantically, a desired object and not the patient or effected object of action. If this verb gives the semantics of its direct object to the VO construction, it would be appropriate for a few other verbs such as *wish*, *need*, and *desire*, but not for the verbs encoding some overt act such as *open*, *cut*, *break*, or *fix* in which, in the phrase of Hopper and Thompson (1980), the action is 'transferred' or 'carried over' from the agent to the patient and makes some change in its status. Lastly, in the grammatical relation of verb with an indirect object, the most frequent verb in parental speech is *tell*, not the expected *give*. *Tell* has a dative object designating the addressee of a speech act, but this event does not involve the transfer of possession of some object to a recipient, as the prototypical semantics of dative objects should have according to the literature. In fact in the speech situation no possession is transferred from one person to another, as no object, possessed or otherwise, is involved in the event. This is not an accidental fact about the verb *tell* but a more general pattern in this grammatical relation, as meanings similar to this make up the majority of tokens generated by frequent verbs; *tell*, *show*, and *ask* account together for 46.3% of all tokens, while the verbs *give*, *get*, and *bring* only account together for 33.7% of all tokens; if we only consider the set of most frequent verbs in parental speech, the aggregate of the meaning 'addressee of communication' is larger among them than that of 'recipient of possession'.

In addition to not bearing the semantic prototypes of the construction, the most frequent items in input are not cut-out to be models for other, less frequent items in the same syntactic pattern for another reason. These frequent items differ from other items in the form-class in their semantics and syntax, often being grammatical verbs or bleached verbs, and in that they are more centrally polysemous and polyvalent than other verbs. It is questionable if frequent verbs can have a role in determining the prototypical meaning of the three core grammatical relations SV, VO, and VI.

The failure of our parental corpus to support the claim that the most frequent verb in each construction is of the expected prototypical semantics is not totally unexpected. Goldberg (2005) and her associates (Sethuraman and Goodman, 2004) have already reported that the pattern of direct objects in parental speech does not provide the required prototypical semantics for the construction to take over. Goldberg also found that *tell* is a contender for the title of the most frequent verb in the dative object pattern, tied with *give* in her sample.[20] Our results largely replicated these findings, adding the third core relation of the subject–verb construction that has not yet been examined by Goldberg and her collaborators. To summarize, in none of the three core grammatical relations is there a most-frequent parental verb that demonstrates prototypical semantics and can thus serve the hypothetical process by which the construction in the abstract gets associated with the relevant prototypical semantics.

To conclude, Construction Grammar does not succeed in accounting for basic syntax in the parental register and children's early speech. Examination of parental speech makes it very clear that the three core grammatical relations subject–verb, verb–object, and verb–indirect object in the linguistic input are not meaningful 'Argument Structure Constructions' but purely formal building blocks of sentence structure, without an associated semantic content of their own. In the SV relation, the great majority of parental tokens were grammatical uses lacking a semantic relation between verb and subject. In the VO relation, some verbs were semi-modal auxiliaries while others received an eventive nominal as an object, appearing in a bleached form that barely contributed any semantics to the combination. In the VI relation there was a meaning split and the construction was associated with at least two major kinds of semantics. Our results thus support the mainstream linguistic opinion according to which core grammatical relations do not constitute meaningful constructions, but, rather, formal patterns to be filled with any kind of semantics (e.g. Jackendoff, 1997; Keenan, 1976; and see section 1.4.2).

In Chapter 1 of this monograph, we described the controversy around the units of syntax between mainstream linguistic theories such as the Minimalist Program or Dependency Grammar on the one hand and Construction Grammar on the other hand, when mainstream linguistics considers Merge/ Dependency couplets as the basic building blocks of syntactic structure, whereas Construction Grammar proposes that the units of structure are meaningful multiword units they name 'constructions'. At the end of Chapter 1, we left the question 'which description is better suited to serve as the framework of a developmental theory?' open, until we had information from this study. We may now conclude that the developmental evidence strongly supports the traditional, mainstream, atomic conception of syntactic building blocks and not the alternative architecture by which multiword schemes are meaningful signals that can take on the role of lexical valency.

Obviously, these results apply only to the three core grammatical relations SV, VO, and VI examined in the present study. It is perfectly possible that other constructions, probably those containing more elements than the word-couplets of the core grammatical relations, are meaningful linguistic signs. It is just the three basic syntactic functions of the clausal core that do not possess meaningfulness of the kind Construction Grammar attributes to multiword constructions.[21] Thus, SV, VO, and VI are not meaningful 'Argument Structure Constructions', nor are they presented to children with their most frequent exemplar representing the prototypical semantics of the construction.

Apparently children have no problem with learning formal grammatical relations without a pure semantic connection between the verb and the complement; as we saw, in Stage I speech the majority of their SV combinations are grammatical uses of the inflected main verbs, and their VO pattern contains Light-Verb Constructions with a rate of use not much lower than in parents' speech. Nor do they appear to be troubled by several different uses of the same verb form in the same syntactic construction. Given the nature of the patterns they are learning, this agrees only with a lexical-specific, item-specific, use-specific, completely local learning process. Interestingly, not only the multiple subcategorization potential of individual verbs are to be learned on an individual basis but, already in this early speech register, the semantics of verb–complement combination is to be computed in the context-specific process of 'semantic tailoring' (Allerton, 1982, pp. 27–8). In this process, the very semantics of the predicate word—verb, adjective, adverb—is not an a priori constant but, rather, it is 'tailored' or adjusted to fit the semantics of its present argument. For instance, the adjective '*old*' means something quite different in the combination '*old friend*' than in the combination '*old relative*'; while the latter refers to a person's age, the former refers to the duration of a relationship. We said above that in a Light-Verb Construction the combination receives its meaning largely from the direct object complement and not from the verb as it would be in a combination built on a 'heavy' verb (Butt, 2003); however, whether a verb is heavy or light, can only be determined in an ad hoc manner, only after examining the complement noun phrase and the possible meaning of its combination with the verb. Given the high frequency of polysemous and idiom-forming verbs in the parental register as well as children's early speech, it is obvious that children are not spared from employment of this complicated means of context-dependent computation of the semantics of word-combinations. Indeed, once you need the verbal context to compute the semantics of word-combinations in some cases, you need it always. Thus, the interactive, complement-dependent, ad hoc process of computing the meaning of multiword expressions by 'semantic tailoring' is apparently the rule and not the exception already in Stage I speech.[22]

As we mentioned in Chapter 2, it has been said repeatedly in developmental texts that syntactic learning is item-specific in the early stages of development. (For some references from the 1970s and the 1980s, see note 6 in Chapter 2.) We have been offered some wonderful studies and illuminative labels for this phenomenon. It is sufficient just to mention the 'verb islands' of Tomasello (1992); the 'word islands' of Nelson (1995); the 'mosaic acquisition' of Rispoli (1991); and the 'lexically-specific acquisition' of Theakston et al. (2002), including the gradual accumulation of different structure- and meaning-specific uses of the same lexeme.

There is, however, a catch in previous approaches. Almost without exception, it is believed that the item-specific learning of the early stages is followed by a second stage of development in which there is abstraction, generalization, scheme formation, categorization, all using semantic similarity. For instance, Theakston et al. (2002) say:

> Constructivists assume children's grammatical knowledge initially consists of con-structions based on high frequency forms in the input (Tomasello, 1992; Pine et al., 1998). Only when they have acquired a number of exemplars of a particular construc-tion will they build the more general schemes, such as the transitive construction (Akhtar and Tomasello, 1997), that underlie adult language use.
>
> Theakston et al. (2002, p. 786)

However, our corpus study of parental speech suggests that adult language use—as far as the three core grammatical relations subject–verb, verb–object, and verb–indirect object are concerned—is no less fragmented, lexical-specif-ic, structure-specific, and mosaic-like than children's Stage I speech. Endstate English is much more like young children's early linguistic system than the highly systematic organization we envisage exists in adults. The schemes, abstractions, and generalization we all look for, may not exist in the funda-mental structures of native English.

This is not a new idea by all means. The notion that language is only par-tially organized was the message in the writings of Bolinger, who wrote in a wonderful phrase: '*In small ways languages are highly patterned, but the total assemblage hangs together by a very weak gravitational force.*' (1975, p. 553).

Bolinger (and Chomsky, 1968, p. 20) also cited on this topic William Dwight Whitney, a highly esteemed linguist of Indo-European languages, for similar sentiments. It is worthwhile citing verbatim a passage directly relevant to our concerns from one of Whitney's books, *Language, and the study of language*:

> [...] even when the process of training which we have described gives general correctness and facility, it is far from conferring universal command of the resources of the English tongue. This is no grand indivisible unity, whereof the learner acquires all or none; it is an aggregation of particulars, and each one appropriates more or less of them, according to his means and ability.
>
> Whitney (1874, p. 17–18)

In our contemporary terminology, syntactic learning might be lexical-specific and structure-specific all the way, because syntactic knowledge is local through and through, dealing with particular structures and meanings. Each of these fragments of structure could be, and probably should be, defined as a meaningful construction, in the manner of Goldberg's (1995) proposals for a Construction Grammar. But, and this is the major conclusion of this corpus based study, the clausal core of English is not composed of 'meaningful argument-structure constructions'. Abstractions with a prototypical meaning, such as the transitive construction mentioned above, do not describe well the goal of development.[23] The clausal core is just three formal slots relative to the verb, no less and no more, and, they need to be learned individually for each verb and each use of each verb.

4.3.1 Form-classes and syntactic categories in a lexicalist system

One question remains unsolved: Is it not the case that children need to form syntactic categories such as Noun (or N), Verb (V), Adjective (A), and so forth? Even if we concede that syntactic behaviour can only be defined for each predicate individually, and hence syntactic and semantic valency is to be acquired in an item-specific manner and stored in the lexicon, it could be claimed that for various purposes in the grammar, there is a need to use the category symbols for form-classes. If true, children would need to form such categories at some point in syntactic development.

However, according to all evidence, the lexicon does not fall into clearly definable form-classes. Form-class category symbols, as formal entities, are hopelessly vague, and, as shall be shown below, virtually impossible to define.

It is a truism that words and grammatical rules do not map to each other uniquely. Instead, the vast majority of grammatical rules in all languages apply to more than a single lexical item,[24] and a single word mostly possesses more than a single grammatical behaviour. Moreover, selected sets of grammatical behaviours tend to be correlated, namely, to be applied to the same items. This means that lexical groups formed by several different grammatical rules and regularities tend to overlap, so that there exist in the lexicon bunches of items sharing clusters of grammatical properties.

However, the order represented by clusters of similar items is only partial; in actuality, the distribution of grammatical rules over the lexicon is more chaotic than ordered. This fundamental complication arises because in natural languages no two grammatical rules possess exactly the same application-class, and no two words are truly identical in their grammatical features. The transparent criterion of 'similar fate' on which we wanted to base form-classes, if applied consistently, generates an impossible number of very small classes.

To see how linguists deal with this issue, we now turn to Beth Levin, the leading authority on verbal subclasses and to David Crystal who is a renowned expert on form-classes in general.

Levin's (1993) monograph on English verbal subclasses is often cited in support of the possibility to identify homogenous subgroups of verbs in the lexicon, similar both in the grammar and in their semantics. Interestingly, Levin herself made it very clear that it is impossible to find groups of verbs that share all their grammatical behaviour. In an attempt to identify the linguistically relevant meaning components which determine verbs' syntax, Levin set up homogenous verb classes with respect to the profile of multiple valency patterns possible with the relevant verbs (more precisely, diathesis alternations), searching for the shared meaning components the different verbs have in common. In her introduction, she explains why the syntactic profile she uses does not contain more than a few of the possible valencies of verbs. She says:

> In this book, I have chosen a level of classification characterized by interesting clustering of verbs that should further the isolation of meaning components [which trigger the linguistic behaviors]. The classification system does not take into account every property of every verb, since such a system would be liable to consist of classes having only one member, a state of affairs that would not provide much insight into the overall structure of the English verb lexicon.
>
> Levin (1993, p. 18)

A rather similar point is made by Crystal (1967), in a chapter on English form-classes. Crystal points out that it is impossible to apply a formal criterion of identical grammatical behaviour when attempting to set up distinct form-classes. He summarizes the complication in the following:

> …very few words have an identical overall formal behaviour, even in a given restricted grammatical environment. One would end up with a multitude of single member classes…
>
> Crystal (1967, p. 28)

To summarize, this avenue is basically unworkable for a linguist, and for a prominent example, see Noam Chomsky. In his book *Theoretical Linguistics*, Lyons (1968) describes the reasons why Chomsky in 1965 gave up using word-classes based on distributional criteria in his grammar:

> It is possible to go a lot further with the distributional subclassification of words than would have been thought feasible, or even desirable, by traditional grammarians. But sooner or later, in his attempts to exclude the definitely unacceptable sentences by means of the distributional subclassification of their component words, the linguist will be faced with a situation in which he is establishing more and more rules, each covering very few sentences; and he will be setting up so many overlapping word-classes that all semblance of generality is lost.
>
> Lyons (1968, p. 152–3)

Lyons continues the text by describing how Chomsky exchanged form-classes with abstract syntactic features. For obvious reasons, this does not work any better than form-classes based on distributional criteria; abstract features are ultimately based on overt grammatical behaviour, and if that is too disorderly to support form-classes in an explicit way, it continues to be so when the connection with abstract features is made only implicitly.

Given that the lexicon cannot be divided into rigid form-classes, our only option is to acknowledge their fundamental fuzziness, as proposed by Bolinger (1975), Hockett (1958), Hopper and Thompson (1984), McCawley (1982), Robins (1964), Ross (1972, 1973), Taylor (1989), and others. Indeed, we shall go one step further and say that form-classes or lexical categories are an optical illusion, and the true structure of the lexicon is not that of a set of mutually exclusive categories (even such fuzzy ones as the prototype categories proposed by some authorities) but that of a network, organized by the pattern of mutual similarities between words.

We do have some interesting hints already what could be the overall structure of the network representing the whole lexicon. We know that multiple grammatical behaviour is amplified in the case of the very frequent items we focused on in this chapter (also see section 4.1.2). The pattern goes beyond verbs; for example, Sinclair (1999) claims that all common words of English have individual patterns of occurrence, and do not fit easily into the general classification into form-classes. This can be translated into the conception that each of these items is at the hub of its own category, arranging other items with respect to it, relative to how similar they are to the core items in meaning and grammatical behaviour. Continuing with this line, we can, if we wish, give up the idea of a few a priori categories altogether, exchanging it with the notion of a complex network in which each and every word is at the hub of its own lexical category, organizing the rest of the lexicon in a perspective relative to itself. If we combine all these self-centred nets, we arrive at a complex lexical network in which different words preserve their uniqueness and unique pattern of similarities to each other. Certainly items possessing many different grammatical behaviours and many different meanings will be at the hub of a dense neighbourhood populated by all the different items with which they have some kind of affinity. Rather than a set of classes, the true structure of the lexicon is thus a complex network, with the frequent, polysemous, and polyvalent items serving as its cores or hubs and defining densely populated areas that we can, if we wish, see as similarity categories defined by the true stars of the system. Such a network-type organization of the lexicon has been proposed by Ferrer i Cancho *et al.* (2003) and Steyvers and Tenenbaum (2005), among others. From our developmental perspective, the lexical network is given automatically as the emergent outcome of item-specific learning that does not need extra steps of acquisition; the task of a child is to learn individual items and their grammatical behaviour, not to form categories.

Appendix A: **Nominal complements in Light Verb Constructions with the verbs *do, give, have, make* and *take***

Note: token frequency is shown in parentheses.

A.1 **Light-Verb Constructions with the verb *do***

A.1.1 Parents: objects of *do*

Poop (12); work (12); picture (9); drawing (7); poo (7); somersault (7); ironing (6); laundry (6); dance (5); cooking (4); exercise (4); washing (4); wee (4); jumping (3); painting (3); shampoo (3); shopping (3); sing (3); bubble (2); cheer (2); curtsy (2); hug (2); pee (2); prayer (2); snap (2); split (2); squiggle (2); talking (2); writing (2); balance (1); blowing (1); boo (1); check (1); circle (1); coloring (1); cough (1); counting (1); cutting (1); cycling (1); drinking (1); drumming (1); eating (1); fighting (1); frying (1); hiccup (1); homework (1); hoovering (1); pause (1); paying (1); peek (1); piddle (1); play (1); playdough (1); powder (1); rattle (1); round (1); running (1); shake (1); speech (1); sweeping (1); telephone (1); tickle (1); whistle (1).

A.1.2 Children: objects of *do*

Picture (2); show (2); weewee (2); drawing (1); drawpainting (1); doo (1); ironing (1); kissing (1); painting (1); plop (1); singsong (1); snowing (1); somersault (1); song (1); trick (1); wake (1); work (1); yukyuk (1).

A.2 **Light-Verb Constructions with the verb** *give*

A.2.1 Parents: objects of *give*

kiss (175); hug (40); ride (22); bath (15); cuddle (8); smile (8); push (4); shot (4); name (3); rest (3); service (3); try (3); bite (2); warning (2); brush (1); clap (1); colouring (1); curl (1); hint (1); look (1); love (1); loving (1); measurement (1); mix (1); pat (1); peekaboo (1); shampoo (1); sigh (1); smack (1); squeeze (1); treat (1); wallop (1); wipe (1).

A.2.2 Children: objects of *give*

Bite (3); kiss (3); brush (1); love (1); ride (1); smile (1).

A.3 **Light-Verb Constructions with the verb** *have*

A.3.1 Parents: objects of *have*

Snack (41); look (37); bite (34); dinner (30); drink (29); nap (21); sleep (18); kick (16); bath (15); breakfast (14); lunch (14); party (14); parade (11); kiss (10); crash (9); ride (9); seat (9); picnic (8); poop (6); cough (5); end (5); hiccups (5); hug (5); stretch (5); talk (4); tantrum (4); ache (2); conversation (3); cuddle (3); dream (3); feeling (3); go (3); sip (3); supper (3); trip (3); wash (3); barbecue (2); call (2); chat (2); dropsy (2); fall (2); hurt (2); rest (2); suck (2); turn (2); wee (2); argument (1); blast (1); change (1); choice (1); cleaning (1); competition (1); dance (1); dindin (1); disagreement (1); discussion (1); drive (1); effect (1); feed (1); fight (1); fixation (1); food (1); game (1); giggle (1); infection (1); lend (1); lick (1); lie (1); mess (1); nosh (1); pee (1); peekaboo (1); picture (1); poopoo (1); practice (1); quietness (1); ramp (1); reaction (1); rummage (1); show (1); sigh (1); sneeze (1); sniff (1); stomachache (1); suspicion (1); syringe (1); taste (1); treat (1); walk (1).

A.3.2 Children: objects of *have*

Drink (18); lunch (6); party (5); ride (5); dinner (4); cough (2); look (2); snack (2); barbecue (1); bath (1); limp (1); nap (1); sleep (1); supper (1).

A.4 **Light-Verb Constructions with the verb** *make*

A.4.1 Parents: objects of *make*

Noise (165); mess (73); picture (61); mark (12); believe (8); bang (4); stack (4); call (3); circle (3); mistake (3); pile (3); sound (3); break (2); melt (2); parade (2); change (1); connection (1); conversation (1); deal (1); detour (1); drawing (1); landing (1); pun (1); race (1); roll (1); sing (1); spark (1); splash (1); suggestion (1); surprise (1); swirl (1); tickle (1).

A.4.2 Children: objects of *make*

Noise (9); mess (7); circle (3); pee (3); picture (2); push (2); mark (1); pick (1); sound (1).

A.5 Light-Verb Constructions with the verb *take*

A.5.1 Parents: objects of *take*

Nap (79); picture (52); bath (41); bite (35); drink (14); look (12); walk (12); care (9); shower (6); sip (6); break (4); ride (3); step (3); turn (3); guess (2); interest (2); peek (2); practice (2); breath (1); breather (1); crawl (1); nosedive (1); notice (1); pause (1); photo (1); rest (1); run (1); seat (1); shake (1); snooze (1); swim (1).

A.5.2 Children: objects of *take*

Bath (7); picture (6); nap (4); ride (4); bite (2); walk (2); care (1); drink (1); peek (1); shower (1); sleep (1).

Notes

1 The Anglo-Saxon stream of English also possesses unique phonetic, prosodic, and morphological features; for example, only native verbs cliticize; there are unique derivational affixes that apply only to Anglo-Saxon roots; native words are stressed on the first syllable while Latinate words have stress on the last or penultimate syllable; all irregular verbs are native; only native words belong to multiple form-classes without marking, namely, exhibit conversion or zero-derivation (see also note 9). These unique features, although probably interact with the syntactic phenomena we are interested in, are beyond the scope of the present book. For some description, see Aronoff (1976), Chomsky and Halle (1968), and Pinker (1989).

2 Sapir (1921, chapter 7) in fact described three kinds of changes or 'drifts' that English has been undergoing. The first is the reduction of the old Indo-European system of syntactic cases; the second is a fixed word-order determined by the syntactic role of the word; the third is the drift toward the invariable word. There is an obvious connection among the three trends pointed out by Sapir, and Robin Lakoff (1972, p. 192) proposed that they can be combined into a single historical shift, underlying the changes to a more analytic grammar in many Indo-European languages. Many other linguists pointed out that English has been undergoing a synthetic-analytic change, among them Robins (1964, p. 337) and Hockett (1958, p. 181). For a recent historical treatment of multiword verbs see Claridge (2000).

3 The changes toward a more analytic type are not unique to English. Similar changes happened to other members of the Indo-European language family (e.g. the Indo-Aryan languages, Masica, 1991), as well in very different language families, unrelated to Indo-Europeans. Ancient Munda and Old Tamil were much more synthetic relative to Modern Dravidian languages (Bright, 1966), and so was the ancient version of the language isolate Georgian. In far-Eastern languages of three different families the same change has been documented, including Japanese, Korean, and Chinese, as well as in the Tibeto-Burman language family in general (Weidert, 1987, p. 370). Moreover, the direction synthetic-to-analytic is not the only direction of change languages undergo. According to theory, this is just part of a universal phenomenon affecting languages by which they undergo a periodic change in their morphosyntactic characteristics. The process is called 'The Linguistic Cycle' (Hodge, 1970). This cycle consists of two alternating periods in which the typological nature of languages changes. One of the periods is a grammaticalization phase in which free lexemes gradually turn into prosodically dependent morphemes and the language becomes morphologically rich (or synthetic). The second kind of period is of an opposite tendency in which morphemes undergo erosion, the language becoming analytic. At this phase, the language compensates for the loss of grammatical morphemes marking various functional contents by generating periphrastic constructions and phrasal lexemes, encoding the same grammatical contents. English is thus thought to be undergoing in documented times merely the synthetic-to-analytic phase of the Linguistic Cycle. For some more treatment see Greenberg (1960).

4 Other categories of such intermediate type of verbs are quasi-modals and semi-auxiliaries (see Coates, 1983; Hermerén, 1986). Quirk *et al.* (1985, pp. 136–7) in particular propose a cline between central modal auxiliaries, through marginal modals and semi-auxiliaries, to main verbs which have a non-finite clause as complement, all of which serve for some grammatical uses.

5 For some more literature on the history of English, see Baugh and Cable (1993), Campbell (1959), Quirk and Wrenn (1958), and Strang (1970).

6 Apart from LVCs, the major pattern of multiword lexemes in Modern English using the Anglo-Saxon verb lexicon are verb-particle constructions, also called phrasal verbs (Bolinger, 1971; Di Sciullo and Williams, 1987; Lipka, 1972; Quirk *et al.*, 1985). In addition, there are other multiword constructions using mainly or only a native verb vocabulary, such as the dative double-object construction we included in

this study of the clausal core (Green, 1974; Grimshaw and Prince, 1986; Gropen *et al.*, 1989; Harley, 2007; Pesetsky, 1995; Pinker, 1989) and the cognate object constructions (Macfarland, 1995). On the phenomenon of multiword or 'dispersed verbs' in English, see Firth (1968, p. 121) and Hopper (1997).

7 The relevant constructions are known by many different names; the terminology is variously *Light-Verb Constructions* (Butt, 2003); *composite predicates* (Cattell, 1984); *complex verbs* (Brinton and Akimoto, 1999); *verbal phrases* (Hiltunen, 1999, p. 133); *stretched verbs* (Allerton, 2001); *expanded predicates* (Algeo, 1995), and others. Allerton (p. 7) lists some further terms and explains some of the different definitions used by researchers.

8 The noun-complement of the Light-Verb Construction is variously called an *eventive object* (Quirk *et al.*, 1985, p. 750), a *verbal noun* (Curme, 1935); a *noun of action or activity noun* (Wierzbicka, 1982); a *process nominal* (Fu *et al.*, 2001); and a *derived nominal* (Laczko, 2000); others use the terms a *predicative noun*, a *complex event nominal*, and so forth.

9 Conversion, functional shift, or zero-derivation is 'the use of a word normally one part of speech or word class as another part of speech, without any change in form' (McArthur, 1992; and see also Jespersen, 1972; Lieber, 1980, and Marchand, 1969). In parenthesis, conversion is yet another phenomenon characteristic of isolating languages, thus it belongs to the special morphological features of the Anglo-Saxon stream of Modern English.

10 See, for example, Allerton (2001) on the regular syntax of light-verb combinations.

11 The term 'light verb' is sometimes mistakenly used in developmental psycholinguistic writings as a designation for verbs with a relatively general meaning, rather than specifically for the use of a verb in the Light-Verb Construction. Obviously, being 'light' is not a fixed feature of verbs appearing in LVCs as the same verbs can and do appear as 'heavy' verbs in other combinations. In addition, there are various other verbs with a relatively general sense, which does not automatically qualify them to appear in LVCs, such as the verb *want* that never does. It is best to leave the technical term 'light verb' for the semantically bleached version of verbs appearing in LVCs, and use some other expression for verbs with relatively general semantics.

12 Oshima-Takane *et al.* (2001) analysed the speech of two children later re-analysed by Barner (2001) with a slightly different methodology, arriving at the same conclusions.

13 Sometimes Ninio (1999a) is cited as if that study found that young children acquiring English or Hebrew begin transitive verb–object combinations with LVCs, using semantically bleached 'light verbs' (e.g. Naigles *et al.*, 2009; Snedeker and Gleitman, 2004). This is a misunderstanding of the proposal made in the article regarding children's earliest verbs that referred to generic verbs and not to light verbs. The point was that many of the earliest verbs children use in transitive verb-combinations, interestingly overlap with the set of generic transitive verbs which are used—in grammaticalized forms including bound morphemes—as markers or inducers of transitivity in various languages of the world. This overlap raised the possibility that these verbs are easy to learn for transitive syntactic patterns because their meaning is apparently close to the semantics of transitivity—a well-known condition on grammaticalization into markers of transitivity. The distinction between generic verbs and semantically bleached light verbs in LVCs is emphasized in note 5 that mentions Hollebrandse and van Hout (1994)'s study on children acquiring Dutch who preferred idiomatic Light-Verb Constructions such as 'give a kiss' or 'make photo' at some relatively early stage of development over their non-idiomatic single-verb alternatives. The text makes an explicit distinction between the results of the Dutch study and the reported findings, saying 'The production of such "light verb constructions", as the authors call them, seems to be a related yet distinct phenomenon from the earliest verb–object combinations discussed in the present paper that were on the whole regular verb–object noun combinations.' (p. 640.)

14 Interestingly, when Ogden (1930) proposed the artificial 'restricted language' Basic English, built on a mere 18 verbs (*be, come, do, get, give, go, have, keep, let, make, may, put, say, see, seem, send, take,* and *will*), all exclusively Anglo-Saxon, the objection to it as a potential international auxiliary language was that the very features that made this language into an efficient communicative tool with such a small vocabulary, also made it extremely complicated to learn. In order to reduce the vocabulary, Ogden heavily utilized the fundamental polysemy of Anglo-Saxon verbs and their ability to head multiword idiomatic combinations such as verb–particle constructions, each of which replaces several simplex verbs; this, however, appeared to the critics to make the learning of this language by foreigners impossibly difficult (e.g. Walsh, 1933).

15 The term is Lichtenberk's (1991) and it signifies a change in the form-class membership of a word with changes in its meaning and use, as a result of grammaticalization.

16 The more frequent a verb, the more it is likely to be a closed-class, grammatical verb (Emonds, 1985, 2000; Kilgarriff, 1997; Pawley, 2006); to be polysemous and ambiguous (Baayen and Moscoso Del Prado Martín, 2005; Dixon, 1991; Jastrzembski, 1981; Köhler, 1986; Pawley, 2006; Zipf, 1945); and to generate phrasal verbs and idioms (Makkai, 1972, 1978; Newman and Rice, 2004; Rundell and Stock, 1994; Sinclair, 1999; Stubbs, 1986; Stubbs and Barth, 2003; Summers, 1996).

17 Indeed, Borg and Comrie (1984) warn against choosing the single more frequent verb as the most prototypical one in a construction:

> [I]n many languages, including Maltese, 'give' is syntactically a very atypical ditransitive verb. This is not particularly surprising: items from the most basic vocabulary are more likely to be anomalous morphologically and syntactically. But this does demonstrate that more care needs to be taken in the choice of the most typical ditransitive verb, selection of 'give' always requiring cross-checking with a variety of other verbs of similar valency.
>
> Borg and Comrie (1984, p. 123)

18 In contrast to our results, Naigles *et al.* (2009) did not find a high use of light verbs in early grammatical use. The reason could be that they unfortunately did not sample in their study three of the five most frequent light verbs in child speech such as *make, do*, and *have*. In addition, they classified *bring* and *want* as 'light verbs' although these verbs do not generate light-verb combinations as a rule.

19 Hopper and Traugott (1993, p. 108) include both auxiliary verbs and 'light' verbs in their cline of grammaticalization, while later publications (Butt, 2003; Traugott, 1999) suggest that 'light' verbs are simply alternative uses of the same-form main verbs, not their grammaticalization. This debate about the diachronic source of 'light' verbs does not affect our conclusions regarding development.

20 Casenhiser and Goldberg (2005, p. 502) considered the possibility that the high token frequency of *tell* relative to *give* is an artefact of the context of observations in the 15-dyad Bates corpus (Bates *et al.*, 1988) from which the data for this analysis were drawn. In this project, a third of the observation time was taken up by book-reading, and 10 of the 11 instances of *tell* the researchers found in maternal speech, directly related to the task of reading a story. We investigated this possibility in the large pooled parental corpus we constructed and it did not check out; very many of the sentences with *tell* in the different corpora included, were requests that the child tell the other parent/grandparent/the investigator about something that happened to the child and were unrelated to joint

bookreading. The relatively higher frequency of *tell* is no artefact; *tell* is indeed more frequent in parental use than *give* over various different observational contexts.

21 Construction Grammar is not the only source of claims about the prototypical semantics of grammatical relations in parental speech. These ideas are quite long-standing, favoured in particular as a component of nativist theories of syntactic development (e.g. Pinker, 1984, 1987, 1989), but not exclusively so. For example, Karmiloff and Karmiloff-Smith (2001), in a recent handbook of language development, take it as an established fact that the linguistic input presents syntax to young children in a simplified variety in which there is a one-to-one mapping of meaning and form:

> Linguistic analyses of child-directed speech show that the notion of an initial proto-type, where the subject is also the agent, does indeed correspond to the structure of the simple sentences mothers use when talking to their toddlers.
>
> Karmiloff and Karmiloff-Smith (2001, p. 116)

Pinker is a central theoretician proposing such ideas, even claiming that the semantics of grammatical relations in English are exceptionally prototypical. His claims have met with much objection, and see for instance Bowerman (1990), Rispoli (1994), and various chapters in the recent collection edited by Mueller-Gathercole (2009).

22 Young children do not seem to find non-literal language difficult in general; see Pearson (1990) for some details.

23 Nor is there, apparently, a role to thematic or semantic similarity in the process of syntactic development, as is sometimes claimed (e.g. Morris *et al.*, 2000; Tomasello, 2000). Studies examining the possible facilitating effect of semantic similarity on transfer of learning in syntactic development, did not find such effects, and transfer of learning between different word-specific syntactic constructions is based, in most probability, purely on similarity of form of expression such as word order, case marking or an identical preposition (Ninio 2005a,b).

24 However, according to Crystal's (1967, p. 37) estimate there are about 400 unique words in English that escape classification to any word-class.

Chapter 5

Frequencies

5.1 Rank-frequency distributions of words

After exploring core grammar in parental and child speech in much detail in the Chapter 4, with a focus on the individual verbs used to generate the three core grammatical relations, in the present chapter we move one level up and examine the total verb use in the two registers. We shall compute the overall distribution of token frequencies of the different verbs in each core grammatical relation in parents' and children's speech, estimate the function with the best fit to the distribution, and compare the two registers on this measure.

The background to this analysis is the so-called Zipf–Mandelbrot law. There is a robust empirical finding that goes under this name, that words' frequency of use does not follow a normal distribution but, rather, it is markedly asymmetrical (Mandelbrot, 1966; Zipf, 1935/1965).[1] If we take a very large text and rank the words in order of their frequency of use, we get a severely skewed distribution, with a few very frequent items and very many infrequent ones. When the frequency of words is plotted as a function of their rank-order in some corpus, the resultant graph follows a typical steeply decreasing graph, and the best mathematical function to fit this graph is the power-law function.[2]

Zipf studied not only the token frequencies of words in large speech samples but looked at various other quantifiable aspects of corpora. In a central publication, Zipf (1949/1972) reported on several distributions derived from natural language that follow power laws; for example, he found that the length of words ranked according to frequency of use has a similar skewed distribution. We already mentioned another finding of his in the last chapter (see note 16 there) according to which the more frequent a word is, the more polysemous it is (Zipf, 1945). Zipf looked at many different aspects of language and it is tempting to generalize that almost anything to do with frequencies in language possesses a power-law distribution. However, he did not analyse the distribution of syntactic form-classes, probably because that would have required parsing the texts for grammar, a labour-intensive task of preparation for this analysis. In fact, nobody has as yet looked at the rank-frequency distribution of syntactic form-classes in large-scale speech corpora.

We already know that tokens of syntactic form-classes in the parental speech register have a skewed distribution. For example, Goldberg *et al.* (2004) analysed English-speaking mothers' utterance tokens in a large corpus and concluded that one specific verb accounts for a large percentage of utterance tokens in different argument structure constructions, among them the Subject–Verb–Oblique Intransitive and the Subject–Verb–Object–Object2 Ditransitive frames. Similar skewed distributions in English maternal speech samples were reported by Naigles and Hoff-Ginsberg (1995), Sethuraman and Goodman (2004), and Theakston *et al.*, (2004); and for Hebrew maternal samples by Ninio (1999a,b). These studies, however, did not go beyond estimating the relative frequency of a few items from the total distribution and did not map the whole range of items and their distribution. The closest to that analysis is Ninio (2006) that presented data on Hebrew maternal speech, finding that the distribution of verbs and adjectives getting an indirect object has a power-law function. As the total number of tokens analysed in this study was only about 7000, it can be seen as a pretest for the present large-scale corpus analysis of English parental form-classes where the number of tokens reaches one to two hundred thousand. The Hebrew study mentioned above also looked at 14 children's first ten different verbs and adjectives with an indirect object and analysed the number of different speakers for each verb, comparing it to the number of different mothers using the verbs. Although there was an interesting similarity between children and mothers, this was not an analysis of token frequency in a corpus and we cannot infer from it how similar the two groups are in the distributions of token frequencies. As there are no other studies of children's early syntax that targeted this question, prior research does not provide information on the question whether children's Stage I syntax possesses the same global features as their parents' core syntax.

A power-law distribution is a severely skewed, unequal distribution, in which there are a few high-value items and many low-value ones. The economist theoretician Vilfred Pareto is credited with the observation that a small segment of the population—the very rich—is in possession of the great majority of the total wealth of the population. The remaining small slice of total wealth is held by a very large number of poor people. For simplicity's sake this phenomenon is often called the 20/80 rule, meaning that the typical degree of inequality is such that 20% of the population holds 80% of all wealth.[3] Basically, the same inequality that Pareto pointed out in the distribution of wealth appears to exist in human lexicons, so that a few popular words are used extremely often, whereas the great majority of the lexicon is used very seldomly by a given language's speakers.

We thus ask whether the phenomenon of power-law-shaped, skewed distribution pointed out by Zipf and Pareto also characterizes the verbs used to construct the basic syntactic relations SV, VO, and VI in parental and child speech. A question of special interest is whether the shape of the token distributions will be similar in the three core syntactic relations, which, as we saw in Chapter 2, have a very unequal number of different verbs. The major question, though, is, whether children recreate parents' distribution of verb tokens in the three grammatical relations, despite being beginning speakers with much smaller verb repertoires. We saw in the previous chapters that even beyond the difference in repertoire size, their use of verbs diverges, at times, considerably from that of parents', and that children's speech does not resemble a random sample of parental speech. If their overall token frequency distribution is similar to that of parents, that is not because they copy a sample of parental utterances and produce them as their own. Instead, a similarity in the overall structure of the syntactic form-classes in parents and children will suggest that despite differences in detail, the global organization of their core syntactic system is very similar to that of parents.

5.2 Zipf curves for parents and children

5.2.1 Method of deriving Zipf curves

For each core syntactic relation we are interested in, we mapped the distribution of tokens generated by the syntactic Heads of the relation, namely, the verbs taking the subject, object, or indirect object as their valency complements. To remind us, we have lemmatized the verbs into their respective stem-groups for frequency analysis, thus *eat, eats, ate, eaten,* and *eating* were all grouped into the stem-group or lemma of *eat*. Suppleted forms for irregular verbs such as *am* and *was* of *be* were also included in the lemma of the relevant stem, disregarding their morphological variation (see Appendix B to Chapter 2).

For each grammatical relation separately, we plotted the token frequency of each verb in a histogram with the verbs ordered according to their rank, from the most frequent to the least frequent. The statistics plotted are number of utterance tokens per verb, when each speech event is counted separately. This plot is a typical rank-frequency Zipf presentation.

5.2.2 Parents' Zipf curves

Figures 5.1–5.3 present the rank-frequency distribution of verbs appearing with a subject, with an object, or with an indirect object, in the parental and child corpus.

The first graph—Figure 5.1—is that of the rank-frequency distribution of the different verbs appearing with a subject, in the parental corpus. As we saw in section 2.5.2, there were in the parental corpus 601 different verb-lexemes in a syntactic subject–verb pattern, together generating a large number of tokens. The following graph represents a total of 195,206 tokens of the SV syntactic relation.

As we can see, these tokens were not distributed uniformly among the different verbs in this form-class. Instead, the token distribution is heavily skewed, with a few verbs responsible for the great majority of tokens produced in this grammatical pattern. The line indicates the closest Zipf-like power-law curve fit to the data. We can observe the very clear power-law distribution; the fit of the power-law curve is excellent ($R^2 = 0.98$, namely, a 98% fit).

Figure 5.2 presents the rank-frequency distribution of 776 different verbs appearing with a direct object in the parental corpus. The graph represents a total of 137,755 tokens of the VO syntactic relation. The fitted power-law curve indicates an excellent fit to the data ($R^2 = 0.97$).

Figure 5.3 presents the rank-frequency distribution of 66 verbs appearing with an indirect object in the parental corpus. The graph represents a total of 6,008 tokens of the VI syntactic relation (direct objects only), and hence it is marginally sufficient to be fitted with a power-law function. The fit of the power-law curve is excellent ($R^2 = 0.97$).

5.2.3 Children's Zipf curves

We repeated the distributional analyses performed on the parental corpus, on the children's corpus. Figures 5.4–5.6 present the rank-frequency distribution

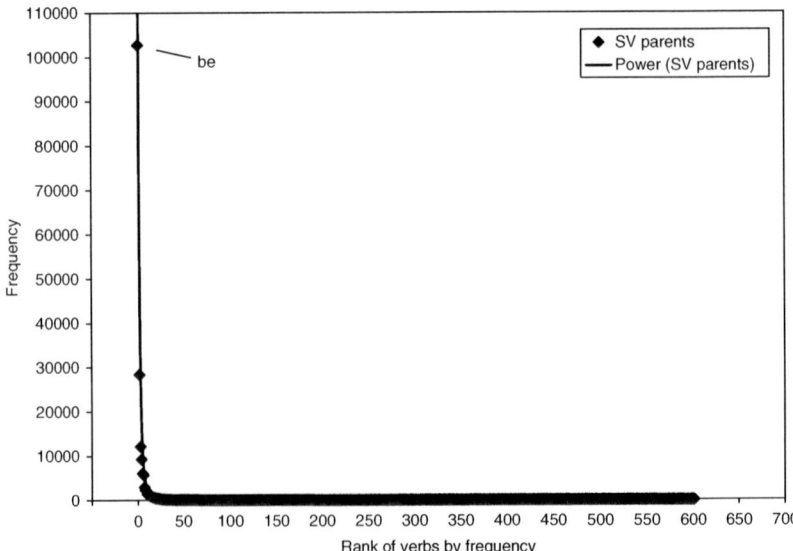

Fig. 5.1 Rank-frequency distribution of parental SV tokens with fitted power-law curve.

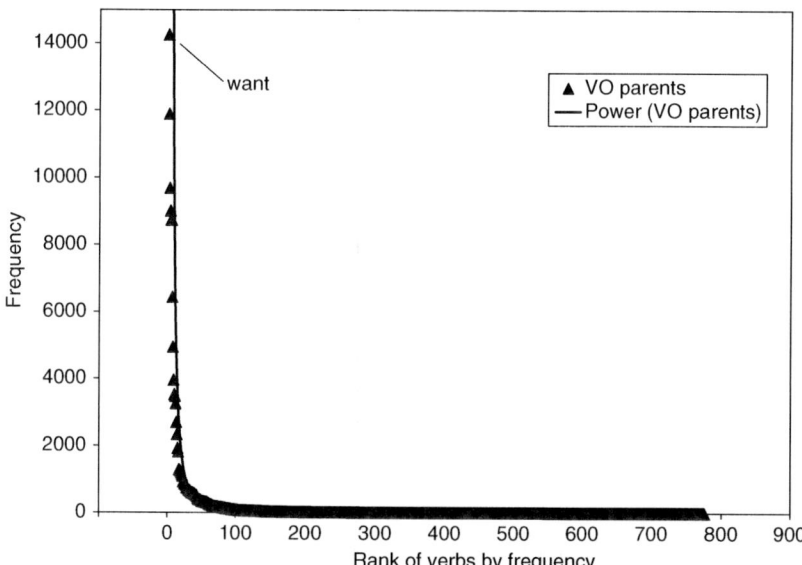

Fig. 5.2 Rank-frequency distribution of parental VO tokens with fitted power-law curve.

of verbs appearing with a subject, with an object, or with an indirect object, in the child corpus. The statistics plotted are number of utterance tokens per verb, when each speech event is counted separately.

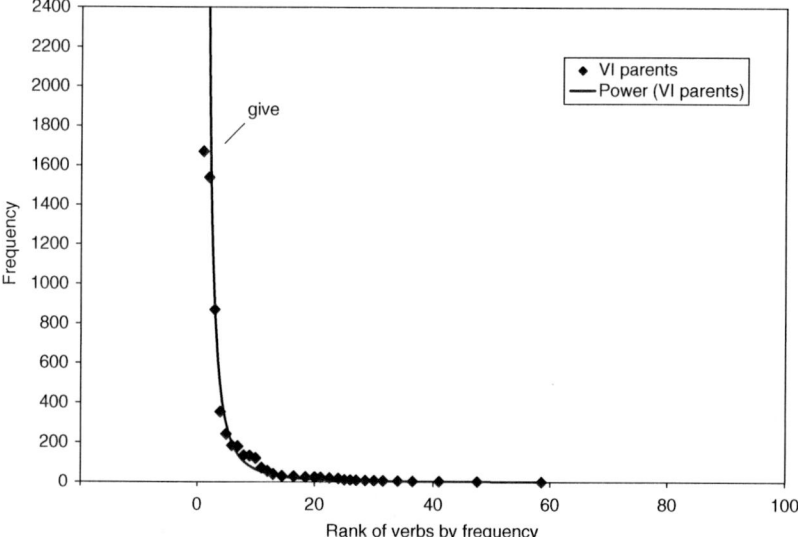

Fig. 5.3 Rank-frequency distribution of parental VI tokens with fitted power-law curve.

As we saw in section 2.5.2, there were 220 different verbs in a syntactic subject–verb pattern in the child corpus. Figure 5.4 presents the rank-frequency distribution of the verbs in SV in the child corpus. The statistics plotted are number of utterance tokens per verb, when each speech event is counted separately. The graph represents a total of 14,375 tokens of the SV syntactic relation.

As before, the line indicates the closest power-law curve that was fitted to the data. The fit of the power-law curve is excellent ($R^2 = 0.98$, namely, a 98% fit).

Figure 5.5 presents the rank-frequency distribution of 238 different verbs appearing with a direct object in the child corpus. The graph represents a total of 11,115 tokens of the VO syntactic relation.

The fit of the power-law curve is $R^2 = 0.95$, namely, a 95% fit.

Figure 5.6 presents the rank-frequency distribution of all the verbs appearing with an indirect object in the child corpus. The graph represents a total of 305 tokens of the VI syntactic relation, involving 24 different verbs.

This sample size is not considered adequate to be fitted with a power-law function, and this curve is presented here only as a rough approximation. Despite the extremely small sample size, the fit of the power-law function is excellent ($R^2 = 0.95$).

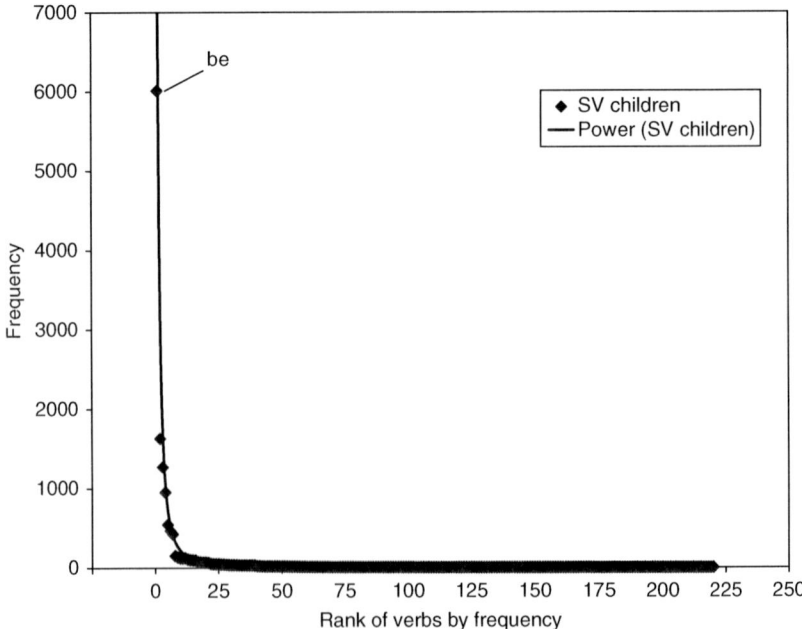

Fig. 5.4 Rank-frequency distribution of children's SV tokens with fitted power-law curve.

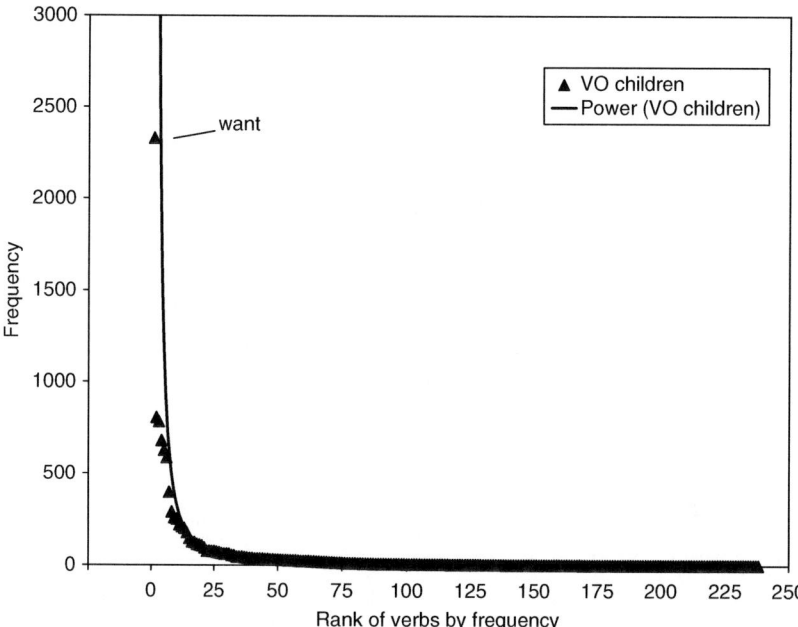

Fig. 5.5 Rank-frequency distribution of children's VO tokens with fitted power-law curve.

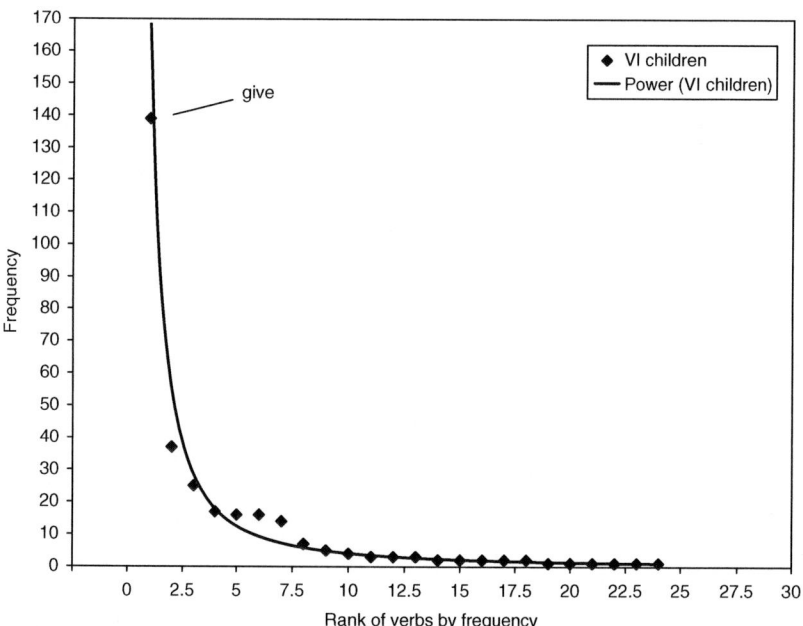

Fig. 5.6 Rank-frequency distribution of children's VI tokens with fitted power-law curve.

5.2.4 **Estimates of power-law exponents**

In order to make a formal comparison among the six token-frequency distributions, we estimated the power-law function best fitting the distribution in each syntactic form-class. Our estimates of the mathematical parameters of the power-law functions are based on the cumulative probability distributions (aka Pareto presentations) and not directly on the Zipf rank-frequency curves we have seen in Figures 5.1–5.6. Mathematically the two are transformations of each other (Adamic, 2009), but the cumulative probability analysis is said to provide a better estimate of the exponent or slope of the power-law function[4] than the Zipf graph (Newman, 2005). The cumulative probability graphs make possible the extraction of reliable (although somewhat low)[5] estimates of the power-law exponents of the relevant distributions. We used the Excel program's best fitting power-law function as the basis for our estimate of the exponents by the least squares method of estimation.

In order to ascertain that we are comparing the children's corpus to the correct parental control, we also performed the analysis on the ten random samples of parental grammar of identical token size to the children's samples. We used the random samples we prepared for the comparison of children's verb repertoires to parents' in Chapter 3 (see section 3.1).

Table 5.1 presents the power-law exponents of the token distribution of verbs in the three syntactic relations, SV, VO, and VI, derived from the cumulative probability distributions by the least squares method of estimation. We present in the same table the results based on the original parental corpus,

Table 5.1 Power-law exponents of the token distribution of verbs in SV, VO, and VI relations in three corpora

Grammatical relation	Total tokens	Types	Power-law exponent
Parental full-sized corpus			
SV	195,206	601	−1.59
VO	137,755	776	−1.58
VI	6,008	66	−1.50
Reduced-sized parental samples, mean value of 10 samples			
SV	14,375	238.6 (7.7)	−1.61 (0.01)
VO	11,115	342.5 (7.8)	−1.71 (0.00)
VI	305	26.6 (2.5)	−1.65 (0.02)
Children's corpus			
SV	14,375	220	−1.66
VO	11,115	238	−1.69
VI	305	24	−1.66

the mean of the ten random parental samples the size of the child corpus, and children's corpus of the three grammatical relations.

The results presented in Table 5.1 are quite remarkable: the three types of grammatical relations are almost exactly identical in their distribution of token frequencies for verbs, both in parents' speech[6] and, even more impressively, also in children's speech. This is so despite large differences in size of sample and of verb repertoire for the three cases in the parental corpus, and a much smaller verb repertoire in the children's corpus. In all six cases, the power-law exponent is about −1.6, the differences are small and can be ignored.

Presenting the distributions of the three grammatical relations and the parental and child data on separate graphs as we did in Figures 5.1–5.6 makes it difficult to be impressed with how similar the distributions are. Although we saw the unequivocal results of the formal comparison involving estimates of the power-law exponent in Table 5.1, we should benefit from an informal comparison of all six distributions on shared set of axes. Figure 5.7 gives such a presentation. In order to make the comparison easier despite large differences in the absolute number of tokens involved, we re-computed the distributions in terms of percentages of total tokens, so that the graph presents from left to right, the highest ranked verb and its percent share in total tokens, followed by the next highest ranked verb and so forth, in the six sets defined by grammatical relation and the corpus analysed.

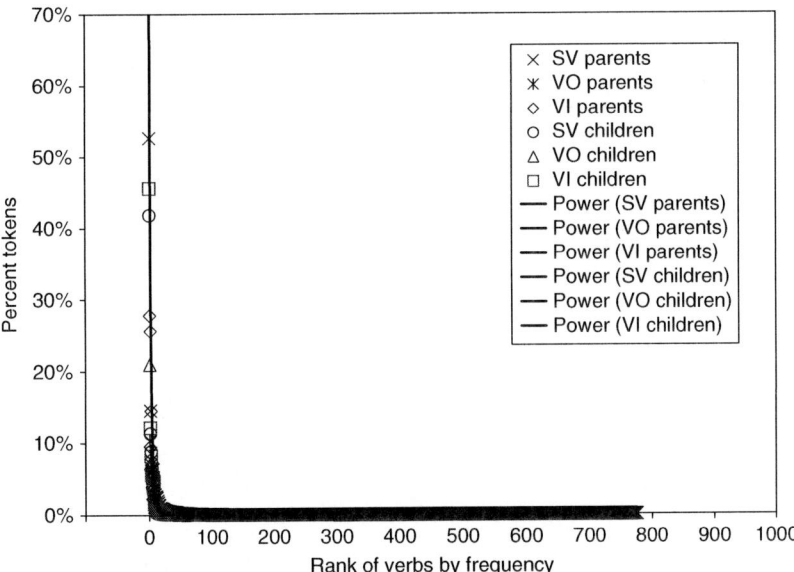

Fig. 5.7 Rank-frequency distribution of three grammatical relations in parents and children (percents).

We fitted six power-law curves to the distributions, one to each set of percentages. In Figure 5.7 only one curve is seen—the reason being that the six fitted curves completely collapsed. As we saw in the formal results of the comparisons, the rank-frequency distributions of verbs in the three grammatical relations, for parents as well as for children, are identical.

5.3 Skewed use patterns in syntactic relations

We saw that verbal form-classes generating the three core grammatical relations in parental speech possess similar highly unequal use patterns. In all three cases, a few verbs account for the great majority of tokens, and many other verbs account for the rest. The high degree of similarity between the subject–verb, verb–object, and verb–indirect object classes on this measure of inequality is surprising as the basic givens of the three grammatical relations and form-classes are far from identical. First, the SV relation takes up 58% of all tokens in the clausal core, the VO relation 40%, and the VI relation just 2% of all tokens, namely, there are serious differences in the relative frequency of the three patterns building up the clausal core. Second, the size of the verb repertoires is quite different, too, so that the SV relation uses 601 different verbs, the VO relation uses 776, and the VI relation, just 66. Despite these differences in the use statistics of the three grammatical relations in parental speech, when we examine their overall pattern of verb use, we arrive at a practically identical exponent representing the degree and shape of inequality—considered the 'scaling parameter' of the power-law distribution (Clauset et al., 2009). Thus, the details are different, but the mathematical estimates of the overall statistical features clearly show a global similarity.

5.3.1 The significance of use frequency in a skewed distribution

It is usually thought that there is a reason for the equivalence of power-law distributions, so that a class of phenomena with a particular 'scaling parameter' probably share the dynamical processes that generate the power-law relation (Barabási and Albert, 1999). In the present case, the dynamics is probably the wish to balance the use of frequent and infrequent verbs, as proposed already by Zipf (1949/1972). Zipf demonstrated that the frequent verbs are qualitatively different from infrequent verbs, and in particular, as we mentioned before, he found that the more frequent a word, the more semantically ambiguous it is. The highly frequent verbs at the start of the rank-frequency distributions we are investigating tend to be highly polysemous indeed.

Zipf thought that the skewed distribution of the use frequency of words is the result of an equilibrium between competing needs and motivations to reduce processing effort:[7] for the speaker, it is easiest to use a small number of highly ambiguous words, as this reduces the effort to pick and choose many specific words to express the same meanings. For the hearer, however, the best is if the message is fully explicit, namely, contains specific words for every meaning conveyed, as it reduces the task of having to resolve ambiguities.[8]

Zipf's equilibrium explanation for the power-law shape of these curves has found empirical support in the work of Ferrer i Cancho and Solé (2001, 2003) who discovered that the Zipf curve of large corpora of multiple speakers shows a division between two sections with different power-law slopes that apparently distinguish between a basic vocabulary shared by all speakers and a residue of more specialized words shared by fewer members of the group.[9] Ferrer i Cancho and Solé claim that the first section of the frequency curve is populated by a small number of very frequent common words which are semantically versatile and polysemous, and the second section, by a very large number of more specific lexemes which are less flexible semantically. This claim matches distinctions made by linguists between a general, polysemous kernel vocabulary and a less polysemous specific vocabulary, for instance by Dixon (1991).

As Dixon showed in his work on the verbal lexicon of English, frequent English verbs are highly polysemous; Dixon points out that these verbs are also syntactically versatile:

> The large *Oxford English Dictionary* lists 27 senses of *have*, 64 of *give* and 94 of *take*. Each of these verbs shows a very varied set of syntactic usages.
>
> Dixon (1991, p. 339)

It appears that parents in our corpus model for young children the English version of balancing between frequent and infrequent verbs, and at the same time, between polysemous general verbs and monosemous specific verbs. The close similarity of the power-law exponents of the three form-classes suggests that the wording of all three grammatical relations strikes a similar balance between general and specific verbs, containing both kernel verbs which are polysemous, semi-grammatical, and versatile, and more specific verbs which tend to be neither. Apparently, both kinds are needed for successful communication in some specific proportion, even in such a simplified speech register as parental speech to young children.

The surprising finding is that the very same inequality of use is present in children's speech already at Stage I of grammatical development. Thus, parents model using a whole range of verbs, frequent as well as infrequent, general as well as specific, polysemous as well as monosemous, and children follow suit and they, too, utilize the verb vocabulary in an identical pattern.

Studies documenting the earliest verb use in languages as different as English, Hebrew, and Estonian revealed that our corpus-based results are not exceptional. Apparently, children start to use a mixture of generic and specific verbs already with the very first verbs used by them in various syntactic patterns (Ninio, 1999a,b; Theakston *et al.*, 2004; Vihman, 1999).[10] This appears to be true even for languages with 'classifying stems' such as the Mayan languages Tzoltil and Tzeltal (Brown, 1998; de Leon, 1999).

For example, Ninio (1999b) documented the first verbs occurring in intransitive word-combinations in the speech of 20 Hebrew-speaking children. Table 3 of this paper presents the verbs in the first seven word-combinations, with the number of different children using them. There were altogether 31 different verbs, showing much overlap between the children; if each child used a different set of verbs, there would be 140 different verbs and not 31. It is obvious that the verbs pattern in a typical Zipf-shaped distribution, with some verbs (the Hebrew equivalents of *come, fall, go, sit*, and *sleep*) used by many children as their earliest verbs, and a very long tail of infrequent verbs (*exit, fly, break, burst, escape, turn, enter*, and so forth) used by just one or two children at this stage of development. The skewed distribution is of course similar to the one we find in our large corpus of English-speaking children for such syntactic patterns as SV and VO; apparently the diversification of the verb vocabulary is an early phenomenon, and thus children do not start word combinations only with generic verbs (a finding that tends to be emphasized because of the large proportion of children using them) but also with specific verbs.

Interestingly, a similar mixture of general and specific is also found in the earliest combining verbs of languages such as the Mayan languages Tzoltil and Tzeltal which are typologically quite dissimilar to the relatively analytical languages English, Hebrew, and Estonian. Both these languages—members of the Tzeltalan subfamily of Mayan—have 'classifying stems', which are verbs whose semantics specifies very strictly the kind of object acted on, whether by shape or type of substance the object is made of. Such verbs in fact supplete for their object, so that, for instance, talking about eating meat requires the use of a different verb than referring to eating tortillas or eating soft things. In several studies exploring Tzeltal and Tzoltil-speaking children's earliest verb use, it was found that they, too, mix generic and specific verbs in a kind of mixture we found for English and Hebrew. De Leon (1999) in an analysis of two children's acquisition of verbs in Tzotzil, shows that the earliest syntactic combinations in one of the children are with the very general verb translating as 'want'; somewhat later, this child too, starts to produce word combinations with more specific verbs. Brown (1998) studied two children, Mik and Xan, acquiring the related language, Tzeltal. One of the children, Mik, used in all his first word combinations general verbs such as the translation equivalents of 'do/make', 'want', 'take in hand', or 'feel', as well as the intransitives 'exist/be located' and 'come'. The other child, Xan, mixed general and specific verbs, using early on both the general verbs 'want', 'exist/be located', 'go', and 'come' and the classifying verbs 'eat tortillas', 'eat soft things', and so forth. The children also used, in addition to the above, some other early general, non-classifying verbs with lexical direct objects such as the translation equivalents of 'give', 'get', and 'receive', which, however, Brown excluded from the database because they appear nearly always in what she deemed as frozen expressions (see also Narasimhan and Brown, 2009). In a summary of the Tzeltal pattern Bohnemeyer *et al.* (2002) conclude:

> Learners of Tzeltal were indeed quick to acquire specific verbs such as *lut* "lodge tightly between objects" (e.g., lips, fork in tree), but learners of both languages [i.e., Tzeltal and Hindi] used general containment terms across a variety of contexts from an early age. If children have any tendency to prefer very narrow, object-specific schemata for their early containment words, this phase is short-lived.
>
> Bohnemeyer *et al.* (2002, p. 124)

It appears Zipf was right, and the mixture of generic and specific verbs is a universal tendency of language use, not excluding even very young speakers in typologically diverse languages. Despite a trend for simplification, parents apparently do not censor themselves from also using semantically more complex, specific verbs. Interestingly, children make use of the semantic diversity of the verb vocabulary parents model for them, closely recreating the parents' statistical pattern of use.

This result joins previous findings of this project in which children are found to be extremely similar to parents in their overall or global use statistics, despite their smaller verbal repertoire and differences in the relative frequency of individual verbs. In Chapter 2 the distribution of the tokens of the three grammatical relations in the core was almost identical in parents' child-directed speech and in young children's speech; about 58% of the clausal core in both registers consists of tokens of the subject–verb relation; 40% is the verb–object relation, and less than 2% are the verb–indirect object relation. In Chapter 3 the proportion of tokens in the clausal core by origin and length was identical in the two corpora: 96% of the tokens are generated by Anglo-Saxon verbs, and 98% by monosyllabic verbs. It seems that child syntax at Stage I is quite similar to parental speech, if we consider the global statistical characteristics of both registers.

It is an intriguing question how children manage to recreate the global characteristics of parental speech despite differences in the concrete details of their own use, including a much smaller verb repertoire. A process by which complex networks such as language develop and keep their global distributions has been offered by Barabási and Albert (1999; see also Newman, 2003). According to this theory, new agents joining an existing network tend to follow a principle called 'Preferential Attachment' by which they connect to nodes that are already highly connected, in preference to nodes with few or no connections. As an example, Preferential Attachment was offered by Barabási and Albert as the process by which the global statistical structure of the Web evolved and by which new users of the Web recreate the same global structure that they found when they joined and even extend its skewedness. This principle is no gross frequency effect as a user will not link to a site just because it is popular overall on the Web but, rather, because it is relatively popular among the sites dealing with the topic she is interested in. In Ninio (2006, chapter 5) I suggested that young children are similar to new users of the Web and come to approximate the overall distributions of their parents' speech through employing Preferential Attachment.[11] The local version of this principle is Pragmatic Matching (Ninio, 1986; Ninio and Wheeler, 1984) children learn novel linguistic forms in order to express some communicative intent which they cannot yet express to their satisfaction, adopting the most frequently modelled form for the expression of such intents in the linguistic environment. For example, in a study of the acquisition of Hebrew it was found that 18-month-old children adopt mothers' single-word expressions of communicative intents in proportions matching the relative frequency of the different expressions in maternal speech, within each type of intent separately. For expression rules modelled by mothers with the greatest relative frequency for their specific intent, the average proportion of children following that rule was 72.6%. For rules ranked second, the mean proportion of children following them dropped to 19.7%; and rules ranked third, 9.6%. The average proportion of children following a rule for rules ranked four or more was only 2.6%. It appears that the most frequently modelled rule for each kind of communicative intent has by far the highest chance of being adopted by children for their own single-word utterances expressing that intent, and the probability sharply decreases for the relatively less frequently modelled rules (Ninio, 1992). In a later study (Ninio, 2009), the overall frequency effect in the same corpus of single-word speech was computed, and it was clear that just being a frequently uttered word does not predict that children would also use that word in large numbers. The most frequent word used by mothers as a single-word utterance was *ken*, 'yes', generating 2675 tokens, and it was also the word most frequently used by the children, with 2540 tokens in the pooled corpus. However, the second most frequent word in that corpus of maternal speech was *yoffi*, 'fine, great', with 1546 tokens, which was barely used by any of the children, with just 17 tokens overall, breaking the frequency correlation. The reason is pragmatic: *yoffi*, 'fine', is used by mothers in almost all instances as praise for children's motor acts, a kind of communicative message mothers emit quite often in dyadic interaction with young children, but it is not one children would have much need of their own to address to their mothers. Just to complete the picture, children's second most frequent word in this single-word set was *lo*, 'no', with 1330 tokens in maternal speech and 1294 tokens in child speech. All three words were the most frequent forms of expression for their respective communicative intents, but the intents of agreeing or refusing were important for children to learn to express whereas the intent of praising was left unlearned until a later age by most.[12] A similar strong input frequency effect on early learning *within* types of communicative intents but not overall was found by Cameron-Faulkner *et al.* (2007) in a study of negation development: the emergence of *no, not*, and *'nt* negation (e.g. *can't, don't*) varied dependent on the pragmatic function of the utterance (e.g. inability, rejection, prohibition) and the frequency with which forms were presented in the input within specific pragmatic functions, but overall frequency was not a good predictor of age of emergence. These studies indicate that the frequency of forms in the input within particular pragmatic functions affects the rate at which structures emerge in children's speech, but overall frequency is fundamentally irrelevant and not part of the selection mechanism. Young children learn to produce language forms that serve their communicative needs and avoid those that they do not require (Ninio and Snow, 1988); Preferential Attachment and similar selective choice mechanisms operate conditional on pragmatic needs and interests.

Our present results show that children's early multiword speech exhibits several of the global statistical features of parents' speech, suggesting that despite being beginning producers of grammatical relations, they manage to retain and reproduce in their speech the major characteristics of adult language. They do not need to match these global features on purpose. The beauty of Preferential Attachment and similar processes is that local decisions translate to global organization without the involved agents having to worry about the big picture. Local decisions such as choosing the most frequently modelled alternative in individual learning situations are sufficient to recreate the global statistical features of the input language. Children at Stage I are apparently very similar to parents in the kind of pragmatic choices they make; differences in details such as a smaller lexicon do not preclude a deep similarity in the overall characteristics of the language they produce.

5.4 **Learning a skewed syntactic system**

We saw in Chapter 4 and earlier in this chapter that the verbal form-classes modelled by parents contain two kinds of verbs: the very frequent that tend to be semantically anomalous, and the rest of the lexicon that tends to be semantically simple but appears rarely in speech. Both types of verbs could pose problems for a young child learning the foundations of clausal syntax; the very frequent verbs because they are multivalent and polysemous, and the very rare, because of low frequency of modelling in the linguistic input. In the present section, we shall trace the fate of both categories of verbs in parental speech, in children's own productions, and interpret our results in terms of the light they shed on the nature of the mechanism by which children acquire syntactic knowledge.

5.4.1 **Learning frequent verbs in syntactic combinations**

The very-frequent section of the Zipf curve apparently contains the so-called *kernel* (Dixon, 1971), *nuclear* (Grimes, 1975), *semi-lexical* (Emonds, 2000), or *basic* vocabulary (Ogden, 1930). This is merely a partial list; these special verbs have received many different characterizations in the linguistic literature (see also note 14, Chapter 4). There are, however, many commonalities in the different approaches. In particular, linguistic descriptions converge on the most conspicuous feature of the very-frequent verbs which is their versatility, both semantic and syntactic. For instance, Dixon (1991) singles out kernel verbs' functioning in light-verb combinations as a kind of syntactic behaviour they do not share with the more specific verbs in their semantic field. Approaching the same phenomenon from a different angle, Butt (2003) and Butt and Geuder (2001) show that light verbs are a semi-lexical category, intermediate between main verbs and auxiliaries, representing the light use of otherwise 'heavy' verbs. Kayne (1993) adopts a similar mono-lexemic treatment of the main verb and auxiliary uses of *have*, pointing out that verbs, in general, can have multiple syntactic valencies. Our analyses in Chapter 4 show that the same multipurpose use and, with it, semantic polysemy, also occur in the case of the very frequent verbs in the parental input. Moreover, the verbs we analysed in detail—namely, *be, have,* and *do* in SV combinations and *do, give, have, make,* and *take* in VO combinations—also appeared in children's speech with the same spread of functions and, often, with the same proportion of multi-use as in parental speech. It seems that children have no great problem learning such ambiguous parental verbs, and when they do, they use them in several different uses and with several different meanings.

It has been speculated that the anomalous semantics of the very frequent parental verbs may actually help children to learn them early in syntactic combinations.

The reason is that because these verbs possess little purely semantic content, all the semantics they have is syntactically-relevant content. Emonds, who mostly discusses auxiliary verbs and their functioning in the SV construction, claims that such verbs lexicalize or 'spell out' certain syntactic features such as types of aspect or tense. He lists as examples the verbs *be, have, get, do, go, come, let,* and *make,* and, possibly *want* and *say* (Emonds, 1985, pp. 164–9). Lehmann (1991, p. 231) considers some very-general verbs lexicalized 'logical predicates' for the syntactic behaviour of their form-class, for example for transitivity. In other words, very frequent verbs may have little specific semantics, but the meaning they do have, reflects in some transparent way the combinatory potential of the relevant class of verbs. The feature of transparency may help young children learn the relevant word-combination with respect to these verbs earlier than for other verbs, although their semantic anomaly appears at first blush to be a considerable hindrance to early acquisition.[13] It is true of course that being a very frequently modelled verb may by itself help with the learning process; in any case, it should be remembered that frequency comes wrapped together with polysemy and polyvalency, and the child's learning task is not unequivocally made easier when a verb is of very high frequency in the input. Interestingly, some psycholinguistic findings make it possible that polysemy actually facilitates rather than complicates cognitive processing. For instance, even at equivalent frequencies, polysemous items allow significantly faster lexical access (Beckwith and Miller, 1990). Core items may not suffer in processing and acquisition from being connected to many different words; dense semantic neighbourhoods appear to help rather than hinder learning.

In general, children learn all the very frequent verbs in parental speech, although it is not quite accurate that relative frequency by itself gives a strong prediction which verb will be taken up by young children and which will not be. In Table 5.2 we present the 30 most frequent verbs in the parental corpus that appear in the SV syntactic relation, with children's tokens for each of these verbs. In Figure 5.8 we present only the first 20 verbs in this set, to ensure legibility.

It is clear that children produce the first seven most frequent verbs in the input, namely *be, can, do, get, go, have,* and *want,* with high frequency in their own speech; in fact these verbs are ranked also as their first seven by token frequency (although not quite in the same order as in parents). This is the point where the frequency match breaks down: parents' next two verbs—*think* and *know*—are considerably less frequent in children's speech, only ranked their 28th and 18th verbs by token frequency. From here on the correlation with parental frequency is practically non-existent, among the set of the first 30 verbs.

Table 5.2 Parents' 30 most frequent verbs in the parental corpus in SV relation, and children's tokens of the verbs in SV

Rank	Verb	Parents' tokens	Child tokens	Rank	Verb	Parents' tokens	Child tokens
1	be	102,700	6,012	16	make	704	95
2	do	28,360	1,268	17	need	678	100
3	can	12,155	544	18	happen	622	42
4	have	9,284	469	19	may	551	22
5	go	6,129	951	20	eat	476	98
6	want	5,773	1,629	21	fall	473	123
7	get	3,013	425	22	take	467	48
8	think	2,357	32	23	tell	377	11
9	know	2,221	71	24	give	337	20
10	like	1,420	134	25	sit	310	123
11	see	1,389	109	26	play	278	66
12	say	1,378	75	27	find	276	47
13	come	1,060	151	28	mean	268	23
14	put	909	123	29	must	245	7
15	look	884	52	30	try	216	8

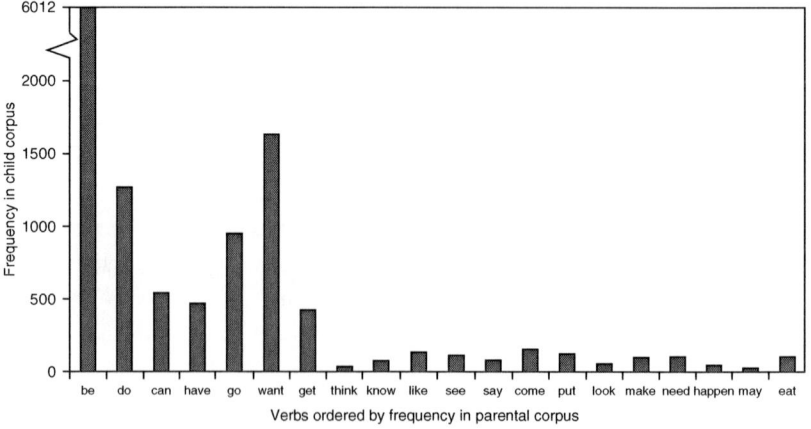

Fig. 5.8 Token frequency in child corpus of verbs in SV combinations by frequency in parental corpus—first 20 most frequent verbs in parents' speech.

This of course reminds us of the same phenomenon in Hebrew single-word speech where the second most frequent word in maternal speech was quite infrequent in child speech. The explanation is probably the same: children use with high frequency at this early stage of development only those verbs that serve their pragmatic needs, and it does not matter if the verbs are presented with a very high frequency (such as the 2370 tokens of *think*); children will produce considerably fewer sentences with such verbs than with a verb such as *see* or *come* that appear with much lower token frequency in the input (1389 and 1060). When we look at the number of different children in the corpus that use the various verbs in the SV combination (data not presented in the figure or table), the pattern repeats: the first seven verbs listed above are used in the SV pattern by at least a third of the children; none of the other verbs are used by more than 15% of the sample. There seems to be a serious preference to generate SV combinations with the extra frequent seven verbs in the input— which happen also to be verbs with grammatical or semi-grammatical uses. As we showed in Chapter 4, it appears that young English-speaking children of Stage I of grammatical development have internalized the principle that subjects belong to auxiliaries, copulae, and semi-auxiliary verbs. This adult-like preference for grammatical Heads of subjects accounts for the popularity of the seven most frequent parental verbs in this pattern; the other relatively frequent verbs do not order themselves in child speech so that they mirror their relative frequency in parental speech.

5.4.2 Learning rare verbs in syntactic combinations

We have seen that children manage quite well with the acquisition of frequent verbs in parental input, we now ask whether they are also capable of learning verbs that appear with low frequency in parental speech. Typically, in a power-law-shaped distribution, about 80% of all items are infrequent, together accounting for about 20% of all tokens. Our parental rank-frequency distributions are no exception. If Zipf's equilibrium theory is correct, the skewed distribution is a necessity, containing as it does both frequent, general, and polysemic verbs and rare, specific, monosemic ones. With such a skewed distribution of the items to learn, it is a crucial question whether children can learn infrequently modelled input items.

The large-sized corpus of parental speech provides a robust database for testing the effects of parental token frequency on children's adoption of the various verbs with a core syntax, in their own productions. Unlike in previous studies, the large parental corpus makes possible an estimate of the absolute frequency of the different verbs in parental speech, without having to worry about sampling limitations biasing our estimates.

As there are no agreed-on norms on what is a rarely used word or word-combination, we opted for a criterion that is often used in corpus linguistics, and that is a frequency below some criterion in a million running words. In our case, we considered any verb in a syntactic combination to be rarely used in that construction if the frequency of its occurrence in the parental corpus in that construction was fewer than 20 tokens in a million running words. This criterion was validated by the distribution of verbs in the parental corpus according to our criterion: the percent of verbs falling into the 'rare' class was 80.0% for SV, 78% for VO, and 77.5% for VI. This is very close to the typical Pareto proportion of 'poor' people which is around 80%.

Using this criterion, we classified all parental verbs in the three types of word-combinations into frequent and rare verbs, and checked each verb for whether it was used by the children in their own productions of the same grammatical relation. Appendix A to this chapter presents the list of all verbs, classified by parental frequency and child use. Table 5.3 presents children's verbs in the three grammatical relations by the frequency class of the verb in the parental corpus.

As we see in Table 5.3, between 35% and 50% of all verbs used by the children in Stage I grammar come from the rare tail of the parental distribution. Namely, 35–50% of all verbs in the verb–subject, object, or indirect object combinations used by children are heard in the input fewer than 20 times in a million words, demonstrating that children are able to learn item-specific syntax on the basis of very little input. Given that we attribute to children a precocious pragmatic principle by which they pick out from the input the form best suiting their communicative intent, it is reassuring that these young children are indeed able to learn verbs with a specific semantics in core syntactic combinations, even if these are not frequently modelled for them.

In addition, the presence of a learning process by which children can acquire item-specific syntactic constructions on the basis of very little input provides considerable support for a lexicalist conception of syntactic knowledge in children.

Table 5.3 Verbs in child corpus used in three grammatical relations, by frequency in parental corpus

Grammatical relation	Verbs	Frequent in parental corpus		Rare in parental corpus	
	Total	Number	Percent	Number	Percent
SV	220	116	52.7%	104	47.3%
VO	238	153	64.3%	85	35.7%
VI	24	12	50.0%	12	50.0%

As described in Chapter 1, a lexicalist syntax such as the current version of the Minimalist Program dictates a process of acquisition and learning which is item-specific and involves the learning of the allowed syntactic pattern of each linguistic item on an item-specific basis. According to such theories of linguistics, syntactic structure is 'projected' from the lexicon, based on the stored valency or subcategorization potential of verbs and other predicate words (Chomsky, 1995a; see also Allerton, 1982). On these grounds, syntactic development is best conceptualized as the accumulation of knowledge on the syntactic behaviour of individual lexical entries (Ninio, 2006). This makes syntactic acquisition into a process that should be quite similar to vocabulary acquisition, namely, a process in which a limited exposure to a new item is sufficient for its acquisition, as long as the mapping (of meaning, of syntactic pattern) to the new form is transparent in the learning context. Our results demonstrate that such a learning process is indeed operating in syntactic development. The syntactic behaviour of individual verbs appears to be learned in a 'fast-mapping' process such as the one observed in vocabulary acquisition.

There have been no previous reports of these rare input models in studies of input effects on acquisition because, in most cases, studies testing for frequency effects omit infrequent items from analysis, both parental and child (e.g. Cameron-Faulkner et al., 2003; Goodman et al., 2008; Lee and Naigles, 2005; Naigles and Hoff-Ginsberg, 1998; Serratrice et al., 2003; and see also Appendix B to this chapter on the methodological issues involved). When we do look at the complete distributions, parental and child, we find that children sample all kinds of verbs parents use and not only their frequent ones, and this is at the early stages of word-combinations. Learning consists of accumulating more and more parental verbs into their own productive use system, without being hindered by low parental frequency. Apparently, syntactic acquisition is indeed quite similar to vocabulary acquisition, namely, a process in which a limited exposure to a new item is sufficient for its acquisition. In most probability, the high proportion of rare input items in children's early word-combinations should be interpreted as evidence that the syntactic behaviour of individual verbs is learned in a 'fast-mapping' process such as has been observed in vocabulary acquisition in general (Carey, 1978), and see more below.

This does not mean that input frequency is not related to order of acquisition. On the whole, frequent items in parental speech do have a greater probability of being used by a larger number of young children than low-frequency items. This kind of conditional probability is usually taken to suggest that learning requires frequent input. However, this conclusion appears to be a mistake; input frequency by itself does not seem to play a part in learning the items since, as we saw, very many low-frequency and even rare verbs get adopted by some children at this early stage of syntactic development. Instead, it is more likely that both parental and child use frequencies represent the relative usefulness of items in talk, and the latter is expected to be similar for parents and children. There are inherent differences between the verbs participating in the syntactic combination which influence their use frequency. Some verbs are more likely than others to be used frequently in parent–child discourse and others are used rarely; different speakers—whether adult or child—have approximately the same magnitude of need for particular verbs in conversation. This kind of similarity does not by itself teach us about the learning process being driven by frequency, only that some verbs—such as *be* and *do*—have many and varied uses in English discourse whereas some others like *clap* and *clean* have more limited usefulness. Even if children learned each verb and its expression in a syntactic pattern with equal ease, there would be a wide variance in use frequencies, counted in speakers or tokens, and these would be similar in different groups of speakers for various lexical, syntactic, and pragmatic reasons. Indeed, distributions are expected to be similar for any two groups of adult speakers of a similar register, although adults cannot be suspected not to know the vocabulary, and their relative frequency of use does not represent order of acquisition or relative difficulty.

5.4.2.1 Rapid learning in vocabulary acquisition and syntactic development

The notion of learning unconstrained by number of trials originated in Learning Theory: single-trial learning was first suggested by Guthrie (1935) who saw it as the general mechanism of learning. Within vocabulary acquisition, rapid or one-trial learning has been proposed by several authors with various names such as 'rare event learning' (Nelson, 1987), 'fast mapping' (Carey, 1978), or 'quick incidental learning of words' (Oetting *et al.*, 1995; and see also Smiley and Huttenlocher, 1995). The gist of these theories of vocabulary acquisition is that young children apparently need very little exposure to novel vocabulary items before they learn them.

The evidence for such processes is quite compelling. Among others, Brainerd and Howe (1978), Carey and Bartlett (1978), and Dollaghan (1985) demonstrated fast mapping in children between two and five years of age. In a recent experimental study using a preferential looking method, Houston-Price *et al.* (2005) extended the findings to children as young as 1;6 and showed that they are able to learn new words on the basis of just three presentations. According to their results, apparently even very young children can learn from very little exposure, possessing an acquisition mechanism capable of dealing with moving as well as static images.

Our findings join these results and demonstrate that the item-specific syntactic behaviour of verbs belongs to the lexical contents which are learned on the basis of very little exposure. Using our large corpus as the basis for robust estimates of input frequencies, we saw that acquisition in children does not seem constrained by some minimal frequency of modelling in the input; rather, they appear to be able to learn verb-complement patterns on the basis of as little input as 20 words in a million. This is not at all surprising if we remember that it is a linguistic commonplace that the lexicon contains the subcategorization potentials of individual verbs, and thus any process that operates in the acquisition of vocabulary items is expected to operate also in the learning of this particular kind of lexical content.

5.5 Similarities and differences between input and output

In the last section we received the impression that children are able to learn any verb-complement combination as long as it is presented in parents' child-directed speech. Indeed, throughout this book we found evidence for the fundamental similarity of young English-speaking children's core grammar to their parents'. We concluded that children seem to have internalized the spirit of the language, recreating in their early grammar many of the special features of native English syntax they heard in parental speech.

However, despite the global similarity between parental and child speech, we also found that there are some serious differences between the child dialect and the parental register. These differences imply that children's learning is also affected by factors which are different from sheer pragmatic choice of what to say in a given communicative situation, guiding parents' choice of words.

First, children may have a similar basic syntactic system as their parents have, but they have less of it. As we saw in Chapter 3, even if we control for sample size, we find that children have fewer verb types in all three grammatical relations; their repertoire is smaller by 40% per same number of tokens as a matched sample of parental speech. Translating this to a factor affecting learning, it is clear that the learning of each new verb in a basic syntactic combination is effortful, and in Stage I grammar children have not yet caught up even with the highly reduced verbal repertoire used by parents in child-directed speech.

Second, verbs used by children are on average significantly simpler morphophonemically than verbs used by parents; as we saw in Chapter 3, a much higher proportion of their verbs are monosyllabic, surpassing parents' proportion by 35–40%. The significance for a learning process is that the articulatory difficulty of verbs affects the chances of children taking them up from the input and using them productively in grammatical relations. Thus, early syntactic development shares with vocabulary development in general a fundamental phonetic factor: easier-to-pronounce monosyllabic verbs will be used by children in syntactic combinations at this stage whereas longer polysyllabic verbs will have to wait for a later stage.

Third, children's verbs in early syntactic combinations are also more likely to be of native origin than verbs used by parents. As we saw in Table 3.5 of Chapter 3, children are less likely to use a Latinate verb than a native one even if they are equal in syllable length. As the native vocabulary tends to be simpler in meaning than the Latinate one, this tendency may reflect children's preference for simple contents.

Lastly, as we saw in Chapter 4, children tend to use in syntactic combination more content verbs than do parents who use a very large percent of functional verbs in subject–verb combinations. Children at Stage I may have come a long way in acquiring the English pattern of using functional verbs for tense, aspect, questioning, and negation, but they are not yet completely over the difficulty such patterns present. Clauses containing periphrastic combinations tend to be longer and their structure and semantics more complex than clauses with direct subject–verb relations in them. Avoiding function verbs is children's way of reducing processing effort, as are the other factors listed above.

Interestingly, our study demonstrates that polysemy and multiple valencies for verbs are not avoided by parents, nor do they seem to pose a special problem for young children. As we saw in Chapter 4, both parents and children use the very frequent verbs in multiple patterns. It appears that Levinson (2000) was quite correct when he commented that articulation is costly for processing while inference is cheap; this certainly seems to be true for learning by young children and colours the features of their earliest syntactic system.[14]

We might summarize that children at Brown's Stage I demonstrate a partial mastery of the core grammar of parental child-directed speech. They appear by this stage to have built a syntactic system which is very much like the system of their parents, and which is practically identical to it in its global features. However, there are considerable quantitative differences between children's grammar and parental grammar: children use fewer and shorter verbs, and probably also simpler verbs, on average, than parents. Development from this stage on should consist of adding more items to children's repertoire: children should add long verbs, rare and Latinate verbs, auxiliary verbs, and copular verbs—and their item-specific syntactic patterns—to their productive repertoire. As far as the clausal core is concerned, children have already got it by Stage I; now they need to finish learning what they are still missing from the basics of English grammar.

If development is a process by which child speech becomes a random sub-sample of parental speech, indistinguishable from the latter, it seems that at Stage I, children have almost achieved the developmental goal for the composition of their core syntax, except for the quantitative difference. The pattern of similarities and differences between input and output can be accounted for by what we know about the abilities and weaknesses of young children. First, children are like parents in their social cognition, at least in what is needed for verbal interaction around shared topics. This probably accounts for the basic similarity in the global features of their core clausal syntax in Stage I. However, social precociousness is not enough for language acquisition, and children are still immature in their ability to learn more than the simplest set of verbs used by their parents. Progress in phonetic and semantic capabilities—needed in all cases of vocabulary acquisition—will probably drive the further elaboration of children's syntactic system as well.

5.6 Conclusions: children are efficient learners of basic syntactic combinations

In the last four chapters of this monograph, we presented the results of a corpus-based study of early syntactic development, switching between levels of analysis, examining the syntax of individual verbs, as well as the global features of various aggregates characterizing the clausal core. We compared children to parents, and used various measures such as randomized virtual samples in order to overcome the statistical problems involved in the comparison. It is clear that we did not use our large corpora for one purpose that corpora are sometimes used for: we did not extract 'slot-and-frame' formulae from our large collection of parental or child sentences, using relative frequency and positional consistency as our sole guide to presumed fixed elements in such formulae, along the lines of Lieven *et al.* (1997) or Bannard *et al.* (2009). Some may say this is a waste of a large corpus; after all, the methods extracting formulae by statistical processes have an excellent field record. For example, Lieven *et al.* reported that a mere 25 'slot-and-frame' formulae discovered in the data by the fixed positioning of the 'frame' items and a number of different 'slot-filling' items following or preceding them, accounted for an average of 60% of child sentences. Bannard *et al.*, using an automatic extraction process allowing a great deal of freedom in the form of the formulae as long as they had at least one fixed word and one variable slot, have arrived at an even higher coverage of 70–80% of all child sentences in two children's corpora.

Our objection to such a research strategy rests on the unmotivated leap between the purely statistical criteria for the discovery of some 'positional pattern' and the assertion that such patterns are the very generalizations on which children's productions are based. The statistical discovery process has no other tool but frequency counts; theoretical issues can be thus decided by simply counting the number of different items following some word in the text, as, for example, was done in Jones *et al.* (2000) in order to decide if only verbs or also nouns and pronouns serve as pivots of lexical-specific 'island' formulae:

> As explained earlier, the data are expected to show that verbs act as frames (taking lots of different common-nouns as slot fillers) whereas common-nouns are not expected to act as frames. Whether this is true can be examined by looking at the number of common-noun types that follow verb types, and vice versa. We operationalise the concept of an "island" as a lexical item which acts as a frame for at least ten different slot fillers (e.g., a verb type would have to have ten different common-noun types as slot fillers). For example, for Anne, the verb "Find" is an island because it is followed by ten common-noun types ("Dolly", "Plate", "Seat", "Welly-boot", "Baby", "Ribbon", "Hat", "Duck", "Pen", and "Bird").[...] Table 3 shows that both pronoun-islands and proper-noun islands exist for Anne, Anne's mother, and MOSAIC. The pronoun-islands are particularly strong (the mean number of slot fillers for pronouns is more than 20 for all three sets of data) and because pronouns take verbs as slot fillers, these islands are problematic for a strict version of the verb-island hypothesis which predicts that only verbs are initially used as frames.
>
> Jones *et al.* (2000, p. 726)

Positional patterns discovered by such criteria are not seen as mere matter of convenience, shortening the way to some underlying order too complicated to arrive at with limited computing resources, as they would be in the typical computer-learning, Natural Language Processing project. Instead, such criteria are seen as sufficient to discover the real generalizations on which children's production is actually based. For example, Pine *et al.* (1998) say:

> [...] we would argue that it is reasonable to assume that a child who produces a criterial number of different instances of a particular pattern has some knowledge of that pattern, provided that (i) the pattern is defined in terms of a particular lexical item (e.g. *can't* + X) rather than an abstract category (e.g. auxiliary verb + X); and (ii) the criterial number is set reasonably high.
>
> Pine *et al.* (1998, p. 811–12)

Similar to Jones *et al.* (2000), Pine *et al.* (1998) also reach the conclusion that not only verbs but also pronouns serve as pivots of productive syntactic patterns used by children to generate multiword utterances. Other texts using the statistical discovery method and proposing the same kind of formulae are, among others, Childers and Tomasello (2001) and Dodson and Tomasello (1998). In some publications (e.g. Tomasello, 2003), frames built around pronouns such as '*he* X-*ed it*' are seen as possibly even more important for syntactic development than ones built around verbs and other predicates. Given that pronouns are considered in symbolic logic to be the quintessential zero-valency items (Reichenbach, 1947), this outcome of the purely statistical method clashes head on with the foundations of valency-based linguistics.

Chapter 1 of this book makes it explicit that mainstream syntactic theory—built on the foundations of the concept of valency and of symbolic logic in general—is seen as the best theoretical option to be adopted as the framework for a study of syntactic development in children. Following this commitment, we opted for the labour-intensive method of hand coding our corpora for three traditional grammatical relations, the subject–verb, verb–object, and verb–indirect object relations, instead of employing some purely statistical discovery process such as the ones discussed above. The outcome of our study is the somewhat mundane-sounding claim that syntactic development is a process fundamentally similar to the acquisition of the lexicon: children learn a vocabulary of verbs together with their syntactic and semantic valency and when they accrue as many verbs as their parents know, they will have finished the job of becoming indistinguishable from adult speakers of their native language.

This description takes it as given that children indeed learn to produce word-combinations of the traditional kind, such as SV or VO, relying on the concepts and units proposed by mainstream theoretical linguistics (the Minimalist Program, Dependency Grammar), typological linguistics, or by traditional linguistics. We did consider an alternative to the formal atomic units of traditional grammar in the form of meaningful multiword constructions possessing prototypical semantics, and showed that the data does not support Construction Grammar in this attempt at exchanging syntactic relations with constructions. However, we did not yet consider the possibility that children learn to produce multiword utterances using frame-and-slot formulae which are altogether unrelated to, and not derived from, the constructs and units proposed by linguistic theorizing.

As explained above, our reluctance to work with purely statistical, rather than linguistic patterns was based on theoretical and not on empirical arguments in favour of the linguistic analysis of sentence structure. Beyond the reluctance to use a system that would provide formats unmotivated by, and even rejected by theoretical linguistics, in Chapter 1 we mentioned several concrete reasons why statistically derived patterns are unlikely to serve children in the course of developing syntactic knowledge. As an example, we discussed a multiword formula mentioned in Cameron-Faulkner *et al.* (2003) and suggested there as one serving development, the '*Are you* ___?' formula. We summarized some of the linguistic arguments against the choice of this schema as the representation of a set of actual sentences said to children, such as 'Are you hungry?' and 'Are you running away from me?', mentioning that the suggested schema covers at least three different sentence types, the copular, the progressive, and the passive, each with a quite different requirement for the fillers of the open slot following 'Are you'. This seemed to us to preclude the learning of 'Are you ___?' as a productive formula by children, as the open slot cannot be filled just anyhow by any words the child would put there. In addition, the meaning of the verb be itself is different in the three uses of this formula, as in one use the verb is a passive auxiliary, in another use it is a progressive aspectual auxiliary, and in the third, it is a copula signalling 'equal to'. In other words, the formula itself, 'Are you ___?', is not a format that could teach a child, just by itself, to generate meaningful sentences. This example was analysed in great detail in Chapter 1 so as to exemplify the pitfalls of statistically extracted formulae and of turning away from the linguistic analyses available in descriptive grammars of English such as Quirk et al. (1985).

This is the time to see if our opting for linguistically derived descriptions of syntactic knowledge is in fact the only way to account for our empirical data. Linguistic arguments aside, it should be possible to actually test the hypothesis that children do or do not learn to produce sentences using formulae and schemas which are not backed by linguistic theory but are suggested as statistical summaries of the input data.

The formula we shall be testing against the linguistic description of our results is the one most often proposed in the developmental literature while most crucially objectionable on linguistic grounds, and that is a lexical formula centred not on verbs but on pronouns as its pivot. In a message discussing the results of the present study, Caroline Rowland (personal communication) suggested that children in Stage I of development have such a large repertoire of verbs used in core syntactic relations not because—as we claimed in section 5.4.2—they learn verbs in some fast-mapping process together with their semantic and syntactic valency, but because they learn verbs as fillers in the slots of lexical frames formed around non-verbs, as proposed in Pine et al. (1998). According to Rowland:

> [...] as soon as you start thinking about lexical frames formed around non-verbs, with verbs in the slots (as we suggested in the 1998 Linguistics paper - Pine, Lieven and Rowland) - then it's quite easy to see how the children could learn a range of verbs very quickly (I like, I want, I have...), though you would predict that they would be able to use them only in a small range of lexical frames.
>
> Rowland (2010, personal communication)

This prediction is possible to test, and we shall turn to it now.

5.6.1 **Spread of verbs in a longitudinal corpus**

First, we checked in a child's longitudinal data whether her rapid spread of verbs over the VO constructions was a result of her learning new verbs in pronoun-centred formulae which are the transitive analogue of the '*I* + X' formula mentioned by Rowland. The data we used are those of Travis, Tomasello's child, whose acquisition data for VO were presented in Ninio (2006) in table 2.2. Travis indeed acquired a large number of new verbs in the VO pattern in a very short time, so that within two months she produced 30 different verbs in the VO pattern. If we look at the age at which she produced each new verb for the first time, we can see that the production of new verbs accelerates from a slow start to a very fast pace by the end of the period covered (see also Ninio, 2006, figure 2.6). If this feat was achieved with the help of for-mulae centred on pronominal objects, we should expect that the majority of Travis's first sentences with a new verb will indeed employ one of a restricted number of accusative pronouns.

Table 5.4 repeats table 2.2 of Ninio (2006) and presents Travis's first sen-tence with each of her first 30 different verbs getting a post-verbal direct object.

We counted the different noun-phrases (NPs) Travis used as direct objects for her novel verbs in the first sentence she used them in, in the VO construc-tion, and found that she used no fewer than 24 different NPs for her first 30 verbs in the VO pattern. She certainly used the pronominal object '*this*' with six different verbs, but in the other 24 cases she used nouns as objects with a novel verb and not pronouns. Just to be on the safe side, we repeated this analysis with the first 19 verbs Travis used in the SVO construction (presented as table 2.1 in Ninio, 2006). In SVO, Travis used 18 different NPs as the direct object in her first sentence with each new verb for the first 19 verbs in this construction.

It appears that this particular well-documented child very quickly acquired a large number of verbs into her transitive syntactic constructions—without, however, showing any evidence that she was learning the verbs in some restrict-ed formula centred around pronoun objects. The variety of noun-phrases employed by Travis in her very first sentences with each of her new verbs in these patterns is in fact impressive. Travis seems to have learned VO and SVO very fast—and with an adult's diversity of complement object terms. There is no evidence whatsoever for her learning new verbs into a pronoun-centred lexical formula; her data support the hypothesis that she learned each verb with its individual semantic and syntactic potential to get a direct object, freely combining it with the appropriate object expression.

Table 5.4 Travis's first sentence with each of her first 30 different verbs getting a post-verbal direct object

Age	Utterance
1;05.01	Get-it hat
1;05.26	Find-it funny (label for picture)
1;05.27	Open door
1;05.27	Yaya (draw) mans
1;05.28	Catch rocks
1;06.01	Ride horsie
1;06.02	Hammer table
1;06.06	Hold Weezer
1;06.06	Get-out kisses
1;06.07	Bite finger
1;06.11	Throw da ball
1;06.13	Got-it Weezer
1;06.16	Touch light
1;06.22	Step-in water
1;06.24	Lock that Lulu
1;06.25	Fix this
1;06.25	Blow balloon
1;06.25	Hit ball
1;06.25	See this
1;06.25	Read this
1;06.29	Maria made this duck
1;06.29	Stop-it bike
1;06.29	Close this
1;06.03	Drop-it ice
1;06.03	Brush-it hair
1;06.03	Watch TV
1;07.00	Clean this
1;07.00	Driving car
1;07.03	Break this
1;07.03	Bring chair

Source: Ninio, 2006, table 2.2, based on Ninio 1999a, Appendix D1.

5.6.2 **Corpus-based analysis of syntactic complement terms**

We could not repeat the same analysis for the children included in the pooled corpus as we had no assurance that the first multiword sentences in the observations stored in the CHILDES archive were actually the child's first sentences with a new verb in SV, VO, or VI patterns. Instead, we collected all verbs in the child corpus with *a single token in the three core relations*, assuming that such rare verbs were the most likely to have been the first and only utterances with this verb by their speaker. If the wide spread of verbs in a particular syntactic construction is accounted for by a pronoun-based formula (as hypothesized by Rowland), we should see for these verbs a high concentration of pronominal complements. Even if the sentences documented for these verbs were not in fact the very first uses for their speakers, the infrequent use marks the verbs as the ones least likely to be habitually used by the children, thus the most likely to require the support of a pronominal format in their production, if such a format indeed serves as a facilitator of new verbs in syntactic combinations.

The results were the following. Among verbs receiving a syntactic subject in the corpus, there were 49 verbs with a single token in the whole corpus. These verbs received 19 different NPs as subjects. The pronoun 'I' appeared with 16 different verbs; the rest of the single-token verbs, namely, 33 verbs, used some other NP as subject, in fact, 18 different ones. The rest of the NPs were *cow, he, it, ma, me, Mommy, Mummy, people, Samantha, Shadow, she, tail, the doctor, the dog, this, we, wheel,* and *you.*

Among verbs getting direct objects, a total of 70 had a single token. These verbs appeared with 39 different object NPs. The pronoun '*it*' appeared with the frequency of 15 in this collection, thus 55 of the single-token verbs had some other NP-complement, 38 different ones. The direct object NPs except for *it* were: *a banana, a cabbage, a dub, a pail of bones, airplane, block, Bonny, car, eating, feet, goodnight, Grandma was here, he hurt his, her, him, letters, matches, me, Mommy, my head, one, somebody, something, that, the bus ticket, the door, the frog, the monkey, the phone, the sheep, the typewriter, them, this, those, what, you, your nose,* and *your pardon.*

Lastly, there were a total of six verbs with a single token among the verbs getting a dative object, and they appeared with four different object NPs. The most frequent was '*me*', with a frequency of two. The other NPs were *lady, Mom,* and *them.*

The results show, again, that even with these rare verbs, children use a great variety of different nominal complements as their subject or object. It is not that Travis and the children of the corpus did not use pronoun subjects (mostly 'I'), objects (mostly '*it*'), and indirect objects ('*me*') with some frequency. They did use them—but alongside these pronoun complements the core syntactic constructions also contained many other nominal expressions. It is impossible to claim on the basis of these data that English-speaking children spread the use of the SV, VO, and VI constructions to many different verbs with the scaffolding of pronominal formulae of the kind proposed by Rowland and suggested in the literature. The large majority of core complements used even with rare verbs are not the favourite pronominal ones. Nor is there evidence for a restricted range of different complement NPs. Recall that Rowland predicted that the acquisition of many new verbs by young children with the help of pronominal formulae would mean that the children would be able to use the relevant verbs only in a small range of lexical frames. Neither in Travis's first verbs in the VO and SVO patterns nor in the rare verbs of the children's corpus do we see a small range of lexical frames for the relevant verbs. This means that the hypothesis of children learning verbs through pronominal frames instead of lexical-specific verb-centred frames is rejected as an explanation for children acquiring such a large repertoire of verbs with core syntax in Stage I of grammar.

We can conclude that pronoun frames do not account for early syntactic development.[15] Instead, children in all probability learn verbs with their syntax in a lexical-specific learning process. This process agrees well with the concepts and units of mainstream linguistics and not with formulae alien to linguistics, derived purely from distributional, statistical analysis of the data.

I do not think that theoretical linguistics needs support from developmental studies such as the present one. It is still reassuring that our results agree so well with the concepts and units of present-day mainstream linguistics, and in particular, with its syntactic atoms in the form of the Merge/Dependency couplet, from which the sentence syntactic structure is build up in a systematic way. Our data does not support the alternative architecture of Construction Grammar in any of the analyses we presented in Chapter 4, and it does not support the non-linguistic, purely frequency-distribution based formulae such as the pronoun-pivot one. Even if researchers are merely interested in a methodological apparatus that provides sustainable empirical generalization, the results of the present large-corpus-based study should encourage them to give Merge/Dependency a chance. There is no such a thing as an a-theoretical descriptive terminology; the moment the researcher engages in any kind of generalization, going beyond the actual sentences to some schema, formula, variable, or slot, this is already a theoretical claim that the formula is a valid entity that structures children's production of sentences. Hence, claiming that there are pronoun-centred frames with variable slots for verbs, such as '*I + X*' does not count as a theory-neutral generalization. Instead, it is a theoretical claim that pronouns can receive verbs as their variables in some kind of systematic unification process in which the semantic role of the verb is determined relative to the meaning of the pronoun. If all known unification-type or valency-type grammars reject this option, choosing instead the predicate and not the pronoun as the semantic and syntactic Head of the word-combination,[16] the choice of such a formula in developmental psycholinguistic research seems ill advised.

Instead of marshalling the linguistic and logical arguments for the regular predicate-centred valency approach, we preferred in this section to show that the pronoun-centred formulae do not succeed in accounting for the empirical developmental data, whereas the verb-centred lexicalist approach does. Even if some researchers would rather prefer not to have to choose a theoretical-linguistic framework for their work, they do not have this option, as any formula, variable, or general schema imply some kind of theoretical choice. We can now return to the question of units of analysis discussed in Chapter 1 of this book and answer it again. At the conclusion of this study, it appears that mainstream theoretical linguistics as well as traditional, typological, and computational linguistics with which it conforms, provide the best theoretical framework for developmental research. Syntactic structure is best described by appealing to the Head–Dependent couplet, with its subtypes which are various distinct grammatical relations. This descriptive apparatus seems to also serve very well the simple speech registers which are parental child-directed speech and children's earliest, Stage I, multiword speech. Our developmental study thus supports the choice of the Minimalist Program and of Dependency Grammar as the linguistic theories providing the most sustainable framework for developmental research.

Using the conventional analytical apparatus of theoretical linguistics in order to explore the beginnings of syntactic development, we found a great deal of similarity between the core syntax of young children and of parents. Children emerge in this project as efficient learners of basic syntactic combinations, their item-specific learning style well suited to the item-specific characteristics of the language they are acquiring. English may not afford a great deal of abstraction, schematization, homogeneous categories, and use of prototypes, especially when it comes to its Anglo-Saxon core; but due to the wonderful self-organizing property of language, out of the fragmented collection of uniquely behaving verbs children acquire, there arises a syntactic system with the same global characteristics as those of the input language. We thus conclude that syntactic development is probably a much simpler process than we had believed it to be: it is a process of learning small pieces of knowledge, their choice driven by pragmatic considerations. Formal syntax is but the means; efficient communication is the end.

Appendix A: **Verbs used by parents, by frequency in the input and use by children**

A.1 **Parents' verbs in the SV relation**

A.1.1 SV: frequent verbs in the input—used by children

Ask; be; belong; bet; bite; blow; break; bring; brush; build; buy; call; can; catch; climb; close; colour; come; count; cry; cut; do; draw; drink; drive; drop; eat; fall; feel; find; finish; fit; fix; fly; forget; get; give; go; guess; happen; have; hear; help; hide; hit; hold; hurt; jump; keep; kick; kiss; knock; know; leave; let; like; live; look; lose; love; make; may; mean; miss; move; must; need; open; pick; play; pop; pour; pull; push; put; read; remember; ride; roll; run; say; scare; see; send; show; sing; sit; sleep; smell; sound; spill; stand; start; stay; stop; swim; take; talk; taste; tell; think; throw; tickle; try; turn; use; wait; wake; walk; want; wash; watch; wear; wish; work; write.

A.1.2 SV: frequent verbs in the input—not used by children

Bless; hope; ought; seem; wonder.

A.1.3 SV: rare verbs in the input—used by children

Bake; bang; bark; bash; beat; bounce; brrmm; bump; burn; burp; carry; change; cheat; check; chew; clap; clean; click; comb; cook; cool; cough; cover; crash; crawl; cross; cuddle; dance; dig; dress; dump; dunk; excuse; feed; fill; grab; hand; hop; hug; hurry; laugh; lay; lick; lie; load; match; melt; mend; mix; nap; pay; pee; peek; pet; pinch; pretend; race; rain; rake; reach; ring; rock; salt; save; scoot; scratch; screw; set; shake; share; shout; shut; ski; slip; smack; smile; smoosh; smooth; snap; speak; spit; splash; spray; squeak; squeeze; squish; steal; step; stick; sting; suppose; sweep; swing; swish; thank; tie; tip; touch; unlock; waste; wet; win; wipe; yell.

A.1.4 SV: rare verbs in the input—not used by children

Abandon; accuse; act; add; agree; ah; answer; apologize; appreciate; arrange; arrive; assert; assume; assure; attach; attack; babysit; back; bag; bath; become; beep; beg; begin; behave; believe; bend; bleach; blend; block; boil; bonk; boo; bother; breathe; bubble; buckle; bug; bully; bust; calm; care; cause; cave; chase; chatter; chip; choke; choose; chop; chuck; chug; clam; clear; cling; clip; clunk; collect; comfort; complain; confuse; connect; continue; control; cooperate; copy; correct; cost; crack; crank; crush; curl; dare; decide; defrost; deliver;

deny; depend; describe; deserve; dial; die; dip; disappear; discover; discuss; dismantle; distort; disturb; dive; doubt; drag; dream; dribble; drill; drip; dry; dust; earn; empty; end; enjoy; erase; escape; exhaust; exist; expect; fail; fancy; fart; fascinate; fetch; fiddle; fight; figure; flap; flash; flatten; flick; flip; float; flop; fold; follow; fool; forbid; forgive; freeze; frighten; fudge; fuss; gather; goof; grease; grow; growl; grunt; hammer; hang; hatch; hate; haul; heat; hitch; hog; holler; honk; hook; hum; hush; ignore; improvise; insist; interest; inter- fere; interpret; interrupt; invite; itch; jiggle; jingle; kid; kill; kneel; knit; land; lead; leak; lean; learn; lend; lift; light; line; list; listen; loan; lock; manage; march; mark; marry; mash; matter; measure; meet; meow; merit; mess; milk; mime; mind; misjudge; mistreat; moan; mow; mumble; name; nibble; nod; notice; offer; ooh; operate; order; owe; own; paddle; paint; pant; park; pass; pat; peck; peekaboo; peel; peep; perform; phone; pipe; plan; plant; please; plug; point; poke; poop; poopoo; pounce; pound; pout; prefer; press; prevent; profile; promise; prompt; propose; protest; prove; punch; quack; quit; raise; rattle; realize; recall; reckon; recognize; recommend; reconsider; record; relax; remind; remove; require; rest; rewind; rhyme; rip; roar; rotate; rub; ruin; rush; sack; saw; scoop; scorch; score; scrape; scream; scrub; seat; sell; serve; settle; sew; shadow; shampoo; sharpen; shatter; shave; shine; shoot; shove; sift; sign; skin; skip; slap; slide; slob; slow; smoke; snatch; sneak; sneeze; snow; soak; sock; sort; sparkle; Spell; spend; spin; split; splodge; spoil; squirm; squirt; stack; stain; stamp; steam; steer; stink; stir; stomp; straighten; stretch; stroke; strug- gle; study; stuff; stumble; style; suck; suffer; suggest; surprise; swallow; swap; swear; switch; tap; tape; teach; tear; tease; teetee; telephone; tend; test; thread; tick; tighten; tire; toot; tread; trick; trip; tumble; twirl; unbuckle; understand; undo; unscrew; untie; unzip; vacuum; vanish; vibrate; visit; volunteer; waddle; warm; warn; water; wave; weed; weigh; whisper; whistle; wiggle; wind; wobble; wrap; wreck; wrinkle; zip; zoom; zuggle.

A.2 Parents' verbs in the VO relation

A.2.1 VO: frequent verbs in the input—used by children

Ask; bang; bash; beat; believe; bet; bite; bless; blow; bounce; break; bring; brush; build; bump; buy; call; carry; catch; change; chase; check; chew; clean; close; colour; comb; cook; count; cover; crack; cut; do; draw; dress; drink; drive; drop; dry; dump; eat; feed; feel; fill; find; finish; fit; fix; fold; forget; get; give; go; grab; guess; hang; have; hear; help; hide; hit; hold; hug; hurt; keep; kick; kiss; knock; know; leave; let; lick; lift; like; look; lose; love; make; mean; mend; mind; miss; mix; move; name; need; open; paint; park; pat; pay; pick; pinch; play; pour; press; pull; push; put; quit; reach; read; remember; ride; rip;

roll; rub; save; say; scare; scratch; see; send; set; shake; share; show; shut; sing; sit; spill; stack; stand; start; stick; stop; suppose; take; taste; tear; tell; thank; think; throw; tickle; tie; tip; touch; try; turn; undo; use; wait; wake; want; wash; watch; wave; wear; wind; wipe; wish; write.

A.2.2 VO: frequent verbs in the input—not used by children

Allow; choke; clap; enjoy; expect; figure; hand; hope; learn; mash; mess; ought; pretend; smell; spit; stir; understand; untie; wonder.

A.2.3 VO: rare verbs in the input—used by children

Answer; bath; beg; bobble; bonk; borrow; bother; brrmm; buckle; burn; cause; climb; cross; cuddle; dial; dig; dunk; empty; fetch; fly; guard; hammer; hook; juggle; jump; lay; lie; lock; mark; match; meet; own; pack; part; pass; peck; peek; peel; pet; plug; poke; post; race; rake; rap; ring; rock; run; salt; scoot; screw; settle; shoot; slide; smack; smoosh; smooth; snap; speak; spin; spoil; squash; squeak; squeeze; squish; steal; swallow; swap; sweep; switch; tape; trick; tuck; twist; type; unbuckle; unlock; visit; walk; waste; wet; whip; wing; work; zip.

A.2.4 VO. rare verbs in the input—not used by children

Abandon; absorb; accept; accuse; add; adjust; admit; adore; afford; afraid; agree; aim; announce; annoy; apply; appreciate; arrange; assert; assume; assure; attach; attack; back; bag; bake; balance; ball; bandage; bead; beep; begin; behave; bend; blame; bleach; blend; blob; block; blot; boil; boo; bop; boss; braid; bruise; bug; buggle; bully; burp; burst; bury; bust; butter; button; bye-bye; calm; camp; care; carve; charge; chip; choose; chop; chuck; circle; clear; click; clip; clobber; clunk; collect; combine; comfort; complain; conduct; confirm; confuse; connect; consider; contain; contemplate; continue; control; cool; coordinate; copy; cornmeal; correct; corrupt; cost; crank; crash; crayon; creep; crumble; crunch; crush; cry; curl; curse; dab; damn; dare; darn; debate; decide; decorate; defrost; defy; deliver; deny; deposit; deprive; describe; deserve; destine; destroy; detect; determine; die; digest; dilute; dip; direct; dirty; discover; discuss; dish; dismantle; displease; disrupt; distort; distract; disturb; doggone; doubt; download; drag; dream; dribble; drill; drip; dry-clean; duck; dust; earn; electrocute; enclose; encourage; end; entertain; entice; erase; establish; evade; excite; exhaust; explain; explore; express; eye; face; fail; fan; fancy; fasten; fence; fight; fish; flap; flatten; flick; flip; flop; flush; follow; foo; fool; force; freeze; frighten; fry; fudge; fun; gain; gather; glue; goad; gobble; grade; grate; grease; grind; grow; gum; guzzle; handle; happen; hasten; hate; haul; head-butt; heat; hitch; hoard; hog; hole; honk; hoover; hop; horn; hum; hunt;

hurry; hush; ice; identify; ignore; imagine; imitate; inch; insult; intend; interest; interrupt; introduce; invent; invite; involve; iron; irritate; itch; jiggle; jog; join; joke; kid; kill; knead; knit; last; latch; leak; lend; light; line; list; listen; live; load; loan; loop; loosen; mail; man; manage; matter; measure; melt; menorah; mention; merit; milk; misjudge; mistreat; mop; mow; muck; mumble; mummy; munch; mush; nag; neglect; nibble; nip; nod; notice; nurse; offer; operate; order; outtalk; overcome; owe; page; paste; pedal; peekaboo; persuade; phone; picture; pile; pin; plan; plant; plaster; please; plunk; point; polish; pop; pound; practice; praise; prefer; prepare; prevent; print; produce; promise; prompt; prop; propose; protect; prove; provide; pry; punch; punish; Quack; quote; raid; rain; raise; ration; rattle; realize; rearrange; recall; reckon; recognize; recommend; reconstruct; record; redo; regret; reload; remedy; remind; remove; repeat; replace; repot; require; rescue; respect; rest; retie; return; rewind; rinse; rotate; round; row; ruin; rush; sack; sail; sample; saw; scalp; scatter; scoop; scorch; score; scrape; scream; scrub; scrunch; seal; seat; sell; separate; serve; sew; shade; shadow; shampoo; sharpen; shatter; shave; shine; shock; shout; shove; shovel; shred; sift; sign; sip; skin; skip; slap; slice; sling; slip; slop; slurp; smash; smear; smoke; smother; smush; snatch; sneak; sniff; soak; soap; sock; soil; sort; spank; spare; spell; spend; splash; split; splodge; spoon; spot; spray; spread; spy; squirt; stab; stain; stamp; stash; stitch; stomp; straighten; strangle; strap; stretch; string; stroke; stroll; stub; stuff; stunt; suck; suggest; suit; support; surprise; sustain; swing; swipe; swoosh; tackle; talk; tan; tap; teach; tease; telephone; tempt; tend; test; thread; threaten; thump; tide; tidy; tighten; tilt; tire; toast; toot; top; torture; toss; trace; trade; trash; tread; treat; trim; trust; tug; turtle; tweak; twirl; unbutton; uncover; undress; unload; unpack; unpeel; unplug; unscrew; unsnap; unstick; unstrap; unthread; unwind; unwrap; unzip; uppie; upset; vacuum; wag; waken; wallop; wang; warm; warn; water; weed; weep; weigh; weight; welcome; whack; wheel; wiggle; win; worry; wrap; wreck; wriggle; wring; wrinkle; yank; yell; zap; zoom.

A.3 **Parents' verbs in the VI relation**

3.1 VI: frequent verbs in the input—used by children

Ask; bring; buy; excuse; feed; get; give; make; read; show; sing; tell.

3.2 VI: frequent verbs in the input—not used by children

Build; find; throw.

3.3 VI: rare verbs in the input—used by children

Draw; fix; leave; listen; pardon; pass; pay; pour; say; talk; want; write.

3.4 VI: rare verbs in the input—not used by children

Allow; bake; bet; cause; cook; cut; deliver; dial; do; drag; encourage; fetch; forgive; hand; have; hold; kiss; learn; lend; loan; mail; offer; owe; paint; persuade; pick; play; promise; put; remember; remind; roll; save; sell; send; serve; take; tape; teach; trade; warn.

Appendix B: **Consequences of the power-law distribution for research**

The skewed nature of word frequency distributions has important consequences for research methodology.

B.1 **Data sparseness problems**

First and most importantly, the skewed distribution of word frequency causes data sparseness problems. Although we built a large-size corpus of parental speech, most of the verbs occurring in it have very low frequency, as may be seen in Figures 5.1–5.3. This is a general phenomenon stemming from the power-law shape of the distribution: No matter how large a corpus is, the majority of lexical elements in it will be observed only rarely. Indeed, in our study a large percentage of all verbs occur in the corpus only once in a given syntactic format. This is not a quirk of parental speech or anything specific to verbal form-classes but a universal feature of vocabulary frequencies in corpora. The existence of words which occur only once in a corpus—the technical term is *hapax legomena*, from the Ancient Greek expression 'said once'—is a major problem feature of all corpora when it comes to statistical treatment, according to Baayen (2001) who is perhaps the leading mathematical theoretician of lexical statistics. The distribution of bigrams and linguistic units larger than the word is even more skewed.

It is a commonplace that generalizations about word meanings and use require multiple examples for reliability, even in simple cases; for example, Sinclair (2005) suggests that a corpus-based linguistic description of unambiguous words should be based on at least 20 examples each. Considerations such as these lead to a research tradition in the study of child language acquisition that focuses on frequent items and excludes the rest from analysis. There have been very many studies with such a methodology, and we shall mention just a few recent ones. Goodman *et al.* (2008) examined the effect of parental frequency on order of acquisition of words across and within lexical categories, including words in the analysis only if 50% or more of the children acquired them by 2;6. Cameron-Faulkner *et al.* (2003) performed a correlational analysis of the relation between the use frequency of maternal sentence-frames and children's adoption of them; they excluded from analysis all frames which were not used by more than half of the children. Serratrice *et al.* (2003) did a similar analysis of past forms, excluding all but the forms that occurred with a high token-frequency in the pooled child data. Truncation of the corpora, however, biases the sample so that it represents only frequent items (that may have specific features not shared by infrequent items), and thus this procedure reduces the generality of research findings. This problem is quite well known in the field, and see for instance Mayor and Plunkett (2009) discussing the problem of estimating infants' vocabulary size beyond the shared, common words included in Communicative Development Inventories (CDIs).

Data sparseness is especially problematic if the analysis a researcher wishes to make, specifically requires multiple instances of given items: even in a very large corpus, very few words will have it. If simple cases require 20 examples each, the numbers obviously increase when the goal of the research is to map variability in grammatical behaviour of words, meaning that only a small portion of the total vocabulary will qualify for study. For the majority of verbs in a corpus, the probabilities of finding multiple syntactic contents is actually zero, as they will be unique in the corpus. This problem is prominent in the methodology of studies exploring the role of multiple syntactic frames on acquisition. For example Naigles and Hoff-Ginsberg (1998) studied the relation between verb frequencies and multiple syntactic frames in parental and child speech. They restricted the analysis to 25 common verbs, presumably because verbs with a low number of tokens in the corpus cannot by definition have a large variety of different syntactic frames. Lee and Naigles (2005) carried out a similar study on the use of multiple syntactic frames in the speech of Mandarin-speaking caretakers. They pointed out that more than 250 of the total 486 different verbs used by the caretakers occur in their sample with a token frequency of less than three; as they see these low-frequency verbs as not informative about the frequency and the diversity of syntactic frames in the input, in this study, too, they analysed only the syntactic behaviour of the most frequent 12% of the verbs produced by the caregivers.

The power-law distribution of tokens in language samples means that with or without truncation of infrequent items, counting the number of different syntactic environments for verbs is extremely problematic as the maximum patterns possible change with total token frequency in the corpus. The number of different patterns that can be found is a function of total number of tokens for the verb; this means that frequent verbs have a high probability to be observed with multiple syntactic contents while infrequent verbs have a much lower probability, the chances decreasing exponentially as the rank of the verb by frequency gets lower. This generates an artefactual correlation between token frequency and syntactic variability, even if in reality there is no such relationship.

This problem is inherent to a power-law skewed distribution and will occur regardless of how many verbs are analysed; it cannot be remedied by statistical means such as computing conditional probabilities in a regression analysis.

B.2 Under-representation by sampling

Another feature of a power-law distribution is the problem of under-representation by sampling. In contrast to a normal distribution, samples do not provide unbiased estimates of the total size of the vocabulary from which the sample is taken. Instead, as the sample size increases, the number of vocabulary items observed keeps increasing (Baayen, 2001). Thus, even large corpora fail to represent the complete population of lexemes in a language. This should be taken into account when generalizing about the characteristics of words in parental language, given the kind of small corpora typically used in the study of child language acquisition which are clearly at risk for under-representing the full range of vocabulary items and their features.

B.3 The problem with number of types

As larger samples have more word types than smaller samples, it is impossible to compare corpora of different magnitudes for estimates of the respective vocabulary sizes, without elaborate statistical corrections. The same is true of measures of vocabulary richness such as the type/token ratio, which, as Baayen (2001) shows, also systematically changes with sample size. This means that it is meaningless to compare the type/token ratio of the three grammatical relations we are investigating in the parent's speech, nor can we compare the vocabulary sizes of children to those of parents on the basis of unequally sized corpora such as the present ones.

In Chapter 3 we made an effort to correct for sample size inequality by estimating the expected verb repertoire size of parents in the SV, VO, and VI patterns if the parental corpus were equal in size to the child corpus. This process halved our estimate of parents' verb vocabulary used in core grammatical combinations and decreased the size differential with children, although the parental verb repertoire was still about 40% larger than children's total verb vocabulary at the relevant early stage of development. Without this correction, we would have said, mistakenly, that children use a mere third of the verb repertoire parents used for core grammar, seriously underestimating children's command of the basic verb repertoire.

B.4 Lack of normality

All statistical treatments of research questions regarding word frequencies require a different set of methods from the ones standardly used in research in the social sciences such as the Pearson product-moment correlation, regression, *t*-test, analysis of variance, or discriminant analysis. A crucial condition for these standard methods which is that the variables involved have a normal distribution, is not satisfied. In other words, in the case of the extremely skewed word frequency data, the 'central limit theorem' fails to guarantee the normality of sample averages, and thus, statistical procedures relying on this assumption cannot be applied with word frequency data. (See also Andriani and McKelvey, 2007.)

In some studies of parental input, researchers attempt to remedy the normality problem by paring off the long tail of infrequent items from the rank-ordered distribution and retain only a small number of very frequent items, assuming that the latter is closer to normal than the complete set. This, however, is a mistake, as the frequent items keep to a skewed and definitely non-normal distribution in which higher-ranked items have about twice as many tokens than their lower-ranked neighbours.

B.5 Central values and their meaning

In psychology as in the social sciences in general, we are used to dealing with phenomena that have a normal, Gaussian distribution, such as people's height or their IQ (intelligence quotient). In a normal distribution—which is a symmetrical distribution—there is a finite variance, namely, a rather small, definitive range of values, and the majority of values huddle around the mean in a symmetrical dispersal. For example, the IQs of a large group of people usually crowd together around a typical central value which is the mean, the median, and also the mode, namely, it is the most frequently occurring value, all other values distribute around it symmetrically, and it is the average of the group's values. There is a meaningfulness or significance to the central value; it is the expected value of the phenomenon and can represent the group as a whole as its typical, representative, average IQ.

In a power-law distribution, the first thing that strikes the observer is that there is no convergence among the three central values as in the normal distribution, and it is much less clear which of the three, if any, can be taken as the representative of the central tendency of the group as a whole. In a corpus such as our parental sentences with subject–verb relations, the median is 3, namely, half of all verbs have a higher frequency than 3 and half, a lower one. The single most frequently encountered value (the mode) for verb frequency is one, namely, the largest group of verbs is that of uniquely occurring ones (*hapax legomena*). Lastly, the mean is much higher than either the median or the mode, because it is influenced by the extremely high frequencies of the upper end of the distribution; in our large corpus, it is 325, but if we had an even bigger corpus, the mean would increase as a large proportion of the new exemplars would join the very-frequent items and thus push the average frequency still more upwards. As the mean changes with sample size, it cannot be taken as a meaningful representative of the population's central tendency, and, obviously, the median and the mode neither, as they tend to be the same low values in all power-law distributions and do not represent anything much about the present object of study.

In fact, a set of values distributed in a power-law pattern is said to have no central tendency as such Instead of means serving as central values and a small variance that ensures most values distribute in a narrow band around the mean, as in a normally distributed variable, power-law distributions are said to be *scale-free* (Barabási, 2002), meaning that they have an infinite variance and cannot be pinned down as to their characteristic range of values.

B.6 **Scale invariance**

Rather than means, in power-law distributions we have a different characteristic value for a distribution. It is the exponent of the power-law function, also called its *signature*. Power-law distributions have *scale invariance*: this is a feature of objects or laws that do not change if size scales (or energy scales) are multiplied by a common factor. Namely, if we multiply the values by some constant (i.e. rescale them), the slope and shape of distribution remain the same.

Scale invariance becomes more visible if we plot a power-law distribution of two variables on a log-log graph. The result is a line with slope k, and multiplying the values by some constant merely shifts the line up or down, but the form of the function and the slope k remain unchanged. All power law distributions with a particular signature or exponent are equivalent except for a constant, and can be seen as scaled versions of each other.

It means that the way to characterize a distribution with a power-law shape—such as the distribution of token frequencies of words in speech samples—is not, as with normal distributions, by specifying its mean and standard deviation, nor its mode or median. Rather, we should calculate its exponent or signature, and compare it to that of other distributions. In our study, the three distributions of token frequency of verbs in the subject–verb, verb–object, and verb–indirect object grammatical relations in parental speech were equivalent because of possessing an almost identical signature. This finding would be invisible if we calculated means and standard deviations of the three sets of data, as these show the expected difference: the mean token frequency per verb of the set with the largest sample (SV) is 325; the mean of the next-largest set (VO) is 178, and the mean of the smallest corpus (VI) is 91. As we said above, this measure (the inverse of type/token ratio) is meaningless in a power-law distribution, merely reflecting the size of the sample but not the characteristic shape of the distribution as a whole. In studies dealing with speech and vocabulary size, only the latter is a mathematically meaningful statistic.

B.7 The problem with productivity measures under a skewed distribution

The notion that token frequency is a criterion of syntactic productivity is an old tradition in the field. For instance, Bloom *et al.* (1975) assumed that children's early word-combinations are generated on the basis of a rule system combining semantic categories such as action and object; they, however, required that the child produce five or more different exemplars in a particular semantic category-combination, in order to consider the semantic rule to be existing in the child's rule system. This meant that in every observational session, if some child utterance did not fall together with at least four others into the same type of semantic combination, it was disregarded by the researchers as functionally nonexistent in that child's productive syntax. As this judgement was made within each observation and they did not accumulate exemplars between observations, a given utterance may be seen as productive on a given date but non-productive on the next, depending on how many others of the same kind the child uttered that day. This obviously penalized all rare types of utterances which were not only not analysed any further but were not even included in the tables listing each observational sessions' transcribed sentences.

In a similar methodology, Lieven, Pine, and their colleagues (Lieven *et al.*, 1997; Pine and Lieven, 1993) pointed out that a mean 60% of young children's tokens of multiword speech were accounted for by just 25 productive syntactic 'slot-and-frame' formulae. The rest of the multiword sentences in that child corpus occurred in patterns with a token frequency of one or two instances, which in these studies was taken as evidence for lack of productivity and even for being a frozen rather than a syntactically constructed word-combination. This means that in these studies, a very large number of low-frequency combination types are deemed non-productive because of their sitting at the low end of a Zipfian power-law distribution.

However, the skewed token distribution in children's syntactic use means that if children are being required to produce multiple exemplars of a verb with the same syntax in order for the verb to qualify for productivity, very few of their verb types they produce word-combinations with, will pass the criterion. As children's distribution is very similar to parents', it is not very easy to dismiss the infrequent verb types as not productive. We would certainly not say that parents are using the majority of their verbs in frozen or rote-learned patterns just because they are used infrequently. We understand that the Zipfian distribution in adults is an outcome of pragmatic factors, representing the balance between using general and specific items existing in the lexicon. In other words, the skewed token distribution is a central and universal feature of speech, and in adults it does not reflect anything else but expected use patterns. It is rather questionable if we should treat the same distribution in children as anything but the reflection of the same pragmatic phenomenon.

Notes

1 Although Zipf's work is much better known, in actuality the first to explore the skewed distribution of words in texts was Estoup (1916).

2 Except for language, power-law-shaped size distributions also characterize many other natural and social phenomena. For a list of 80 different examples, see Andriani and McKelvey (2007).

3 Pareto's distribution is also a power-law one, but it is a continuous cumulative distribution rather than a discrete one like Zipf's rank/frequency one.

4 The exponent of the power-law function is often symbolized by the Greek letter *gamma*.

5 For a more detailed discussion of this problem, see Goldstein *et al.* (2004) and Newman (2005).

6 We repeated the analysis using the maximum-likelihood method with the algorithms provided by Clauset *et al.* (2009). Reassuringly, the estimates we got are very similar to the least squares estimates derived with the Microsoft Excel program: −1.50, −1.51, −1.50 for SV, VO, and VI. We shall continue to use the more accessible least squares method for further analyses.

7 Zipf (1949/1972) thought that all behaviour, including that of speakers, is motivated by the Principle of Least Effort, and that this principle accounted for the power-law shape of the use distributions. The mathematical model and proof for this intuitive theory was provided by Mandelbrot (1953), who is considered the joint creator of the Zipf–Mandelbrot Law. Interestingly, a similar idea of a principle of least effort is also the fundamental motivation attributed to language users in the Minimalist Program (Chomsky, 1995a).

8 On the explanation for the skewed shape of vocabulary frequencies in a Zipf curve in terms of a need to employ words with different degrees of

specificity for efficient communication, see also Ferrer i Cancho (2005) and Manin (2008).

9 Similar findings were presented by Ninio (2005c) on Hebrew verbal form-classes.

10 It may be relatively easy, when acquiring transitive syntactic patterns, to learn a generic verb that is so close to transitiveness that it is a cross-linguistic candidate for getting grammaticalized as a transitive marker (as suggested by Ninio, 1999a). However, being a generic verb for past tense or completive aspect has no possible relevance for learning transitive syntax. This is the reason why Theakston *et al.* (2004) did not in fact test the hypothesis that genericness is a facilitating factor in acquisition, as they mixed various generic verbs for tense and aspect, taken from Bybee *et al.*'s (1994) book on the development of the morphology of tense, aspect and modality, into a list of generic verbs for transitivity, in a study of the acquisition of transitive syntax in children. Obviously a verb which is a candidate for turning into a morpheme for past tense or completive aspect (such as '*stop*'), will not therefore be easier to learn with a direct object than other verbs.

11 This is a possible formalization of Nelson *et al.* (2003)'s notion that young children 'enter a community of minds'.

12 See Ninio and Snow (1996) on divergences between maternal and child pragmatic interests and roles in the dyadic interaction that account for differences in relative frequency of various speech uses.

13 In Chapter 4 we discussed the proposal that very frequent verbs impart their lexical semantics to the construction to become the latter's prototypical semantics (e.g. Goldberg, 1995, 2005). Somewhat different are suggestions that some frequent verbs are generic expressions of the relevant grammatical relations, and hence may be easily learned in those patterns (Clark, 1978; Hershberg and Ninio, 2004; Ninio, 1999a,b; and Powers, 2001).

14 This conclusion is the reverse of the one reached by Naigles (2002), who says: 'It is argued that in language acquisition, learning form is easy but learning meaning, and especially linking meanings and forms, is hard.' The disagreement may stem from a difference of methodology. I concur with Tomasello and Akhtar (2003) who question whether the intermodal preferential looking studies and other methods not involving production that Naigles refers to in her paper are indeed measures of syntactic knowledge.

15 Pronouns may well have some role in the process of syntactic development. For example, in Ninio (1994b) it was suggested that Travis and some other children acquiring English may treat cliticized object pronouns such as *it* as transitiveness markers, helping them master the concept of predicates. The objection in this section is merely to pronoun-centred 'slot-and-frame' formulae being used by researchers instead of the linguistically motivated verb-complement ones.

16 Verb-centred grammars and parsers are, for example, Bresnan (2001), Covington (1990), Hellwig (1986), McCord *et al.* (1992), Pollard and Sag (1987), and Sleator and Temperley (1991).

References

Abbot-Smith, K. and Behrens, H. (2006). How known constructions influence the acquisition of other constructions: the German passive and future constructions. *Cognitive Science*, **30**, 995–1026.

Akhtar, N., Jipson, J., and Callanan, M. (2001). Learning words through overhearing. *Child Development*, **72**, 416–30.

Adamic, L. A. (2009). Zipf, Power-laws, and Pareto - a ranking tutorial. (http://www.hpl.hp.com/research/idl/papers/ranking/ranking.html)

Aho, A. V., Sethi, R., and Ullman, J. D. (1986). *Compilers: Principles, techniques, and tools.* Reading, MA: Addison-Wesley.

Akhtar, N., Jipson, J., and Callanan, M. (2001). Learning words through overhearing. *Child Development*, **72**, 416–30.

Albert, R. and Barabási, A.-L. (2002). Statistical mechanics of complex networks. *Review of Modern Physics*, **74**, 47–97.

Algeo, J. (1995). Having a look at the expanded predicate. In B. Aarts and C. F. Meyer (eds), *The verb in contemporary English* (pp. 203–17). Cambridge: Cambridge University Press.

Allen, S. E. M. (1998). Categories within the verb category: learning the causative in Inuktitut. *Linguistics*, **36**, 627–32.

Allerton, D. J. (1982). *Valency and the English verb.* London: Academic Press.

Allerton, D. J. (2001). *Stretched verb constructions in English.* London/ New York: Routledge.

Alsina, A. (2001). Is case another name for grammatical function? Evidence from object asymmetries. In W. D. Davies and S. Dubinsky (eds), Objects and other subjects: Grammatical functions, functional categories and configurationality (pp. 77–102). Dordrecht: Kluwer Academic Publishers.

Alsina, A., Bresnan, J., and Sells, P. (eds). (1997). *Complex predicates.* Stanford, CA: CSLI Publications.

Anderson, J. R. (1976). *Language, memory, and thought.* Hillsdale, NJ: Lawrence Erlbaum.

Andrews, A. (1985). The major functions of the noun phrase. In T. Shopen (ed), Language typology and syntactic description, Vol. 1: Clause structure (pp. 62–154). Cambridge: Cambridge University Press.

Andriani, P. and McKelvey, B. (2007). Beyond Gaussian averages: Redirecting organization science toward extreme events and power laws. *Journal of International Business Studies*, **38**, 1212–30.

Anglin, J. M. (1993). Vocabulary development: A morphological analysis. *Monographs of the Society for Research in Child Development*, **58**, 238.

Ariel, M. (2008). A review of A. E. Goldberg (2006). Constructions at work: The nature of generalizations in language. Oxford: Oxford University Press. *Language*, **84**, 632–6.

Aronoff, M. (1976). *Word formation in generative grammar*. Cambridge, MA: MIT Press.

Autret, J. (1945). The verbal idea in Anglo-Saxon verbs with prepositions, and its translation into Romance languages. *The French Review*, **18**, 350–4.

Baayen, R. H. (2001). *Word frequency distributions*. Dordrecht: Kluwer Academic Publishers.

Baayen, R. H. and Moscoso Del Prado Martín, F. (2005). Semantic density and past-tense formation in three Germanic languages. *Language*, **81**, 666–98.

Bacchielli, R. (1993). Syntheticity and analyticity in the syntactic make-up of English.
In M. Gotti (ed), *English diachronic syntax* (pp. 55–66). Milano: Angelo Guerini.

Baddeley, A. D. (1999). Essentials of human memory. Hove: Psychology Press.

Bak, P. (1997). *How nature works: The science of self-organized criticality*. Oxford: Oxford University Press.

Baker, C. L. (1979). Syntactic theory and the projection problem. *Linguistic Inquiry*, **10**, 533–81.

Baltin, M. R. (1989). Heads and projections. In M. R. Baltin and A. S. Kroch (eds), *Alternative conceptions of phrase structure* (pp. 1–16). Chicago, IL: University of Chicago Press.

Bannard, C., Lieven, E., and Tomasello, M. (2009). Modeling children's early grammatical knowledge. *Proceedings of the National Academy of Sciences*, **106**, 17284–9.

Barabási, A.-L. (2002). *Linked: The new science of networks*. Cambridge, MA: Perseus.

Barabási, A. -L. and Albert, R. (1999). Emergence of scaling in random networks. *Science*, **286**, 509–12.

Barner, D. (2001). Light verbs and the flexible use of words as noun and verb in early language learning. M.Sc. thesis, McGill University, Montreal, Canada.http://digitool.library.mcgill.ca/R/?func=dbin-jump-fullandobject_id=32752andlocal_base=GEN01-MCG02

Bates, E., Bretherton, I., and Snyder, L. (1988). *From first words to grammar: Individual differences and dissociable mechanisms.* New York: Cambridge University Press.

Bates, E. and MacWhinney, B. (1987). Competition, variation, and language learning. In B. MacWhinney (ed), *Mechanisms of language acquisition* (pp. 157–93). Hillsdale, NJ: Lawrence Erlbaum.

Baugh, A. C. and Cable, T. (1993). *A history of the English language (4th edn).* Englewood Cliffs, NJ: Prentice Hall.

Becker, M. (2004). Is Isn't Be. *Lingua*, **114**, 399–418.

Beckwith, R. and Miller, G. A. (1990). Implementing a lexical network. In G. A. Miller, R. Beckwith, C. Fellbaum, D. Gross, K. Miller, and R. Tengi (eds), Five papers on WordNet. CSL Report 43 (pp. 65–74). Princeton, NJ: Cognitive Science Laboratory, Princeton University. Reprinted in International Journal of Lexicography, **3**, 302–12. Available at http://ijl.oxfordjournals.org/cgi/reprint/3/4/302

Bellinger, D. and Gleason, J. (1982). Sex differences in parental directives to young children. *Journal of Sex Roles*, **8**, 1123–39.

Bernstein, N. (1982). *Acoustic study of mothers' speech to language-learning children: An analysis of vowel articulatory characteristics.* Unpublished doctoral dissertation. Boston University.

Bernstein-Ratner, N. (1984). Patterns of vowel modification in motherese. *Journal of Child Language*, **11**, 557–78.

Biber, D. (1995). *Dimensions of register variation: a cross-linguistic comparison.* Cambridge: Cambridge University Press.

Biber, D., Conrad, S., and Reppen, R. (1998). *Corpus linguistics: Investigating language structure and use.* New York: Cambridge University Press.

Biber, D., Johansson, S., Leech, G., Conrad, S., and Finegan, E. (eds). (1999). *Longman grammar of spoken and written English.* London: Longman.

Bliss, L. (1988). The development of modals. *The Journal of Applied Developmental Psychology*, **9**, 253–61.

Bloom, L. (1970). *Language development: form and function in emerging grammars.* Cambridge, MA: MIT Press.

Bloom, L. (1973). *One word at a time: The use of single-word utterances before syntax.* The Hague: Mouton.

Bloom, L., Lightbown, P., and Hood, L. (1975). Structure and variation in child language. *Monographs of the Society for Research in Child Development,* **40**, 160.

Bloom, L., Merkin, W., and Wootten, J. (1982). Wh-questions: Linguistic factors that contribute to the sequence of acquisition. *Child Development,* **53**, 1084–92.

Bloom, L., Rispoli, M., Gartner, B., and Hafitz, J. (1989). Acquisition of complementation. *Journal of Child Language,* **16**, 101–20.

Bloom, L., Tackeff, J., and Lahey, M. (1983). Learning to in complement constructions. *Journal of Child Language,* **10**, 391–406.

Bloomfield, L. (1933). *Language.* London: George Allen and Unwin.

Bock, J. K. (1982). Toward a cognitive psychology of syntax: Information processing contributions to sentence formulation. *Psychological Review,* **89**, 1–47.

Bohnemeyer, J., Kelly, A., and Abdel Rahman, R. (eds), (2002). Annual Research Report, Max Planck Institute for Psycholinguistics, Nijmegen, The Netherlands. http://www.mpi.nl/institute/annual-reports/archive-annual-reports/MPI-Anrep-2002-print.pdf

Bolinger, D. (1971). *The phrasal verb in English.* Cambridge, MA: Harvard University Press.

Bolinger, D. (1975). *Aspects of language (2nd edn).* New York: Harcourt Brace Jovanovich.

Borg, A. J. and Comrie, B. (1984). Object diffuses in Maltese. In F. Plank (ed), *Objects: Towards a theory of grammatical relations* (pp. 109–26). London: Academic Press.

Bowerman, M. (1973). *Early syntactic development: a crosslinguistic study with special reference to Finnish.* Cambridge: Cambridge University Press.

Bowerman, M. (1976). Semantic factors in the acquisition of rules for word use and sentence construction. In D. Morehead and A. Morehead (eds), Directions in normal and deficient child language (pp. 99–179). Baltimore, MD: University Park Press.

Bowerman, M. (1990). Mapping thematic roles onto syntactic functions: are children helped by innate linking rules? *Linguistics,* **28**, 1253–89.

Bowerman, M. and Brown, P. (eds). (2008). *Crosslinguistic perspectives on argument structure: Implications for learnability.* Mahwah, NJ: Lawrence Erlbaum.

Braine, M. D. S. (1963). The ontogeny of English phrase structure: The first phase. *Language*, **39**, 1–14.

Brainerd, C. J. and Howe, M. L. (1978). The origins of all-or-none learning. *Child Development*, **49**, 1028–34.

Brent, M. R. and Siskind, J. M (2001). The role of exposure to isolated words in early vocabulary development. *Cognition*, **81**, 31–44.

Bresnan, J. (1982). Control and complementation. In J. Bresnan (ed), The mental representation of grammatical relations (pp. 282–390). Cambridge, MA: MIT Press.

Bresnan, J. (2001). *Lexical-Functional Syntax*. Oxford: Blackwell.

Bright, W. (1966). Dravidian metaphony. *Language*, **42**, 311–23.

Bright, W. (1997). Social factors in language change. In F. Coulmas (ed), The handbook of sociolinguistics (pp. 81–91). Oxford: Blackwell.

Brinton, L. J. (2005). *Where grammar and lexis meet: The take a walk construction in English*. Paper presented at the Colloquium Series of the Department of Linguistics, Simon Fraser University.

Brinton, L. J. and Akimoto, M. (eds). (1999). Collocational and idiomatic aspects of composite predicates in the history of English. Amsterdam: John Benjamins.

Broen, P. (1972). The verbal environment of the language-learning child. *American Speech and Hearing Association Monograph*, No. **17**.

Brown, P. (1998). Children's first verbs in Tzeltal: Evidence for an early verb category. *Linguistics*, **36**, 713–53.

Brown, R. (1973). *A first language: the early stages*. Cambridge, MA: Harvard University Press.

Brown, R. and Fraser, C. (1963). The acquisition of syntax. In C. N. Cofer and B. S. Musgrave (eds), *Verbal behavior and learning: problems and processes* (pp. 158–97). New York: McGraw-Hill.

Butler, C. S. (1985). *Systemic linguistics: Theory and applications*. London: Batsford Academic and Educational.

Butt, M. (2003). The Light Verb jungle. *Harvard Working Papers in Linguistics*, **9**, 1–49.

Butt, M. and Geuder, W. (2001). On the (semi)lexical status of light verbs. In N. Corver and H. van Riemsdijk (eds), *Semi-lexical categories: The function of content words and the content of function words* (pp. 323–70). New York: Mouton de Gruyter.

Bybee, J. (1985). *Morphology: a study of the relation between meaning and form*. Amsterdam: Benjamins.

Bybee, J., Perkins, R., and Pagliuca, W. (1994). *The evolution of grammar: Tense, aspect, and modality in the languages of the world.* Chicago, IL: University of Chicago Press.

Cameron-Faulkner, T., Lieven, E. V., and Theakston, A. (2007). What part of 'no' do children not understand? *Journal of Child Language,* **33,** 251–82.

Cameron-Faulkner, T., Lieven, E. V. M., and Tomasello, M. (2003). A construction based analysis of child directed speech. *Cognitive Science,* **27,** 843–73.

Campbell, A. (1959). *Old English grammar.* Oxford: Clarendon Press.

Carey, S. (1978). The child as word learner. In M. Halle, J. Bresnan, and G. Miller (eds), *Linguistic theory and psychological reality* (pp. 264–93). Cambridge, MA: MIT Press.

Carey, S. and Bartlett, E. (1978). Acquiring a single new word. *Papers and Reports on Child Language Development,* **15,** 17–29.

Carlson-Luden, V. (1979). *Causal understanding in the 10-month-old.* Unpublished Ph.D. thesis. University of Colorado at Boulder, CO.

Carnie, A. (2008). *Constituent structure.* Oxford: Oxford University Press.

Casenhiser, D. and Goldberg, A. E. (2005). Fast mapping between a phrasal form and meaning. *Developmental Science,* **8,** 500–8.

Cassidy, K. W. and Kelly, M. H. (1991). Phonological information for grammatical category assignments. *Journal of Memory and Language,* **30,** 348–69.

Cattell, R. (1984). *Syntax and semantics, Vol. 17: Composite predicates in English.* New York: Academic Press.

Chambers, J. K. (1995). *Sociolinguistic theory.* Oxford: Blackwell.

Chametzky, R. (2000). *Phrase structure: from GB to Minimalism.* Malden, MA: Blackwell.

Chametzky, R. (2003). Phrase structure. In R. Hendrick (ed), Minimalist syntax (pp. 192–235). Oxford: Blackwell.

Childers, J. B. and Tomasello, M. (2001). The role of pronouns in young children's acquisition of the English transitive construction. *Developmental Psychology,* **37,** 730–48.

Chomsky, N. (1957). *Syntactic structures.* The Hague: Mouton.

Chomsky, N. (1965). *Aspects of the theory of syntax.* Cambridge, MA: MIT Press.

Chomsky, N. (1968). *Language and mind.* New York: Harcourt, Brace Jovanovich.

Chomsky, N. (1981). *Lectures on government and binding.* Dordrecht: Foris.

Chomsky, N. (1995a). *The Minimalist Program.* Cambridge, MA: MIT Press.

Chomsky, N. (1995b). Bare phrase structure. In G. Webelhuth, (ed), Government and Binding Theory and the Minimalist Program (pp. 383–439). Oxford: Blackwell.

Chomsky, N. (2000). *New horizons in the study of language and mind.* Cambridge: Cambridge University Press.

Chomsky, N. (2001). Derivation by phase. In M. Kenstowicz (ed), Ken Hale: a life in language (pp. 1–52). Cambridge, MA: MIT Press.

Chomsky, N. and Halle, M. (1968). *The sound pattern of English.* New York: Harper and Row.

Christiansen, M. H. and Monaghan, P. (2006). Discovering verbs through multiple-cue integration. In K. Hirsh-Pasek and R. M. Golinkoff (eds), Action meets word: How children learn verbs (pp. 88–107). Oxford: Oxford University Press.

Claridge, C. (2000). *Multi-word verbs in Early Modern English: A corpus-based study. Language and computers: studies in practical linguistics, 32.* Amsterdam and Atlanta, GA: Rodopi.

Clark, E. V. (1978). Discovering what words can do. Papers from the Parasession on the Lexicon, CLS 14 (pp. 34–57). Chicago, IL: University of Chicago Press.

Clark, E. V. (1993). *The lexicon in acquisition.* Cambridge: Cambridge University Press.

Clark, E. V. (1996). Early verbs, event types, and inflections. In C. E. Johnson and J. H. V. Gilbert (eds), Children's language, Vol. 9 (pp. 61–73). Mahwah, NJ: Lawrence Erlbaum.

Clark, E. V. and Kelly, B. (eds). (2006). *Constructions in acquisition.* Stanford, CA: CSLI Publications.

Clauset, A., Shalizi, C. R., and Newman, M. E. J. (2009). Power-law distributions in empirical data. *SIAM Review, 51*, 661–703.

Coates, J. (1983). *The semantics of the modal auxiliaries.* London: Croom Helm.

Cole, P. and Sadock, J. M. (eds). (1977). *Syntax and semantics 8: Grammatical relations.* New York: Academic Press.

Collins, C. (2002). Eliminating labels. In S. D. Epstein and D. Seely (eds), Derivation and explanation in the Minimalist Program (pp. 42–64). Oxford: Blackwell.

Comrie, B. (1989). *Language universals and linguistic typology (2nd edn).* Chicago, IL: The University of Chicago Press.

Corkum, V. and Dunham, P. (1996). The Communicative Developmental Inventory-WORDS Short Form as an index of language production. *Journal of Child Language, 23*, 515–28.

Cormack, A. and Smith, N. (2001). Don't move! *University College London Working Papers in Linguistics*, **13**, 215–41.

Covington, M. A. (1990). Parsing discontinuous constituents in dependency grammar. *Computational Linguistics*, **16**, 234–6.

Croft, W. (1990). *Typology and universals*. Cambridge: Cambridge University Press.

Croft, W. (2001). *Radical Construction Grammar: Syntactic theory in typological perspective*. Oxford: Oxford University Press.

Croft, W. (2003). Lexical rules vs. constructions: a false dichotomy. In H. Cuyckens, R. Dirven, and K-U. Panther (eds), Motivation in language (pp. 49–68). Amsterdam: Benjamins.

Croft, W. (2009). Constructions and generalizations. *Cognitive Linguistics*, **20**, 157–66.

Crystal, D. (1967). Word classes in English. *Lingua*, **17**, 24–56.

Crystal, D. (1987). The Cambridge encyclopedia of language. Cambridge: Cambridge University Press.

Culicover, P. and Jackendoff, R. (2005). Simpler syntax. Oxford: Oxford University Press.

Curme, G. O. (1935). Parts of speech and accidence. Vol. 2 of G. O. Curme and H. Kurath (eds), A grammar of the English language. Boston, New York: D.C. Heath.

Dabrowska, E. (2000). From formula to schema: The acquisition of English questions. *Cognitive Linguistics*, **11**, 83–102.

De Leon, L. (1999). The development of transitivity in early Tzotzil (Mayan): Language-specific patterns vs. *universal predictions. International Journal of Bilingualism*, **3**, 219–39.

De Schutter, G. and Gillis, S. (1990). *Structurele aspecten van het Nederlandse lexicon* (Vol. 64). Antwerp: University of Antwerp.

Demetras, M. (1989a). *Changes in parents' conversational responses: A function of grammatical development*. Paper presented at ASHA, St. Louis, MO.

Demetras, M. (1989b). *Working parents' conversational responses to their two-year-old sons*. Unpublished doctoral dissertation. University of Arizona.

Di Sciullo, A. M. and Williams, E. (1987). *On the definition of word*. Cambridge, MA: MIT Press.

Dik, S. C. (1978). *Functional grammar*. Amsterdam, New York: Elsevier/ North-Holland.

Dik, S. C. (1997). *The theory of functional grammar, Part 1*. Berlin: Mouton de Gruyter.

Dixon, R. M. W. (1971). A method of semantic description. In D. D. Steinberg and L. A. Jakobovits (eds), Semantics: an interdisciplinary reader in philosophy, linguistics and psychology (pp. 436–71). Cambridge: Cambridge University Press.

Dixon, R. M. W. (1991). *A new approach to English grammar, on semantic principles.* Oxford: Oxford University Press.

Dodson, K. and Tomasello, M. (1998). Acquiring the transitive construction in English: The role of animacy and pronouns. *Journal of Child Language,* **25**, 555–74.

Dollaghan, C. (1985). Child meets word: 'Fast mapping' in preschool children. *Journal of Speech and Hearing Research,* **28**, 449–54.

Dowty, D. R. (1982). Grammatical relations and Montague Grammar. In P. Jacobson and G. K. Pollum (eds), The nature of syntactic representation (pp. 79–130). Dordrecht: Reidel.

Dowty, D. R. (1991). Thematic proto-roles and argument selection. *Language,* **67**, 547–619.

Dryer, M. (1986). Primary objects, secondary objects and antidative. *Language,* **62**, 808–45.

Emonds, J. E. (1985). *A unified theory of syntactic categories.* Dordrecht: Foris.

Emonds, J. E. (2000). *Lexicon and grammar: The English syntacticon.* Berlin: Mouton de Gruyter.

Epstein, S. D., Groat, E. M., Kawashima, R., and Kitahara, H. (1998). *A derivational approach to syntactic relations.* Oxford: Oxford University Press.

Epstein, S. D. (1999). Un-principled syntax: the derivation of syntactic relations. In S. D. Epstein and N. Hornstein, (eds), Working minimalism (pp. 317–45). Cambridge, MA: MIT Press.

Erman, B. and Warren, B. (2000). The idiom principle and the open choice principle. *Text,* **20**, 29–62.

Estoup, J. B. (1916). *Gammes stenographiques.* Paris: Gauthier Villars.

Feldman, A. (1998). *Constructing grammar: fillers, formulas, and function.* Unpublished doctoral dissertation, University of Colorado, Boulder.

Fenson, L., Dale, P. S., Reznick, J. S., Bates, E., Thal, D. J., and Pethick, S. J. (1994). Variability in early communicative development. *Monographs of the Society for Research in Child Development,* **59**, 242.

Ferguson, C. A. (1977). Baby talk as a simplified register. In C. E. Snow and C. A. Ferguson (eds), *Talking to children: Language input and acquisition* (pp. 205–39). New York: Cambridge University Press.

Fernando, C. (1996). *Idioms and idiomaticity.* Oxford: Oxford University Press.

Ferrer i Cancho, R. (2005). The variation of Zipf's law in human language. *The European Physical Journal B*, **44**, 249–57.

Ferrer i Cancho, R. and Solé, R. V. (2001). Two regimes in the frequency of words and the origins of complex lexicons: Zipf's law revisited. *Journal of Quantitative Linguistics*, **8**, 165–73.

Ferrer i Cancho, R. and Solé, R. V. (2003). Least effort and the origins of scaling in human language. *Proceedings of the National Academy of Sciences of the USA*, **100**, 788–91.

Ferrer i Cancho, R., Solé, R. V., and Köhler, R. (2003). Universality in syntactic dependency networks. *Santa Fe Institute Working Paper #03-06-042.*

Fillmore, C. J., Kay, P., and O'Connor, C. (1988). Regularity and idiomaticity on grammatical constructions: The case of let alone. *Language*, **64**, 501–38.

Finkenstaedt, T. and Wolff, D. (1973). *Ordered profusion: studies in dictionaries and the English lexicon.* Heidelberg: Winter.

Firth J. R. (1968). A new approach to grammar. In F. R. Palmer (ed), Selected papers of J. R. Firth, 1952-59 (pp. 114–25). London: Longman. (Original work published 1952–1959.)

Foley, W. and Olson, M. (1985). Clausehood and verb serialization. In J. Nichols and A. Woodbury (eds), Grammar inside and outside the clause (pp. 17–60). Cambridge: Cambridge University Press.

Foley, W. A. and Van Valin, R. D. Jr. (1984). *Functional syntax and universal grammar.* Cambridge: Cambridge University Press.

Foley, W. A. and Van Valin, R. D. Jr. (1985). Information packaging in the clause. In T. Shopen (ed), *Language typology and syntactic description, Vol. 1* (pp. 282–364). Cambridge: Cambridge University Press.

Forner, M. (1979). The mother as LAD: Interaction between order and frequency of parental input and child production. In F. R. Eckman and A. J. Hastings (eds), Studies in first and second language acquisition (pp. 17–44). Rowley, MA: Newbury House.

Francis, W. N. and Kučera, H. (1979). *Brown corpus manual of information to accompany a standard corpus of present-day American English, revised and amplified.* Providence, RI: Brown University, Department of Linguistics.

Francis, W. N. and Kučera, H. (1982). *Frequency analysis of English usage: Lexicon and grammar.* Boston, MA: Houghton Mifflin.

Fraser, B. (1970). Idioms within a transformational grammar. *Foundations of Language*, **6**, 22–42.

Fraser, N. M. (1993). *Dependency parsing.* Unpublished Ph.D. thesis, University College London, London.

Fraser, C. and Roberts, N. (1975). Mothers' speech to children of four different ages. *Journal of Psycholinguistic Research*, **4**, 9–16.

Frege, G. (1960). On sense and reference (M. Black, Trans.). In P. Geach and M. Black (eds), Translations from the philosophical writing of Gottlob Frege (pp. 56–78). Oxford: Basil Blackwell. (Original work published 1892).

Fu, J., Roeper, T. and Borer, H. (2001). The VP within process nominals: evidence from adverbs and VP anaphor do-so. *Language and Linguistic Theory*, **19**, 549–82.

Furrow, D. and Nelson, K. (1986). A further look at the motherese hypothesis: A reply to Gleitman, Newport and Gleitman. *Journal of Child Language*, **13**, 163–76.

Furrow, D., Nelson, K., and Benedict, H. (1979). Mothers' speech to children and syntactic development: Some simple relationships. *Journal of Child Language*, **6**, 423–42.

Gallagher, R. and Appenzeller, T. (eds). (1999). *Special edition of Science about complex systems, 284*, No. 5411.

Gazdar, G., Klein, E., Pullum, G., and Sag, I. (1985). *Generalized Phrase Structure Grammar*. Oxford: Blackwell.

Givón, T. (1979). *On understanding grammar*. New York: Academic Press.

Givón, T. (1997). Grammatical relations: an introduction. In T. Givón (ed), Grammatical relations: A functionalist perspective (pp. 1–84). Amsterdam: John Benjamins.

Gleitman, L. R. (1990). The structural sources of verb learning. *Language Acquisition*, **1**, 3–35.

Gneuss, H. (1991). The Old English language. In M. Godden and M. Lapidge (eds), The Cambridge companion to Old English literature (pp. 23–54). Cambridge: Cambridge University Press.

Goldberg, A. E. (1995). *Constructions: a Construction Grammar approach to argument structure*. Chicago, IL: University of Chicago Press.

Goldberg, A. E. (1996). Jackendoff and construction-based grammar. *Cognitive Linguistics*, **7**, 3–19.

Goldberg, A. E. (1999). The emergence of argument structure semantics. In B. MacWhinney (ed), The emergence of language (pp. 197–213). Hillsdale, NJ: Lawrence Erlbaum.

Goldberg, A. E. (2003). Constructions: a new theoretical approach to language. *Trends in Cognitive Science*, **7**, 219–24.

Goldberg, A. E. (2005). *Constructions at work: the nature of generalization in language*. Oxford: Oxford University Press.

Goldberg, A. E., Casenhiser, D. M., and Sethuraman, N. (2003). A lexically based proposal of argument structure meaning. *In Proceedings from the Annual Meeting of the Chicago Linguistic Society*, **39**, 67–81.

Goldberg, A. E., Casenhiser, D. M., and Sethuraman, N. (2004). Learning argument structure generalizations. *Cognitive Linguistics*, **15**, 289–316.

Goldberg, A. E. and Jackendoff, R. (2004). The English Resultative as a family of constructions. *Language*, **80**, 532–68.

Goldenberg, G. (1985). Al torat hapoal vehapoal haivri [On the theory of the verb and the Hebrew verb]. In M. Bar-Asher (ed), Mexkarim Balashon, Vol. 1 (pp. 295–348). Jerusalem: The Hebrew University.

Goldenberg, G. (1989). The contribution of semitic languages to linguistic thinking. *Ex Oriente Lux*, **30**, 107–15.

Goldstein, M. L., Morris, S. A., and G. G. Yen (2004). Problems with fitting to the power-law distribution. *The European Physical Journal B - Condensed Matter and Complex Systems*, **41**, 255–8.

Goodman, J. C., Dale, P. S., and Li, P. (2008). Does frequency count? Parental input and the acquisition of vocabulary. *Journal of Child Language*, **35**, 515–31.

Green, G. M. (1974). *Semantics and syntactic regularity*. Bloomington, IN: Indiana University Press.

Green, G. M. (1997). *Modelling grammar growth: Universal grammar without innate principles or parameters*. Paper presented at GALA97 Conference on Language Acquisition, Edinburgh.

Green, T. M. (1990). *The Greek and Latin roots of English*. New York: Ardsley House.

Greenberg, J. H. (1960). A quantitative approach to the morphological typology of language. *International Journal of American Linguistics*, **26**, 178–94 (Reprint of a 1954 article).

Greenberg, J. (1966). Language universals. In T. A. Sebeok (ed), *Current trends in linguistics, volume III: Theoretical foundations* (pp. 61–112). The Hague: Mouton.

Grimes, J. E. (1975). *The thread of discourse*. The Hague: Mouton.

Grimshaw, J. and Prince, A. (1986). *A prosodic account of the to-dative alternation*. Unpublished manuscript, Brandeis University.

Grimshaw, J. and Mester, A. (1988). Light verbs and theta-marking. *Linguistic Inquiry*, **19**, 205–32.

Grishman, R., Macleod, C., and Meyers, A. (1994). Complex syntax: Building a computational lexicon. In Proceedings of the 15th international conference on computational linguistics (COLING 94) (pp. 268–72). Kyoto, Japan.

Gropen, J., Pinker, S., Hollander, M., Goldberg, R., and Wilson, R. (1989). The learnability and acquisition of the dative alternation in English. *Language*, **65**, 203–57.

Guthrie, E. R. (1935). *The psychology of learning*. New York: Harper.

Haken, H. (2000). *Information and self-organization: a macroscopic approach to complex systems*. Berlin: Springer-Verlag.

Halliday, M. A. K. (1964). Comparison and translation. In M. A. K. Halliday, M. McIntosh, and P. Strevens (eds), The linguistic sciences and language teaching (pp. 111–34). London: Longman.

Halliday, M. A. K. (1977). Text as semantic choice in social contexts. In T. A. Dijk and J. S. Petofi (eds), Grammars and descriptions (pp. 176–225). New York: Walter de Gruyter.

Halliday, M. A. K. (1978). *Language as social semiotic: the social interpretation of language and meaning*. Edward Arnold: London.

Harley, H. (2007). *The bipartite structure of verbs cross-linguistically, or Why Mary can't exhibit John her paintings*. Paper presented at the 2007 ABRALIN Congres in Belo Horizonte, Brazil.

Hayes, D. P. and Ahrens, M. G. (1988). Vocabulary simplification for children: a special case of 'motherese'. *Journal of Child Language*, **15**, 395–410.

Hayes, D. P. (2000). *The Cornell Corpus*. Ithaca, NY: Cornell University.

Hellwig, P. (1986). Dependency Unification Grammar (DUG). In Proceedings of the 11th International Conference on Computational Linguistics (pp. 195–98). Bonn.

Henning, A., Striano, T., and Lieven, E. (2005). Maternal speech to infants at 1 and 3 months of age. *Infant Behavior and Development*, **28**, 4, 519–36.

Hermerén, L. (1986). Modalities in spoken and written English: an inventory of forms. In G. Tottie and I. Backlund (eds), English in speech and writing: a symposium (pp. 57–91). Stockholm: Almquist and Wiksell International.

Hershberg, U. and Ninio, A. (2004). Optimal exemplar learning in cognitive systems. *Cognitive Systems (ESSCS)* **6**, 181–8.

Higginson, R. P. (1985). *Fixing-assimilation in language acquisition*. Unpublished doctoral dissertation. Washington State University.

Hiltunen, R. (1999). Verbal phrases and phrasal verbs in Early Modern English. In L. J. Brinton and M. Akimoto (eds), Collocational and idiomatic aspects of composite predicates in the history of English (pp. 133–66). Amsterdam: John Benjamins.

Hirsh-Pasek, K. and Golinkoff, R. M. (1996). *The origins of grammar: evidence from early language comprehension*. Cambridge, MA: MIT Press.

Hockett, C. F. (1958). *A course in modern linguistics.* New York: Macmillan.

Hodge, C. T. (1970). The linguistic cycle. *Language Sciences,* **13**, 1–7.

Hollebrandse, B. and van Hout, A. (1994). Light verb learning in Dutch. In *Papers from the Dutch-German Colloquium on Language Acquisition, University of Groningen, September 1-2, 1994. Amsterdam Series in Child Language Development 3.* Amsterdam: Publications of the Institute for General Linguistics.

Holmes, J. and Hudson, R. (2005). Constructions in Word Grammar. In J-O. Östman and M. Fried (eds), Construction Grammars: cognitive grounding and theoretical extensions (pp. 243–72). Amsterdam: Benjamins.

Hopper, P. J. (1997). Discourse and the category 'verb' in English. *Language and Communication,* **17**, 93–102.

Hopper, P. J. and Thompson, S. A. (1980). Transitivity in grammar and discourse. *Language,* **56**, 251–99.

Hopper, P. J. and Thompson, S. A. (1984). The discourse basis for lexical categories in universal grammar. *Language,* **60**, 703–52.

Hopper, P. J. and Traugott, E. C. (1993). *Grammaticalization.* Cambridge: Cambridge University Press.

Hornby, A. S. (1945). *A guide to patterns and usage in English.* London: Oxford University Press.

Houston-Price, C., Plunkett, K., and Harris, P. (2005). 'Word-learning wizardry' at 1;6. *Journal of Child Language,* **32**, 175–89.

Howe, C. (1981). *Acquiring language in a conversational context.* New York: Academic Press.

Huddleston, R. (1980). On Palmer's defence of the distinction between auxiliaries and main verbs. *Lingua,* **50**, 101–15.

Hudson, R. (1984). *Word Grammar.* Oxford: Blackwell.

Hudson, R. (1990). *English Word Grammar.* Oxford: Blackwell.

Hudson, R. (1995). *Word meaning.* London: Routledge.

Hudson, R. (1998). *English grammar.* London: Routledge.

Hudson, R. (2008). Word Grammar and Construction Grammar. In G. Trousdale and N. Gisborne (eds), Constructional approaches to English grammar (pp. 257–302). Berlin, New York: Mouton de Gruyter.

Huttenlocher, J., Haight, W., Bryk, A., Seltzer, M., and Lyons, T. (1991). Early vocabulary growth: Relation to language input and gender. *Developmental Psychology,* **27**, 236–48.

Jaakkola, R. and Akhtar, N. (2000). Assessing children's knowledge word order with familiar and novel verbs. In E. Clark (ed), The Proceedings of the Thirteenth Annual Child Language Research Forum (pp. 33–40). Stanford, CA: CSLI Publications.

Jackendoff, R. S. (1996). Conceptual semantics and cognitive semantics. *Cognitive Linguistics*, **7**, 93–129.

Jackendoff, R. S. (1997). Twistin' the night away. *Language*, **73**, 534–59.

Jastrzembski, J. E. (1981). Multiple meanings, number of related meanings, frequency of occurrence, and the lexicon. *Cognitive Psychology*, **13**, 278–305.

Jespersen, O. (1965). *A modern English grammar on historical principles*: volume VI: Morphology. London: Allen and Unwin.

Jespersen, O. (1972). Growth and structure of the English language (9th edn). Oxford: Blackwell.

Johansson, R. and Nugues, P. (2008). Extended Constituent-to-Dependency conversion for English. http://www.lucas.lth.se/lt/pennconverter

Johansson, S. and Hofland, K. (1989). *Frequency analysis of English vocabulary and grammar based on the LOB Corpus*. Oxford: Clarendon Press.

Johansson, S., Leech, G., and Goodluck, H. (1978). *Manual of information to accompany the Lancaster-Oslo/Bergen Corpus of British English, for use with digital computers*. Oslo: Department of English, University of Oslo.

Johnson, D. E. (1977). On relational constraints on grammars. In P. Cole and J. M. Sadock (eds), Syntax and Semantics 8: Grammatical relations (pp. 151–78). New York: Academic Press.

Johnson, D. E. and Postal, P. M. (1980). *Arc Pair Grammar*. Princeton, NJ: Princeton University Press.

Jones, G., Gobet, F. and Pine, J. M. (2000). A process model of children's early verb use. In L. R. Gleitman and A. K. Joshi (eds), Proceedings of the 22nd Annual Meeting of the Cognitive Science Society in Philadelphia, PA (pp. 723–8). Mahwah, NJ: Erlbaum.

Jones, L. V. and Wepman, J. (1966). *A spoken word count*. Chicago, IL: Language Research Association.

Karmiloff, K. and Karmiloff-Smith, A. (2001). *Pathways to language: From foetus to adolescent*. Cambridge, MA: Harvard University Press.

Kavanaugh, R. D. and Jirkovsky, A. M. (1982). Parental speech to young children: A longitudinal analysis. *Merrill–Palmer Quarterly*, **28**, 297–311.

Kay, P. (1996): Argument structure: causative ABC constructions. Unpublished lecture notes, Berkeley University, Berkeley, CA. http://www.icsi.berkeley.edu/~kay/bcg/5/lec05.html

Kaye, K. (1980). Why don't we talk 'baby talk' to babies. *Journal of Child Language*, **7**, 489–507.

Kayne, R. (1993). Toward a modular theory of auxiliary selection. *Studia Linguistica*, **47**, 3–31.

Kearns, K. (1988). Light Verbs in English. Unpublished manuscript, Cambridge, MA: MIT. http://www.ling.canterbury.ac.nz/documents/lightverbs.pdf

Kearns, K. (1998). Extraction from make the claim constructions. *Journal of Linguistics*, **34**, 53–72.

Keenan, E. L. (1976). Towards a universal definition of 'subject'. In C. N. Li (ed), Subject and topic (pp. 303–33). New York: Academic Press.

Keenan, E. L. (1979). On surface form and logical form. Studies in the Linguistic Sciences, 8, 163–203. Reprinted in E. L. Keenan (ed), (1987). Universal Grammar: fifteen essays (pp. 375–428). London: Croom Helm.

Keenan, E. L. (1984). The functional principle: generalizing the notion of 'subject of'. In M. W. La Gally, R. Fox, and A. Bruck (eds), Papers from the Tenth Regional Meeting of the Chicago Linguistic Society (pp. 298–309). Chicago, IL: Chicago Linguistic Society.

Keenan, E. L. and Comrie, B. (1977). NP accessibility and universal grammar. *Linguistic Inquiry,* **8**, 63–100.

Keren-Portnoy, T. (2006). Facilitation and practice in verb acquisition. *Journal of Child Language*, **33**, 487–518.

Keren-Portnoy, T., Vihman, M. M., DePaolis, R. A., Whitaker, C., and Williams, N. M. (in press). The role of vocal practice in constructing phonological working memory. *Journal of Speech, Language, and Hearing Research*

Kibrik, A. E. (1997). Beyond subject and object: toward a comprehensive relational typology. *Linguistic Typology*, **1–3**, 279–346.

Kiekhoefer, K. (2002). *The acquisition of the ditransitive construction.* Paper presented at the Joint meeting of the 9th International Congress of the International Association of the Study of Child Language and the 23rd Annual Symposium on Research in Child Language Disorders (IASCL/ SRCLD), Madison, WI.

Kilgarriff, A. (1997). Putting frequencies in the dictionary. *International Journal of Lexicography*, **10**, 135–55.

Kiparsky, P. (1968). Tense and mood in Indo-European syntax. *Foundations of Language*, **4**, 30–57.

Klima, E. S. and Bellugi-Klima, U. (1966). Syntactic regularities in the speech of children. In J. Lyons and R. J. Wales (eds), Psycholinguistics papers (pp. 183–208). Edinburgh: Edinburgh University Press.

Köhler, R. (1986). *Zur linguistischen Synergetik: Struktur und Dynamik der Lexik.* Bochum, Germany: Brockmeyer.

Korman, M. (1984). Adaptive aspects of maternal vocalizations in differing contexts at ten weeks. *First Language*, **5**, 44–5.

Koskenniemi, I. (1977). On the use of verbal phrases of the type 'to take revenge' in English Renaissance drama. *Poetica*, **7**, 80–90.

Krug, M. G. (2000). *Emerging English modals: a corpus-based study of grammaticalization (Topics in English Linguistics, No 32)*. Berlin, New York: Mouton de Gruyter.

Kuczaj, S. (1976). -ing, -s and -ed: *A study of the acquisition of certain verb inflections*. Unpublished doctoral dissertation, University of Minnesota.

Kuczaj, S. A. and Brannick, N. (1979). Children's use of the Wh question model auxiliary placement rule. *Journal of Experimental Child Psychology*, **28**, 43–67.

Laakso, A. (2005). On parsing CHILDES. Paper presented at the 2nd Midwest Computational Linguistics Colloquium (MCLC), The Ohio State University - Columbus, Ohio, May 14–15, 2005. http://cogprints.org/4204/1/parsing-childes.pdf

Laczko, T. (2000). Derived nominals, possessors and Lexical Mapping Theory. In M. Butt and T. H. King (eds), Argument realization (pp. 189–227). Stanford, CA: CSLI Publications.

Lakoff, G. (1977). Linguistic gestalts. *Chicago Linguistics Society*, **13**, 236–87.

Lakoff, R. T. (1972). Another look at drift. In R. P. Stockwell and R. K. S. Macaulay (eds), Linguistic change and generative theory (pp. 172–98). Bloomington, IN: Indiana University Press.

Lambek, J. (1958). The mathematics of sentence structure. *American Mathematics Monthly*, **65**, 154–70.

Landau, B. and Gleitman, L. R. (1985). *Language and experience: Evidence from the blind child*. Cambridge, MA: Harvard University Press.

Langacker, R. W. (1987). *Foundations of cognitive grammar*, Volume I. Stanford, CA: Stanford University Press.

Larson, R. K. (1988). On the Double Object Construction. *Linguistic Inquiry*, **19**, 335–91.

Lee, J. N. and Naigles, L. R. (2005). Input to verb learning in Mandarin Chinese: A role for syntactic bootstrapping. *Developmental Psychology*, **41**, 529–40.

Lehmann, C. (1991). Predicate classes and participation. In H. Seiler and W. Premper (eds), Partizipation: Das sprachliche Erfassen von Sachverhalten (pp. 183–239). Tubingen: Gunter Narr Verlag.

Levin, B. (1993). *English verb classes and alternations*. Chicago, IL: Chicago University Press.

Levinson, S. C. (2000). *Presumptive meanings: The theory of generalized conversational implicature*. Cambridge, MA: MIT Press.

Lichtenberk, F. (1991). Semantic change and heterosemy in grammaticalization. *Language*, **67**, 475–509.

Lieber, R. (1980). Morphological conversion within a restrictive theory of the lexicon. In M. Moortgat, H. V. D. Hulst, and T. Hoekstra (eds), The scope of lexical rules (pp. 161–200). Holland: Foris Publications.

Lieberman, E., Michel, J-B., Jackson, J., Tang, T., and Nowak, M. A. (2007). Quantifying the evolutionary dynamics of language. *Nature*, **449**, 713–16.

Lieven, E. V. M., Pine, J. M., and Baldwin, G. (1997). Lexically-based learning and early grammatical development. *Journal of Child Language*, **24**, 187–219.

Lipka, L. (1972). *Semantic structure and word-formation: Verb-particle constructions in contemporary English.* Munich: Wilhelm Fink.

Lyons, J. (1968). *Introduction to theoretical linguistics.* Cambridge: Cambridge University Press.

Macfarland, T. (1995). *Cognate objects and the argument/adjunct distinction in English.* Unpublished Ph.D. thesis, Northwestern University, Evanston, Illinois.

Macnamara, J. (1982). *Names for things. A study of human learning.* Cambridge, MA: MIT Press.

MacWhinney, B. (1975). Pragmatic patterns in child syntax. *Stanford Papers and Reports on Child Language Development*, **10**, 153–65.

MacWhinney, B. (1982). Basic syntactic processes. In S. A. Kuczaj (ed), Language development: Vol. 1. Syntax and semantics (pp. 73–136). Hillsdale, NJ: Lawrence Erlbaum.

MacWhinney, B. (2000). *The CHILDES project: Tools for analyzing talk* (3rd edn). Mahwah, NJ: Lawrence Erlbaum.

MacWhinney, B. and Snow, C. (1985). The Child Language Data Exchange System. *Journal of Child Language*, **12**, 271–95.

MacWhinney, B. and Snow, C. (1990). The Child Language Data Exchange System: An update. *Journal of Child Language*, **17**, 457–72.

Mainzer, K. (1996). *Thinking in complexity: the complex dynamics of matter, mind, and mankind* (2nd edn). New York: Springer-Verlag.

Makkai, A. (1972). *Idiom structure in English.* The Hague: Mouton.

Makkai, A. (1978). Idiomaticity as a language universal. In J. H. Greeenberg (ed), *Universals of human language*, Vol. 3: Word structure (pp. 401–48). Stanford, CA: Stanford University Press.

Mandelbrot, B. B. (1953). An information theory of the statistical structure of language. In Jackson, W. (ed), *Communication theory* (pp. 503–12). New York: Academic Press.

Mandelbrot, B. B. (1966). Information theory and psycholinguistics: A theory of word frequencies. In P. Lazarsfeld and N. Henry (eds), Readings in mathematical social science (pp. 350–68). Cambridge, MA: MIT Press.

Manin, D. Y. (2008). Zipf's Law and avoidance of excessive synonymy. *Cognitive Science*, **32**, 1075–98.

Manning, C. D. (1996). *Ergativity: argument structure and grammatical relations.* Stanford: CSLI Publications.

Marantz, A. (1984). *On the nature of grammatical relations.* Cambridge MA: MIT Press.

Maratsos, M. (1983). Some current issues in the study of the acquisition of grammar. In P. H. Mussen (ed), Handbook of child psychology: Formerly Carmichael's manual of child psychology (4th edn) (pp. 707–86). New York: Wiley.

Marchand, H. (1969). *The categories and types of present-day English word formation: a synchronic-diachronic approach* (2nd edn). Munich: Verlag C. H. Beck.

Marcus, M. P., Santorini, B., and Marcinkiewicz, M. A. (1993). Building a large annotated corpus of English: The Penn Treebank. *Computational Linguistics*, **19**, 313–30.

Masica, C. (1991). *The Indo-Aryan languages: Cambridge language surveys.* Cambridge: Cambridge University Press.

Matsumoto, M. (1999). Composite predicates in Middle English. In L. J. Brinton and M. Akimoto (eds), Collocational and idiomatic aspects of composite predicates in the history of English (pp. 59–96). Amsterdam: John Benjamins.

Matthews, P. H. (2007). *Syntactic relations.* Cambridge: Cambridge University Press.

Mayor, J. and Plunkett, K. (2009). A mathematical insight into the size of infant vocabularies. In: N. Taatgen and H. van Rijn (eds), Proceedings of the 31st Annual Cognitive Science Society (pp. 437–42). Austin, TX: Cognitive Science Society.

McArthur, T. (1992). Conversion. In T. McArthur, T. B. McArthur and F. McArthur (eds), The Oxford companion to the English language (pp. 263). Oxford: Oxford University Press.

McCawley, J. D. (1982). *Thirty million theories of grammar.* Chicago, IL: The University of Chicago Press.

McCord, M., Bernth, A., Lappin, S., and Zadrozny, W. (1992). Natural language processing within a Slot Grammar framework. *International Journal on Artificial Intelligence Tools*, **1**, 229–77.

McEnery, T. and Wilson, A. (1996). *Corpus linguistics.* Edinburgh: Edinburgh University Press.

Mel'cuk, I. A. (1979). *Studies in dependency syntax.* Ann Arbor, MI: Karoma.

Mel'cuk, I. A. (1988). *Dependency syntax: Theory and practice.* Albany, NY: State University of New York Press.

Miller, P. H. (1999). *Strong generative capacity.* Stanford, CA: CSLI Publications.

Mindt, D. (2000). *An empirical grammar of the English verb system.* Berlin: Cornelsen Verlag.

Monaghan, P., Chater, N., and Christiansen, M. H. (2005). The differential role of phonological and distributional cues in grammatical categorisation. *Cognition,* **96,** 143–82.

Morisset, C. E. (1991). *Environmental influences on language development of high social risk toddlers.* Unpublished Ph.D. thesis, University of Washington, Washington.

Morris, W. C., Cottrell, G. W., and Elman, J. L. (2000). A connectionist simulation of the empirical acquisition of grammatical relations. In S. Wermter and R. Sun (eds), Hybrid neural symbolic integration (pp. 175–93). Berlin: Springer-Verlag.

Mueller-Gathercole, V. C. (ed). (2009). *Routes to language: Studies in honor of Melissa Bowerman.* New York: Psychology Press.

Müller, S. (2006). Phrasal or lexical constructions? *Language,* **82,** 850–83.

Naigles, L. R. (2002). Form is easy, meaning is hard: Resolving a paradox in early child language. *Cognition,* **86,** 157–99.

Naigles, L. R. and Hoff, E. (2006). Verbs at the very beginning: Parallels between comprehension and input. In K. Hirsh-Pasek and R. Golinkoff (eds), Action meets word: How children learn verbs (pp. 336–63). New York: Oxford University Press.

Naigles, L. R. and Hoff-Ginsberg, E. (1995). Input to verb learning: evidence for the plausibility of syntactic bootstrapping. *Developmental Psychology,* **31,** 827–37.

Naigles, L. R. and Hoff-Ginsberg, E. (1998). Why are some verbs learned before other verbs? Effects of input frequency and structure on children's early verb use. *Journal of Child Language,* **25,** 95–120.

Naigles, L. R., Hoff, E., and Vear, D. (2009). Flexibility in early verb use: Evidence from a multiple-N diary study. *Monographs of the Society for Research in Child Development,* **74,** 293.

Narasimhan, B. and Brown, P. (2009). Getting the inside story: Learning to talk about containment in Tzeltal and Hindi. In V. C. Mueller-Gathercole (ed),

Routes to language: Studies in honor of Melissa Bowerman (pp. 97–132). New York: Psychology Press.

Nelson, K. (1973). Structure and strategy in learning to talk. *Monographs of the Society for Research in Child Development*, **141**, 38.

Nelson, K. (1995). The dual category problem in the acquisition of action words. In Tomasello, M. and Merriman, W. E. (eds), Beyond names for things: young children's acquisition of verbs (pp. 223–49). Hillsdale, NJ: Lawrence Erlbaum.

Nelson, K. E. (1987). Some observations from the perspective of the rare event cognitive comparison theory of language acquisition. In K. E. Nelson and A. Van Kleeck (eds), Children's language, Vol. 6 (pp. 289–331). Hillsdale, NJ: Lawrence Erlbaum.

Nelson, K. E., Denninger, M. M., Bonvillian, J. D., Kaplan, B. J., and Baker, N. (1984). Maternal input adjustments and non-adjustments as related to children's linguistic advances and to language acquisition theories. In A. D. Pellegrini and T. D. Yawkey (eds), The development of oral and written language in social contexts: Readings in developmental and applied linguistics (pp. 31–56). Norwood, NJ: Ablex.

Nelson, K., Hampson, J., and Shaw, L. K. (1993). Nouns in early lexicons: evidence, explanations and implications. *Journal of Child Language*, **20**, 61–84.

Nelson, K., Plesa Skwerer, D., Goldman, S., Henseler, S., Presler, N., and Fried Walkenfeld, F. (2003). Entering a community of minds: An experiential approach to 'Theory of Mind'. *Human Development*, **46**, 24–46.

Newman, J. (1996). *Give: a Cognitive Linguistic study*. Berlin, New York: Mouton de Gruyter.

Newman, J. and Rice, S. (2004). Patterns of usage for English SIT, STAND, and LIE: A cognitively inspired exploration in corpus linguistics. *Cognitive Linguistics*, **15**, 351–96.

Newman, M. E. J. (2003). The structure and function of complex networks. *SIAM Review*, **45**, 167–256.

Newman, M. E. J. (2005). Power laws, Pareto distributions and Zipf's law. *Contemporary Physics*, **46**, 323–51.

Newport, E. L., Gleitman, H., and Gleitman, L. R. (1977). Mother, I'd rather do it myself: Some effects and non-effects of maternal speech style. In C. E. Snow and C. A. Ferguson (eds), Talking to children: Language input and acquisition (pp. 109–49). Cambridge: Cambridge University Press.

Nichols, J. (1986). Head-marking and dependent-marking grammar. *Language*, **62**, 56–119.

Nickel, G. (1968). Complex verbal structures in English. *International Review of Applied Linguistics*, **6**, 1–21.

Ninio, A. (1985). The meaning of children's first words: Evidence from the input. *Journal of Pragmatics*, **9**, 527–46.

Ninio, A. (1986). The direct mapping of function to form in children's early language. *Journal of Psycholinguistic Research*, **15**, 559 (Abstract).

Ninio, A. (1988). On formal grammatical categories in early child language. In Y. Levy, I. M. Schlesinger, and M. D. S. Braine (eds), Categories and processes in language acquisition (pp. 99–119). Hillsdale, NJ: Lawrence Erlbaum.

Ninio, A. (1992). The relation of children's single word utterances to single word utterances in the input. *Journal of Child Language*, **19**, 87–110.

Ninio, A. (1994a). Predicting the order of acquisition of three-word constructions by the complexity of their dependency structure. *First Language*, **14**, 119–52.

Ninio, A. (1994b). *Words with holes: The acquisition of the predicateness of predicates. Emory Conference on Cognitive and Functional Approaches to Grammatical Development*, Emory University, Atlanta, Georgia.

Ninio, A. (1995). Compiler Grammar: A dependency-oriented minimalist approach. *Theoretical Linguistics*, **21**, 159–95.

Ninio, A. (1996). A proposal for the adoption of dependency grammar as the framework for the study of language acquisition. In G. Ben Shakhar and A. Lieblich (eds), Volume in honor of Shlomo Kugelmass (pp. 85–103). Jerusalem: Magnes.

Ninio, A. (1999a). Pathbreaking verbs in syntactic development and the question of prototypical transitivity. *Journal of Child Language*, **26**, 619–53.

Ninio, A. (1999b). Model learning in syntactic development: intransitive verbs. *International Journal of Bilingualism*, **3**, 111–31.

Ninio, A. (2003). No verb is an island: Negative evidence on the Verb Island hypothesis. *Psychology of Language and Communication*, **7**, 3–21.

Ninio, A. (2005a). Testing the role of semantic similarity in syntactic development. *Journal of Child Language*, **32**, 35–61.

Ninio, A. (2005b). Accelerated learning without semantic similarity: indirect objects. *Cognitive Linguistics*, **16**, 531–56.

Ninio, A. (2005c). Kernel vocabulary and Zipf's Law in maternal input to syntactic development. Paper presented at the 30th Annual Boston University Conference on Language Development. Printed in D. Bamman, T. Magnitskaia and C. Zaller (eds), BUCLD 30: Proceedings of the 30th annual Boston University Conference on Language Development (pp. 423–31). Somerville, MA: Cascadilla Press.

Ninio, A. (2006). *Language and the learning curve: A new theory of syntactic development*. Oxford: Oxford University Press.

Ninio, A. (2009). *Local decisions and global similarity in language development*. Talk given at the Colloquium of the Department of Psychology, The Hebrew University of Jerusalem.

Ninio, A. and Snow, C. E. (1988). Language acquisition through language use: The functional sources of children's early utterances. In Y. Levy, I. Schlesinger, and M. D. S. Braine (eds), Categories and processes in language acquisition (pp. 11–30). Hillsdale, NJ: Lawrence Erlbaum.

Ninio, A. and Snow, C. E. (1996). *Pragmatic development*. Boulder, CO: Westview Press.

Ninio, A. and Wheeler, P. (1984). Functions of speech in mother-infant interaction. In L. Feagans, G. J. Garvey and R. M. Golinkoff (eds), The origins and growth of communication (pp. 196–207). Norwood, NJ: Ablex.

Noonan, M. (1985). Complementation. In T. Shopen (ed), Language typology and syntactic description, Vol. 2 (pp. 42–140). Cambridge: Cambridge University Press.

Ochs, E. (1982). Talking to children in Western Samoa. *Language in Society*, **11**, 77–104.

Ogden, C. K. (1930). *Basic English: a general introduction with rules and grammar*. London: Kegan Paul.

Oetting, J. B., Rice, M. L., and Swank, L. K. (1995). Quick incidental learning (QUIL) of words by school-age children with and without SLI. *Journal of Speech and Hearing Research*, **38**, 434–45.

Online Etymological Dictionary http://www.etymonline.com/.

Oshima-Takane, Y., Barner, D., Elsabbagh, M., and Guerriero, S. (2001). Learning of deverbal nouns. In Proceedings for the VIIIth Congress of the International Association for the Study of Child Language, San Sebastian, Basque Country (pp. 1155–72).

Palmer, F. R. (1990). *Modality and the English modals* (2nd edn). London: Longman.

Parks, R. (1999). The Wordsmyth educational dictionary-thesaurus. http://www.wordsmyth.net/

Pawley, A. (2006). Where have all the verbs gone? Remarks on the organisation of languages with small, closed verb classes. Paper presented at the 11th Binnenial Rice University Linguistics Symposium.

Perlmutter, D. (ed) (1983). *Studies in Relational Grammar*. Chicago, IL: The University of Chicago Press.

Perlmutter, D. M. and Postal, P. M. (1983). Some proposed laws of basic clause structure. In D. M. Perlmutter (ed), Studies in Relational Grammar (pp. 81–128). Chicago, IL: The University of Chicago Press.

Pesetsky, D. (1995). *Zero syntax: Experiencers and cascades.* Cambridge, MA: MIT Press.

Phillips, J. (1973). Syntax and vocabulary of mothers' speech to young children: Age and sex comparisons. *Child Development,* **44,** 182–5.

Phillips, J. D. (1999). Divergence, convergence and self-organization in landscapes. *Annals of the Association of American Geographers,* **89,** 466–88.

Pike, K. L. and Pike, E. (1982). *Grammatical analysis.* Arlington, TX: Summer Institute of Linguistics.

Pine, J. M. and Lieven, E. V. M. (1993). Reanalyzing rote-learned phrases: Individual differences in the transition to multi-word speech. *Journal of Child Language,* **20,** 551–71.

Pine, J. M. and Lieven, E. V. M. (1997). Slot and frame patterns in the development of the determiner category. *Applied Psycholinguistics,* **18,** 123–38.

Pine, J. M., Lieven, E. V. M., and Rowland, C. F. (1998). Comparing different models of the development of the English verb category. *Linguistics,* **36,** 807–30.

Pine, J. M. and Martindale, H. (1996). Syntactic categories in the speech of young children: The case of the determiner. *Journal of Child Language,* **23,** 369–95.

Pinker, S. (1984). *Language learnability and language development.* Cambridge, MA: Harvard University Press.

Pinker, S. (1987). The bootstrapping problem in language acquisition. In B. MacWhinney (ed), Mechanisms of language acquisition (pp. 399–441). Hillsdale, NJ: Lawrence Erlbaum.

Pinker, S. (1989). *Learnability and cognition: the acquisition of argument structure.* Cambridge, MA: MIT Press.

Plank, F. (ed). (1984). *Objects: towards a theory of grammatical relations.* London: Academic Press.

Pollard, C. and Sag, I. (1987). *Information-based syntax and semantics,* Vol. 1, Fundamentals. Stanford, CA: Center for the Study of Language and Information.

Post, K. (1992). *The language learning environment of laterborns in a rural Florida community.* Unpublished doctoral dissertation. Harvard University.

Powers, S. M. (2001). Children's semi-lexical heads. In N. Corver and H. van Riemsdijk (eds), Semi-lexical categories: The function of content words and the content of function words (pp. 97–126). New York: Mouton de Gruyter.

Powers, S. M. (2002). Merge as a basic mechanism of language: Evidence from language acquisition. In E. Witruk and A. D. Friederici (eds), Basic functions of language, reading and reading disability (pp. 105–117). Dordrecht, Netherlands: Kluwer.

Pustejovsky, J. (1995). *The generative lexicon.* Cambridge, MA: MIT Press.

Pylkkänen, L. and McElree, B. (2006). The syntax-semantics interface: On-line composition of sentence meaning. In M. Traxler and M.A. Gernsbacher (eds), Handbook of psycholinguistics (2nd edn) (pp. 537–77). New York: Elsevier.

Quirk, R. (1974). *The linguist and the English language.* London: Arnold.

Quirk, R., Greenbaum, S., Leech, G., and Svartvik, J. (1985). *A comprehensive grammar of the English language.* London: Longman.

Quirk, R. and Wrenn, C. L. (1958). *An Old English grammar* (2nd edn). London: Methuen.

Radford, A. (1990). *Syntactic theory and the acquisition of English syntax.* Oxford: Blackwell.

Reichenbach, H. (1947). *Elements of symbolic logic.* New York: Macmillian.

Rescorla, L., Alley, A., and Christine, J. (2001). Word frequencies in toddlers' lexicons. *Journal of Speech, Language, and Hearing Research,* **44,** 598–609.

Rind, D. (1999). Complexity and climate. *Science,* **284,** 105–7.

Rispoli, M. (1991). The mosaic acquisition of grammatical relations. *Journal of Child Language,* **18,** 517–51.

Rispoli, M. (1994). Structural dependency and the acquisition of grammatical relations. In Y. Levy (ed), Other children, other languages: Issues in the theory of language acquisition (pp. 265–302). Hillsdale, NJ: Lawrence Erlbaum.

Ritter, E. and Rosen, S. T. (1993). Deriving causation. *Natural Language and Linguistic Theory,* **11,** 519–55.

Roark, B. and Demuth, K. (2000). Prosodic constraints and the learner's environment: a corpus study. In S. C. Howell, S. A. Fish, and T. Keith-Lucas, (eds), Proceedings of the 24th Annual Boston University Conference on Language Development (Vol. 2, pp. 597–608). Somerville, MA: Cascadilla Press.

Roberts, K. (1983). Comprehension and production of word order in Stage I. *Child Development,* **54,** 443–9.

Robins, R. H. (1964). *General linguistics: An introductory survey.* London: Longmans.

Robinson, P. (1986). Constituency or dependency in the units of language acquisition? An approach to describing the learner's analysis of formulae.

Lingvisticae Investigationes, International Journal of French Linguistics and General Linguistics, **10**, 417–37.

Roland, D., Dick, F., and Elman, J. L. (2007). Frequency of basic English grammatical structures: A corpus analysis. *Journal of Memory and Language*, **57**, 348–79.

Rollins, P. R. (2003). Caregivers' contingent comments to 9-month-old infants: Relationships with later language. *Applied Psycholinguistics*, **24**, 221–34.

Rosen, S. (1990). *Argument structure and complex predication*. New York: Garland.

Ross, J. R. (1972). The category squish: Endstation Hauptwort. In Papers from the Eighth Regional Meeting, Chicago Linguistic Society (pp. 316–28). Chicago, IL: Chicago Linguistic Society.

Ross, J. R. (1973). Nouniness. In O. Fujimura (ed), Three dimensions of linguistic theory (pp. 137–258). Tokyo: TEC.

Rowland, C. F. (2010). Personal communication, 11 March, 2010

Rowland, C. F. and Fletcher, S. L. (2006). The effect of sampling on estimates of lexical specificity and error rates. *Journal of Child Language*, **33**, 859–77.

Rundell, M. and Stock, P. (1994). The corpus revolution. *English Today*, **30**, 9–17; 31, 21–38; 32, 45–51.

Sachs, J. (1983). Talking about the there and then: The emergence of displaced reference in parent-child discourse. In K. E. Nelson (ed), Children's language (Vol. **4**, pp. 1–28). Hillsdale, NJ: Lawrence Erlbaum.

Sachs, J., Brown, R., and Salerno, R. A. (1976). Adults' speech to children. In W. von Raffler-Engel and Y. Lebrun (eds), Baby talk and infant speech (pp. 240–45). Lisse: Swetz and Zeitlinger.

Sag, I. A., Baldwin, T., Bond, F., Copestake, A., and Flickinger, D. (2002). Multiword expressions: A pain in the neck for NLP. In Proceedings of the Third International Conference on Intelligent Text Processing and Computational Linguistics (CICLing'02) (pp. 1–15).

Sagae, K., Lavie, A., and MacWhinney, B. (2004a). Adding syntactic annotations to transcripts of parent-child dialogs. Proceedings of the Fourth International Conference on Language Resources and Evaluation (LREC 2004). Lisbon, Portugal, May 2004.

Sagae, K., MacWhinney, B., and Lavie, A. (2004b). Automatic parsing of parental verbal input. *Behavior Research Methods, Instruments and Computers*, **36**, 113–26.

Sagae, K., Davis, E., Lavie, A., MacWhinney, B., and Wintner, S. (2010). Morphosyntactic annotation of CHILDES transcripts. *Journal of Child Language*, **37**, 705–29.

Sapir, E. (1921). *Language: an introduction to the study of speech*. New York: Harcourt Brace Jovanovich.

Sapir, E. (1931). The function of an international auxiliary language. *Psyche*, **11**, 4–15.

Schachter, P. (1977). Reference-related and role-related properties of subjects. In P. Cole and J. M. Saddock (eds), Syntax and semantics 8: Grammatical relations (pp. 279–306). New York: Academic Press.

Schlesinger, I. (1995). On the semantics of the object. In B. Aarts and C. F. Meyer (eds), The verb in contemporary English (pp. 54–74). Cambridge: Cambridge University Press.

Schutze, C. (2002). *The non-omission of nonfinite be. Paper presented in the Workshop on First Language Acquisition at the 19th Scandinavian Conference of Linguistics*, Tromso, Norway.

Seiler, H. (1988). *The dimension of participation*. Translated and edited by F. Leal (Función, 7). Guadalajara, Mexico: Universidad de Guadalajara.

Serratrice, L., Joseph, K. L., and Conti-Ramsden, G. (2003). The acquisition of past tense in preschool children with specific language impairment and unaffected controls: regular and irregular forms. *Linguistics*, **41-42**, 321–49.

Sethuraman, N. and Goodman, J. C. (2004). Children's mastery of the transitive construction. In E. V. Clark (ed), Online proceedings of the 32nd session of the Stanford Child Language Research Forum (pp. 60–7). Stanford, CA: CSLI Publications. http://www-csli.stanford.edu/pubs

Sherrod, K. B., Friedman, S., Crawley, S., Drake, D., and Devieux, J. (1977). Maternal language to prelinguistic infants: Syntactic aspects. *Child Development*, **48**, 1662–5.

Sichel, H. S. (1986). Word frequency distributions and type-token characteristics. *The Mathematical Scientist*, **11**, 45–72.

Siewierska, A. and Bakker, D. (in press). Three takes on grammatical relations: a view from the languages of Europe and North and Central Asia. In B. Comrie and V. Solovyev (eds), *Argument structure in the languages of Northern Eurasia*. Amsterdam: John Benjamins.

Sinclair, J. (1991). *Corpus, concordance and collocation*. Oxford: Oxford University Press.

Sinclair, J. (1999). A way with common words. In H. Hasselgard and S. Oksefjell (eds), Out of corpora (pp. 157–79). Amsterdam: Rodopi.

Sinclair, J. (2005). Corpus and text: Basic principles. In M. Wynne (ed), Guide to good practice in developing linguistic corpora. Was accessed at http://ahds.ac.uk/litlangling/linguistics/index.html

Skeat, W. W. (1917). *A primer of English etymology*. Oxford: Clarendon Press.

Sleator, D. and Temperley, D. (1991). Parsing English with a Link Grammar. *Carnegie Mellon University Computer Science technical report (CMU-CS-91-196, October 1991)*.

Slobin, D. I. (1985). Crosslinguistic evidence for the language-making capacity. In D. I. Slobin (ed), *The crosslinguistic study of language acquisition* (Vol. 2, pp. 1159–249). Hillsdale, NJ: Lawrence Erlbaum.

Slocum, J. and Lehmann, W. P. (2009). Old English Online; Series Introduction. http://www.utexas.edu/cola/centers/lrc/eieol/engol-0-X.html

Smiley, P. and Huttenlocher, J. (1995). Conceptual development and the child's early words for events, objects, and persons. In M. Tomasello and W. E. Merriman (eds), *Beyond names for things: Young children's acquisition of verbs* (pp. 21–62). Hillsdale, NJ: Lawrence Erlbaum.

Snedeker, J. and Gleitman, L. R. (2004). Why it is hard to label our concepts. In G. Hall and S. Waxman (eds), Weaving a lexicon (pp. 257–93). Cambridge, MA: MIT Press.

Snow, C. E. (1972). Mothers' speech to children learning language. *Child Development*, **43**, 549–65.

Snow, C. E. (1977a). Mothers' speech research: from input to interaction. In C. E. Snow and C. Ferguson (eds), Talking to children (pp. 31–49). Cambridge: Cambridge University Press.

Snow, C. E. (1977b). The development of conversation between mothers and babies. *Journal of Child Language*, **4**, 1–22.

Snow, C. E. (1986). Conversations with children. In P. Fletcher and M. Garman (eds), *Language acquisition* (2nd edn, pp. 363–75). New York: Cambridge University Press.

Snow,C. E. and Ferguson, C. (eds) (1977). *Talking to children*. Cambridge: Cambridge University Press.

Snow, C. E., Pan, B., Imbens-Bailey, A., and Herman, J. (1996). Learning how to say what one means: A longitudinal study of children's speech act use. *Social Development*, **5**, 56–84.

Solé, R. V., Corominas Murtra, B., Valverde, S., and Steels, L. (2005). Language networks: their structure, function and evolution. Santa Fe Institute Working Paper 05-12-042.

Starosta, S. (1988). *The case for Lexicase*. London: Pinter.

Steedman, M. J. (1988). Combinators and grammars. In R. T. Oehrle, E. Bach, and D. Wheeler (eds), Categorial grammars and natural language structures (pp. 417–42). Dordrecht: Reidel.

Stern, D. N., Spieker, S., Barnett, R. K. and MacKain, K. (1983). The prosody of maternal speech: infant age and context related changes. *Journal of Child Language*, **10**, 1–15.

Steyvers, M. and Tenenbaum, J. (2005). The large-scale structure of semantic networks: Statistical analyses and a model of semantic growth. *Cognitive Science*, **29**, 41–78.

Storkel, H. L. (2004). Do children acquire dense neighborhoods? An investigation of similarity neighborhoods in lexical acquisition. *Applied Psycholinguistics*, **25**, 201–21.

Strang, B. M. H. (1970). *A history of English*. London: Methuen.

Stubbs, M. (1986). Language development, lexical competence and nuclear vocabulary. In K. Durkin (ed), Language development in the school years (pp. 34–56). London: Croom Helm.

Stubbs, M. and Barth, I. (2003). Using recurrent phrases as text-type discriminators: A quantitative method and some findings. *Functions of Language*, **10**, 61–104.

Summers, D. (1996). Computer lexicography: The importance of representativeness in relation to frequency. In J. Thomas and M. Short (eds), Using corpora for language research (pp. 260–66). London: Longman.

Suppes, P. (1974). The semantics of children's language. *American Psychologist*, **29**, 103–14.

Svartvik, J. (1990). *The London-Lund corpus of spoken English: description and research*. Lund Studies in English, **82**. Lund: Lund University Press.

Svartvik, J. (ed). (1992). *Directions in Corpus Linguistics: Proceedings of Nobel Symposium 82*. Berlin: Mouton de Gruyter.

Szabolcsi, A. (1986). Indefinites in complex predicates. *Theoretical Linguistic Research*, **2**, 47–83.

Tardif, T., Gelman, S.A., and Xu, F. (1999). Putting the 'Noun Bias' in context: A comparison of English and Mandarin. *Child Development*, **70**, 620–35.

Taylor, J. R. (1989). *Linguistic categorization: Prototypes in linguistic theory*. Oxford: Clarendon.

Taylor, J. R. (1998). Syntactic constructions as prototype categories. In M. Tomasello (ed), The new psychology of language: Cognitive and functional approaches to language structure (pp. 177–202). Mahwah, NJ: Lawrence Erlbaum.

Tesnière, L. (1959). *Éléments de syntaxe structurale*. Paris: Klincksieck.

Theakston, A. L., Lieven, E. V. M., Pine, J. M., and Rowland, C. F. (2001). The role of performance limitations in the acquisition of verb-argument structure: an alternative account. *Journal of Child Language*, **28**, 127–52.

Theakston, A. L., Lieven, E. V. M., Pine, J. M., and Rowland, C. F. (2002). Going, going, gone: the acquisition of the verb 'go'. *Journal of Child Language*, **29**, 783–811.

Theakston, A. L., Lieven, E. V. M., Pine, J. M., and Rowland, C. F. (2004). Semantic generality, input frequency and the acquisition of syntax. *Journal of Child Language*, **31**, 61–99.

Tomasello, M. (1992). *First verbs: A case study of early grammatical development*. Cambridge: Cambridge University Press.

Tomasello, M. (2000). The item-based nature of children's early syntactic development. *Trends in Cognitive Sciences*, **4**, 156–63.

Tomasello, M. (2003). *Constructing a language: A usage-based theory of language acquisition*. Cambridge, MA: Harvard University Press.

Tomasello, M. (2006). Acquiring linguistic constructions. In W. Damon, R. M. Lerner, D. Kuhn and R. S. Siegler (eds), Handbook of child psychology, Volume 2, Cognition, perception, and language (pp. 255–98). New York: Wiley.

Tomasello, M., and Akhtar, N. (2003). What paradox? A response to Naigles. *Cognition*, **88**, 317–23.

Tomasello, M. and Brandt, S. (2009). Flexibility in the semantics and syntax of children's early verb use. Commentary on Naigles, Hoff and Vear (2009), Flexibility in early verb use: Evidence from a multiple-N diary study. Monographs of the Society for Research in Child Development, **74**, 293.

Traugott, E. C. (1999). A historical overview of complex predicates. In L. J. Brinton and M. Akimoto (eds), Collocational and idiomatic aspects of composite predicates in the history of English (pp. 239–60). Amsterdam: John Benjamins.

Valian, V. (1991). Syntactic subjects in the early speech of American and Italian children. *Cognition*, **40**, 21–81.

Van Houten, L. (1986). *Role of maternal input in the acquisition process: The communicative strategies of adolescent and older mothers with their language learning children*. Paper presented at the Boston University Conference on Language Development, Boston.

Van Langendonck, W. (1987). Word Grammar and child grammar. *Belgian Journal of Linguistics*, **2**, 109–32.

Van Valin, R. D. Jr. (1993). A synopsis of Role and Reference Grammar. In R. D. Van Valin (ed), Advances in Role and Reference Grammar (pp. 1–164). Amsterdam: John Benjamins.

Van Valin, R. D. Jr. (2004). Semantic macroroles in Role and Reference Grammar. In R. Kailuweit and M. Hummel (eds), Semantische Rollen (pp. 62–82). Tübingen: Narr.

Van Valin, R. D. Jr. and LaPolla, R. (1997). *Syntax: structure, meaning and function*. Cambridge: Cambridge University Press.

Venneman, T. (1977). Konstituenz und Dependenz in einigen neueren Grammatiktheorien. [Constituency and dependency in a new theory of grammar] *Sprachwissenschaft*, **2**, 259–301.

Verplaetse, H. (2003). What you and I want: a functional approach to verb complementation of the modal WANT TO. In R. Facchinetti, M. G. Krug and F. R. Palmer (eds), Modality in Contemporary English (pp. 151–89). Berlin/New York: Mouton de Gruyter.

Vihman, M. M. (1999). The transition to grammar in a bilingual child: Positional patterns, model learning, and relational words. *International Journal of Bilingualism*, **3**, 267–301.

Vihman, M. M., Kay, E., de Boysson-Bardies, B., Durand, C., and Sundberg, U. (1994). External sources of individual differences? A cross-linguistic analysis of the phonetics of mothers' speech to 1-year-old children. *Developmental Psychology*, **30**, 651–62.

von Raffler-Engel, W. and Lebrun, Y. (eds). (1976). *Baby talk and infant speech*. Lisse: Swetz and Zeitlinger.

Walsh, C. (1933). The verb system in Basic English. *American Speech*, **8**, 137–43.

Wardhaugh, R. (1992). *An introduction to sociolinguistics*. Oxford: Blackwell.

Warren-Leubecker, A. (1982). *Sex differences in speech to children*. Unpublished doctoral dissertation. Georgia Institute of Technology.

Warren-Leubecker, A. and Bohannon, J. N. (1984). Intonation patterns in child-directed speech: Mother-father speech. *Child Development*, **55**, 1379–85.

Watts, D. J. and Strogatz, S. H. (1998). Collective dynamics of 'small-world' networks. *Nature*, **393**, 440–2.

Weidert, A. (1987). *Tibeto-Burman tonology*. Amsterdam: John Benjamins.

Wells, C. G. (1981). *Learning through interaction: The study of language development*. Cambridge: Cambridge University Press.

Whitney, W. D. (1874). *Language, and the study of language: Twelve lectures on the principles of linguistic science*, 5th edition. New York: Scribner.

Reprinted in M. Silverstein (ed), (1971). Whitney on language. Cambridge, MA: MIT Press.

Wierzbicka, A. (1982). Why can you have a drink when you can't *have an eat? *Language*, **58**, 753–99.

Williams, J. M. (1975). *Origins of the English language, a social and linguistic history*. New York: Free Press.

Wilson, J. and Henry, A. (1998). Parameter setting within a socially realistic linguistics. *Language in Society*, **27**, 1–21.

Wilson, B. and Peters, A. M. (1988). What are you cookin' on a hot?: Movement constraints in the speech of a three-year-old blind child. *Language*, **64**, 249–73.

Zamuner, T. S. (2009). The structure and nature of phonological neighbour-hoods in children's early lexicons. *Journal of Child Language*, **36**, 3–21.

Zamuner, T. S., Gerken, L. A. and Hammond, M. (2005). The acquisition of phonology based on input: A closer look at the relation of cross-linguistic and child language data. *Lingua*, **10**, 1403–26.

Zipf, G. K. (1945). The meaning-frequency relationship of words. *Journal of General Psychology*, **33**, 251–6.

Zipf, G. K. (1965). *Psycho-biology of language: an introduction to dynamic phi-lology*. Cambridge, MA: MIT Press. (Original work published 1935.)

Zipf, G. K. (1972). *Human behaviour and the principle of least effort: An introduction to human ecology*. New York: Hafner. (Original work published 1949.)

Zwicky, A. and Pullum, G. K. (1986). Two spurious counterexamples to the principle of phonology-free syntax. *OSU Working Papers in Linguistics*, **32**, 92–9.

Author index

Subject index

Note: page numbers in *italics* refer to Figures and Tables.